TOP-DOWN STRUCTURED PROGRAMMING TECHNIQUES

TOP-DOWN STRUCTURED PROGRAMMING TECHNIQUES

Clement L. McGowan
John R. Kelly
BROWN UNIVERSITY

FIRST EDITION

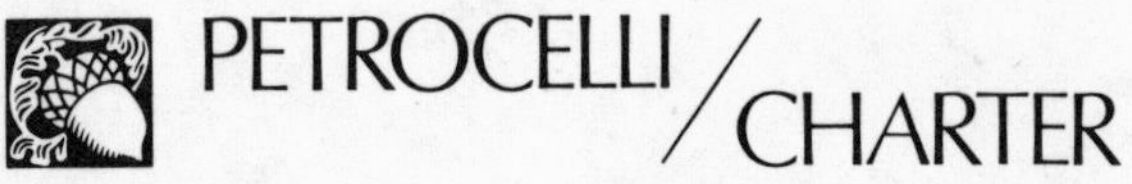

NEW YORK 1975

Published simultaneously in the United Kingdom by Mason/Charter Publishers, Inc., London, England.

First Printing

Printed in the United States of America

Library of Congress Cataloging in Publication Data

McGowan, Clement L 1942-
Top-down structured programming techniques.

(Computer science series)
1. Electronic digital computers--Programming.
I. Kelly, John R., 1944- joint author. II. Title.
QA76.6.M318 1975 001.6'42 74-30427
ISBN 0-88405-304-0

CONTENTS

TOP-DOWN STRUCTURED PROGRAMMING TECHNIQUES

1. INTRODUCTION

This book is addressed to programmers—not to beginners in the computer field and not to mathematicians. Its principal topic is structured programming. Daniel McCracken in the December 1973 issue of *Datamation* calls structured programming "a major intellectual invention, one that will come to be ranked with the subroutine concept or even the stored program concept."[1]

There is no question that structured programming (whatever it is) is an "in" thing. It is currently advocated by many leading computer scientists at major North American and European universities, by the Federal Systems Division (FSD) of IBM, and by a growing number of commercial software companies. Anything such a diverse computing group can agree upon is worthy of attention.

In this chapter we mention the "software crisis" and imply the need for better programming practices. We then propose a preliminary answer to the question, What is structured programming? The chapter concludes with an overview of the book's contents.

This is not a textbook, but major portions of it have been used in software engineering courses at Brown University and at the University of California, Los Angeles. Some mathematical concepts and some technical details appear herein simply because computer programming involves both intimately. Not every reader will profit from every single page, but we do expect (and hope) that every reader will become a better programmer for having read this book.

1.1 SOFTWARE: THE RATE-DETERMINING STEP

Software dominates computing, and future prospects are for much more of the same. A recent Rand Corporation study of computer systems found software to be "the major source of difficult future problems and operational penalties."[2] This study, with projections into the 1980s, contained many fascinating facts, among them:

Software costs in the United States now exceed $10 billion per year.

For the U.S. Air Force the current software/hardware ratio of total ADP system cost is greater than 65/35 and will swell to 90/10 by 1985.

Programmers in large software projects typically spend their time as follows: 45–50 percent in program checkout, about one third in program design, and less than 20 percent in actually coding.

"The software crisis" is not a hollow phrase. We commonly assume that large computer systems in production still contain errors. This attitude is solidly grounded in experience. Horror stories abound about a system becoming useless after a key programmer quits. There is a feeling that modern computing systems have reached the practical limit of complexity with which man can deal. They are so large that they can no longer fit inside one person's head. For many programmers, truly reliable software, which is error-free and easy to modify and to maintain, belongs in a category with the Holy Grail.

For example, IBM's operating system OS/360 contained hundreds of errors when it was released. In fact, two years after issuing OS/360 RELEASE 18 the ratio of maintenance costs to development costs was more than 3:1. This reflects a growing software reality. More and more the goals of reliability, maintainability, and modifiability are given precedence over the traditional performance goals of space and time optimization (which, of course, are still very important).

The trend in software development now seems to place efficiency considerations subordinate to clear, logical structuring. We would like to "modularize" programs so that an individual module could be replaced by a functionally equivalent but better (usually more efficient) module. After such a replacement the system's performance might be improved but its capabilities should be preserved.

A recent empirical study found that in a typical FORTRAN program "only 3 percent of the statements make up 50 percent of the program's execution time."[3] One would expect a similar pattern for other programming languages. This suggests the following coding strategy: first, write the program straightforwardly, emphasizing clarity and reliability; then, after the program is working, rewrite and optimize the time-consuming code (usually within inner loops). Such a tack should help a programmer to invest his time more profitably.

This touches upon another major software problem, programmer productivity. The significant trend in hardware is toward cost reductions. In the next decade hardware performance should increase by a factor of at least ten. Can improvement of an order of magnitude be made in programmer productivity? If not, then a software/hardware cost ratio of 9:1, as projected for the U.S. Air Force by 1985, might well be representative of future computer systems.

Consider a large production programming project. When all overhead is included, the typical programmer averages only about ten debugged source statements per person-day. Clearly coding ten statements takes but a few minutes of an eight-hour day. But the programmers on this large production project appear to be very busy and to be working very hard. So, what are they doing?

Besides coding and designing, production programmers are typically engaged in such activities as writing driver routines for testing purposes, integrating program units, debugging, attending meetings to resolve various program interfaces, and recoding to meet newly determined interfaces. Programmers also shoulder an invisible clerical burden: They personally submit and collect their own jobs; they maintain current program listings; they perform necessary program editing themselves; and they also must produce documentation as an activity separate from programming. Moreover, today's compilers and operating systems comprise a powerful but complex set of software tools. And large production projects often have their less experienced programmers making major technical decisions on how these tools will be used.

Program reliability and programmer productivity are inextricably bound. Edsger Dijkstra in his classic 1972 ACM Turing Award Lecture made the following observation:

> Software seems to be different from many other products, where as a rule a higher quality implies a higher price. Those who want really reliable software will discover that they must find means of avoiding the majority of bugs to start with, and as a result the programming process will become cheaper. If you want more effective programmers, you will discover that they should not waste their time debugging—they should not introduce the bugs to start with. In other words, both goals point to the same change.[4]

In this connection Harlan Mills of IBM's FSD notes:

> Errors in either syntax or logic should be extremely rare, because you can prevent them from entering into your programs by positive actions on your part. Programs do not

> acquire bugs as people do germs—just by hanging around other buggy programs. They acquire bugs only by having programmers insert them.[5]

Some recent indications are that the program production process can be brought under better control. Mills, in describing the development for *The New York Times* of an on-line information system with over 80,000 source lines, wrote:

> Although this development was conducted under commercial pressures for high programming productivity (some 10,000 lines per programmer manyear), the system came down only once from a software error in its first year of operation (although a few other errors were detected not causing system failure). All in all, the rate of detected errors produced by the principal programmers was about one error per manyear of effort.[6]

This remarkable achievement level—10,000 lines and one error per year—can be attributed to several factors, including the skills of the principal programmers and IBM's innovative Chief Programmer Team (CPT) approach.

The CPT approach introduces a major reorganization of both the personnel and the procedures involved in a production programming project. This approach entails a promising new form for project organization and management, the rigid separation of clerical tasks from programming tasks, and the explicit use of top-down structured programming. By all accounts top-down structured programming was a major factor in achieving the astounding reliability and productivity levels for *The New York Times* information bank project.

1.2 A NEW PROGRAMMING METHODOLOGY

Reliability is the sine qua non of software systems. There is really no point in engaging in efficiency considerations for unreliable systems. And to achieve reliability you should make your code correct and clear before you try to make it faster or more compact. Structured programming is a technical elaboration of this basic point of view.

The formal counterpart of reliability is the notion of "correctness." We say a program is correct if it actually does what it purports to do. Formally proving various programs correct is an active area of computer science research. To rigorously prove the correctness of a program you have written is a challenging (but impractical) undertaking. However, we can regard structured programming as a practical payoff from formal correctness studies.

Dijkstra proposed that we take a "constructive" approach to the problem of program correctness by controlling "the process of program generation such as to produce a priori correct programs."[7] To facilitate this process we limit the rules for program composition to those which are well understood. We would like to informally establish that our program is correct *as* we are designing and coding it.

A program is a static representation of an algorithm. The execution of a program is a dynamically changing activity. When we use a program text to reason about a program's execution, we are crucially concerned with the program's flow of control. In structured programming only three forms of control structures are permitted. These forms are simple sequencing or concatenation of statements, selecting the next statement(s) to be executed by the result of a test (often with a true or false answer), and conditional iteration. The restriction to these three means of program composition is far from arbitrary; rather, it is based directly upon considerations of program correctness.

Each of the forms has the property that it is single entry/single exit. As such, they provide alternative ways to structure or to decompose a one-in/one-out "black box." When expanded into code, the forms can be read from top to bottom with no jumping around in the program text. Moreover, each of the permissible control structures corresponds to a standard mathematical pattern of reasoning, namely, linear reasoning or substitution, case analysis, and induction. By building program control logic out of nested permissible forms, we are designing software which can be directly translated into code and into mathematics.

Böhm and Jacopini in a 1966 paper[8] first showed that statement sequencing, IF-THEN-ELSE conditional branching, and DO-WHILE conditional iteration would suffice as a set of control structures for expressing *any* flow-chartable program logic. Thus, when programming in a language (like PL/I or ALGOL) which contains the IF-THEN-ELSE and the DO-WHILE constructs, it is theoretically possible to avoid ever using an explicit GO TO statement. And in, say, FORTRAN the use of GO TO's could be restricted (again theoretically) to hand compiling instances of IF-THEN-ELSE and of DO-WHILE into equivalent FORTRAN sequences with GO TO's.

Dijkstra introduced and developed the concept of structured programming in a series of publications beginning in 1968. In a sense he advocated that the theoretically possible (as established by Böhm and Jacopini) should become actual programming practice. The motivation was to make programs more intellectually manageable by using a proof-of-correctness approach to their construction.

In 1971 Harlan Mills and F. Terry Baker of IBM's FSD demonstrated that there can be a practical payoff by applying structured programming techniques in a production environment. The dramatic success of *The New York Times'* on-line information-retrieval system project and, more recently, the Skylab mission-simulation system has led to a major commitment by FSD for using structured programming.

Many others have contributed to the complex of ideas that we group under the term *structured programming.* And some of the basic ideas, as with most basic ideas, have appeared before. But the entrance into the real world of production programming is quite recent and, it seems, is destined to grow.

Exactly what is structured programming? A variety of meanings have been associated with the concept. Certainly both a design method and a coding technique are implied. The design aspects often embrace the phrases "levels of abstraction," "top-down expansion," and "stepwise refinement." The coding features include restriction to a set of single-entry/single-exit control structures, often with explicit formatting conventions to promote readability. And top-down coding is sometimes considered to be a part of structured programming.

We find it convenient first to specify what we mean by a structured program and then to characterize structured programming as a group of methodologies for producing structured programs. We will later detail one particular methodology—top-down, segmented structured programming.

We say a program is *structured* with respect to a set S of one-in/one-out flow-of-control figures if the program's flowchart can be realized by some nested combination of figures from S. For example, consider the set S_1 of three flow-of-control patterns given by Fig. 1.1. If Fig. 1.2 represented the flowchart of a program SP, then the sequence from Fig. 1.3 through Fig. 1.7 shows that SP is a structured program with respect to the set S_1 of one-in/one-out flow-of-control figures.

In the sequence from Fig. 1.3 through Fig. 1.7, each time we recognize an instance of a control structure from the set S_1 we replace that instance with a simple one-in/one-out function box. We continue this process until only a single function box remains. Flowcharts that cannot be reduced in this way to just a sole one-in/one-out box are said to be *not* structured with respect to the set S_1. Fig. 1.8 gives a flowchart which cannot be realized as some nested combination of figures from S_1. If Fig. 1.8 represented the flowchart for a program U, then U would be an unstructured program with respect to the flow-of-control patterns given by S_1 in Fig. 1.1.

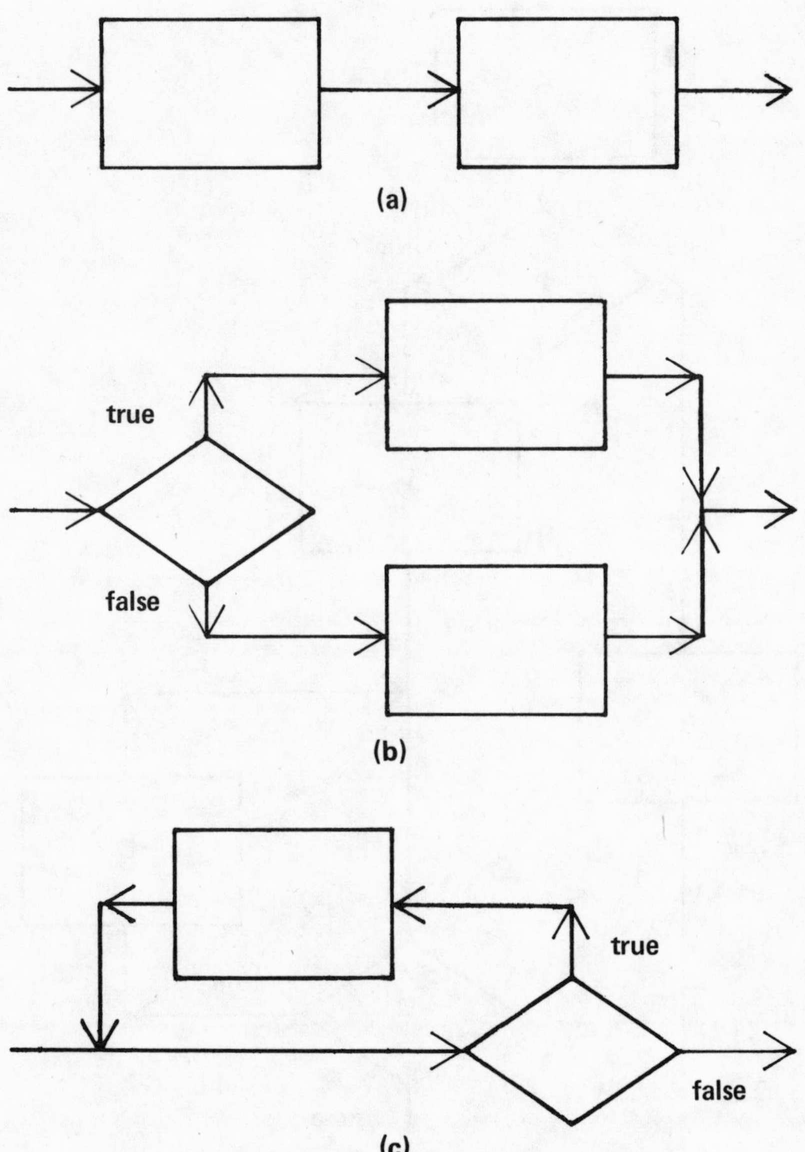

FIG. 1.1 A set S_1 of one-in/one-out flow-of-control figures

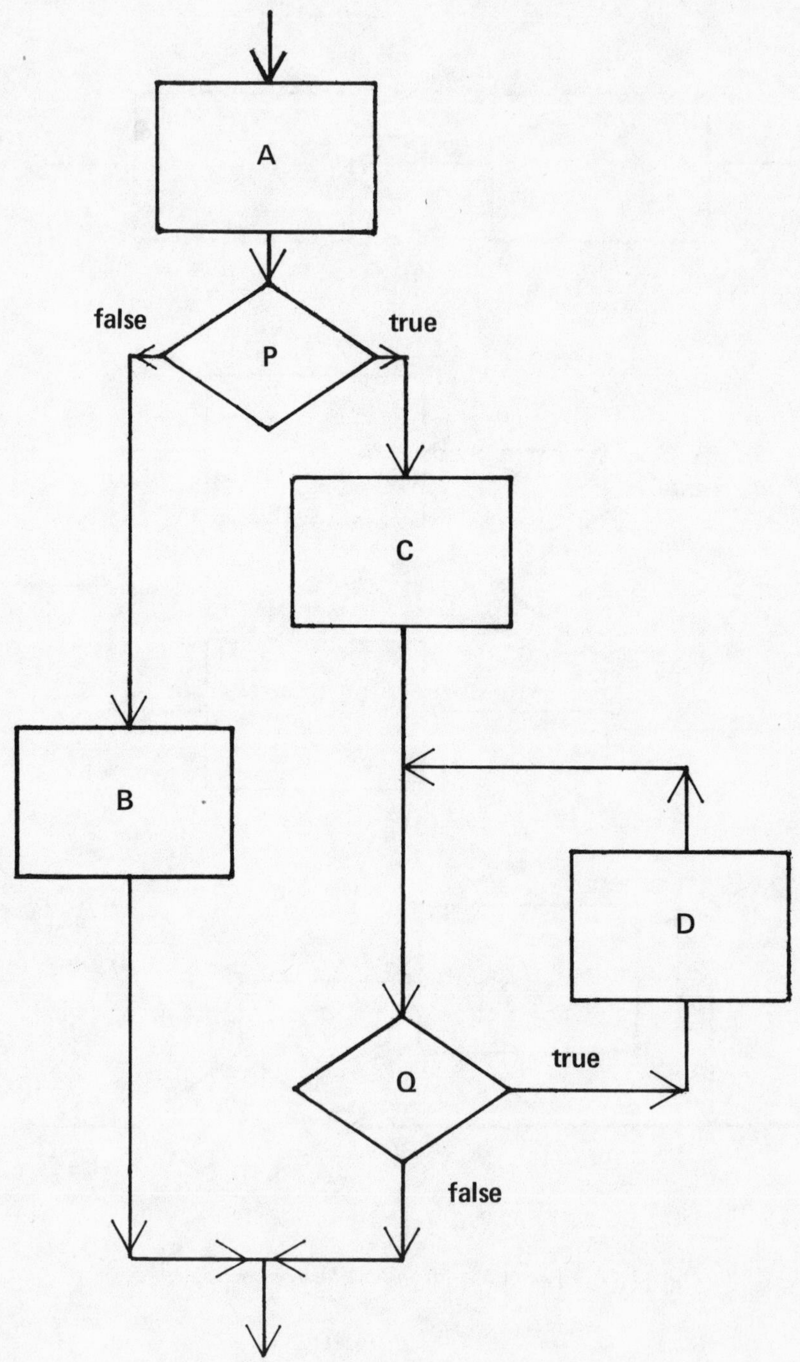

FIG. 1.2 Sample program flowchart

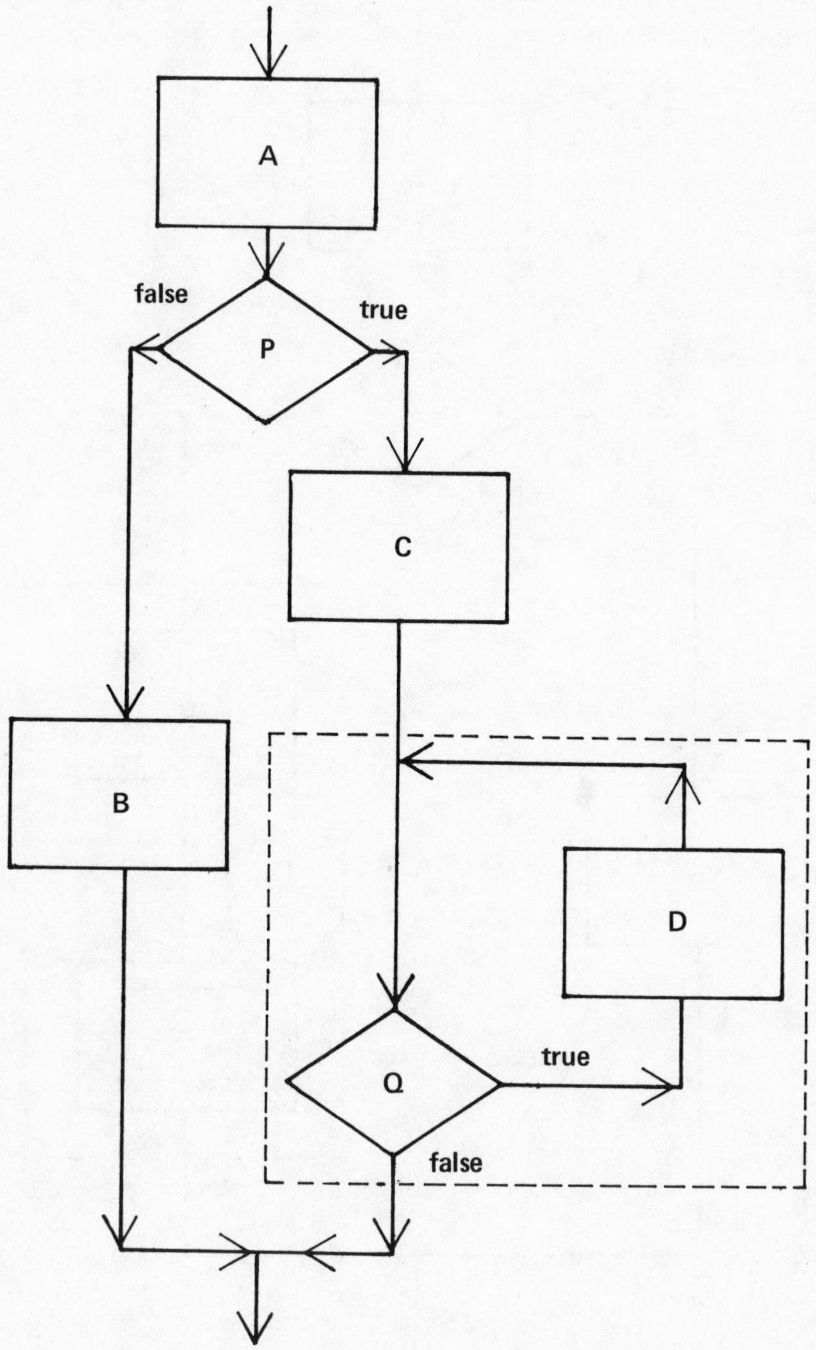

FIG. 1.3 Instance of Fig. 1.1(c) nested within a flowchart

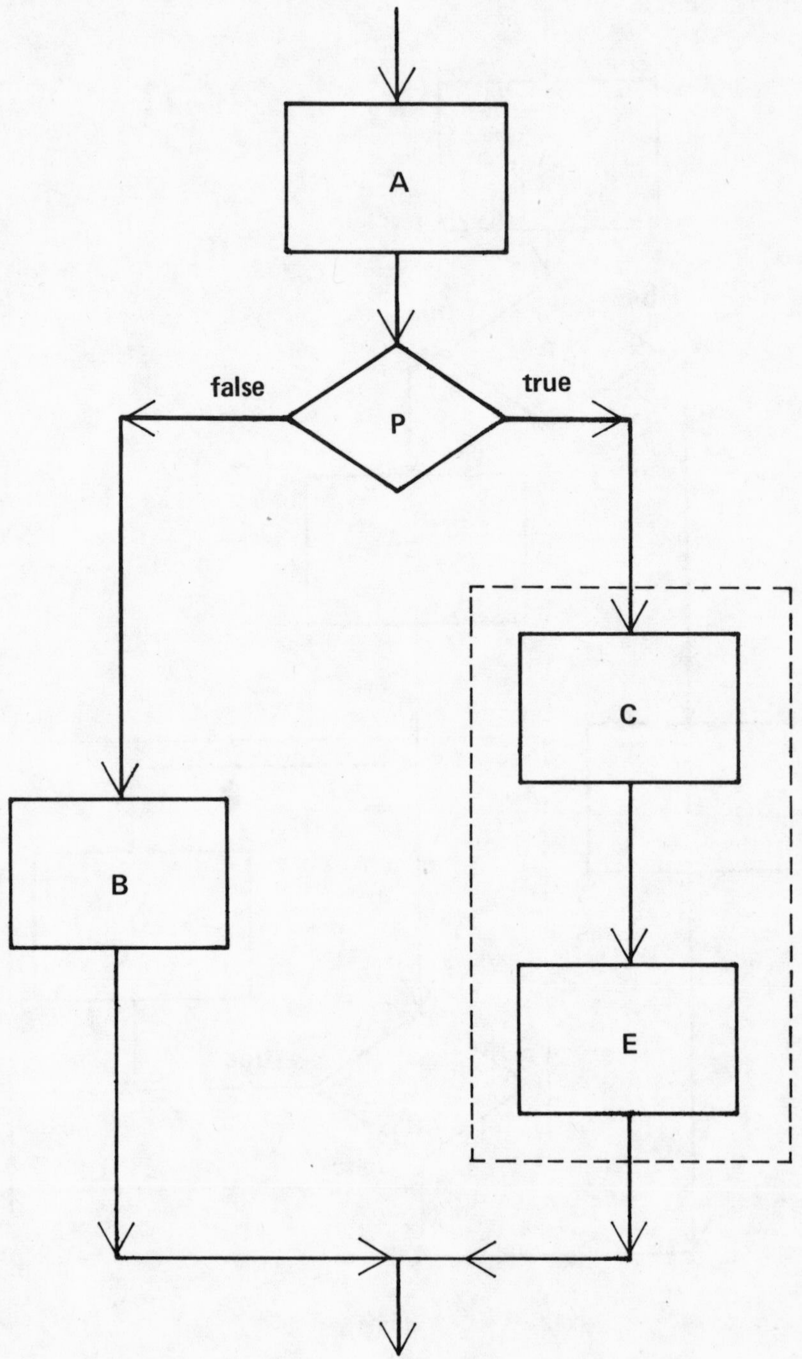

FIG. 1.4 Instance of Fig. 1.1(a) nested within a flowchart

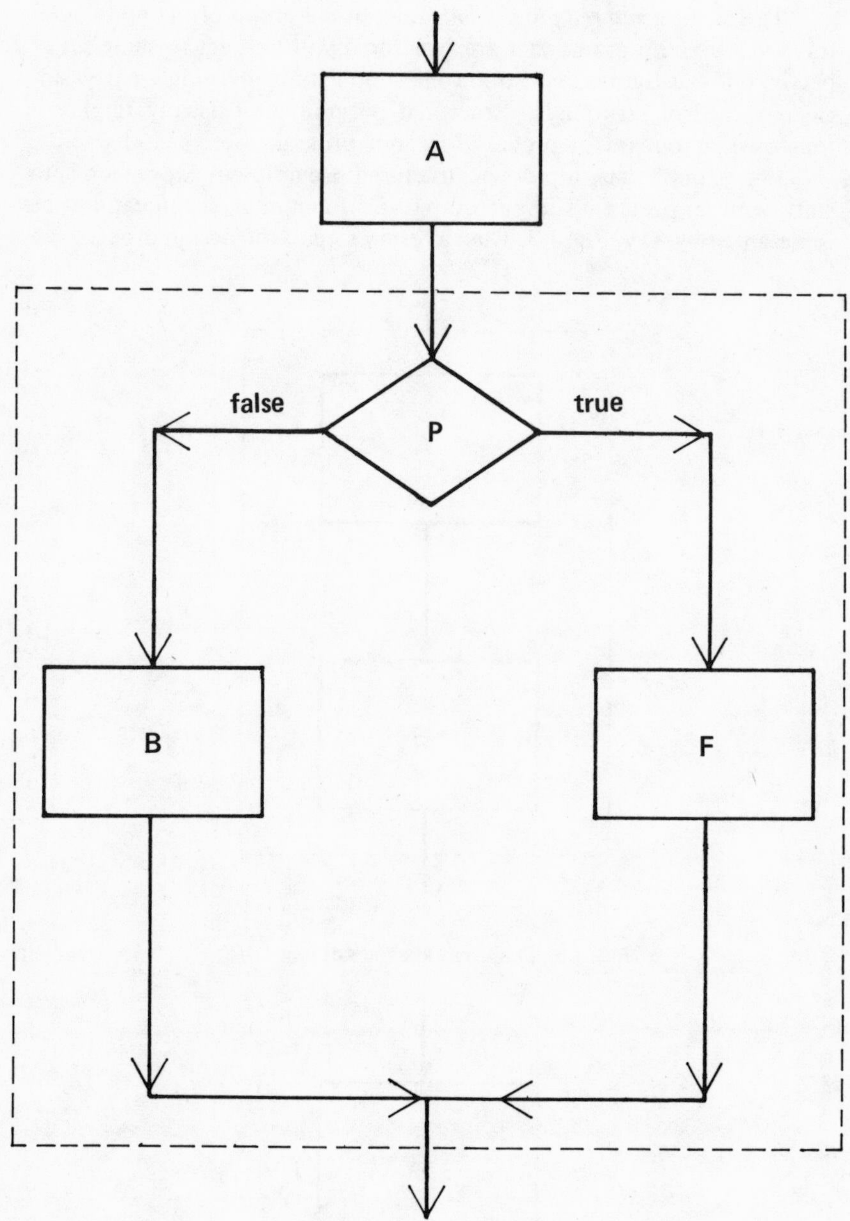

FIG. 1.5 Instance of Fig. 1.1(b) nested within a flowchart

The term *structured programming* denotes a group of methodologies for developing programs that are structured with respect to some set of one-in/one-out figures. To exploit the simplicity of the single-entry/single-exit control structures, structured programming usually implies a top-down or outside-in process for both program design and coding.

For example, one top-down structured programming approach is to start with a program's input/output or functional specifications as represented by, say, Fig. 1.7. Then at every step of the design process you

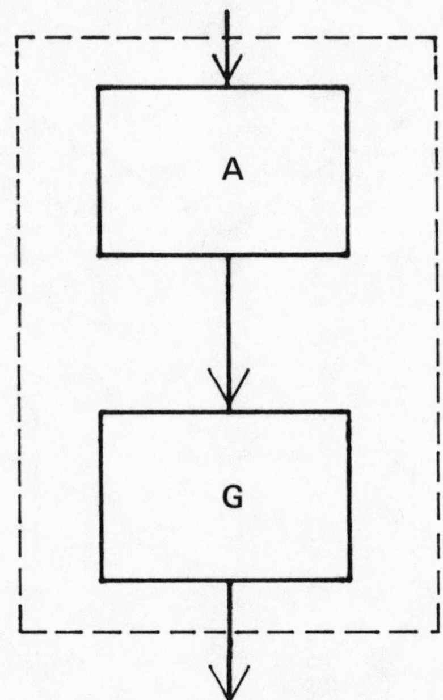

FIG. 1.6 Flowchart instance of Fig. 1.1(a)

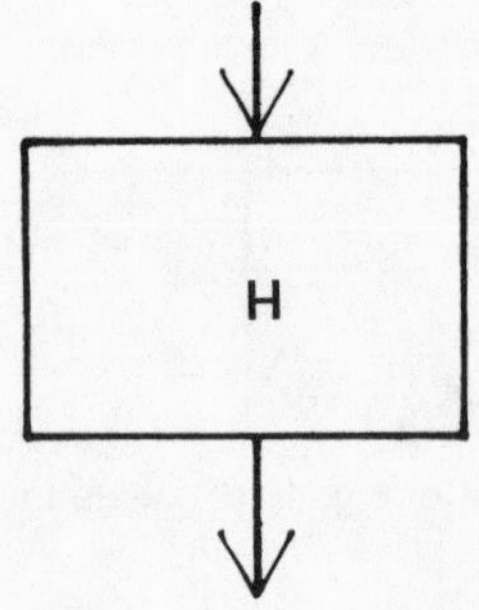

FIG. 1.7 Simple one-in/one-out function box

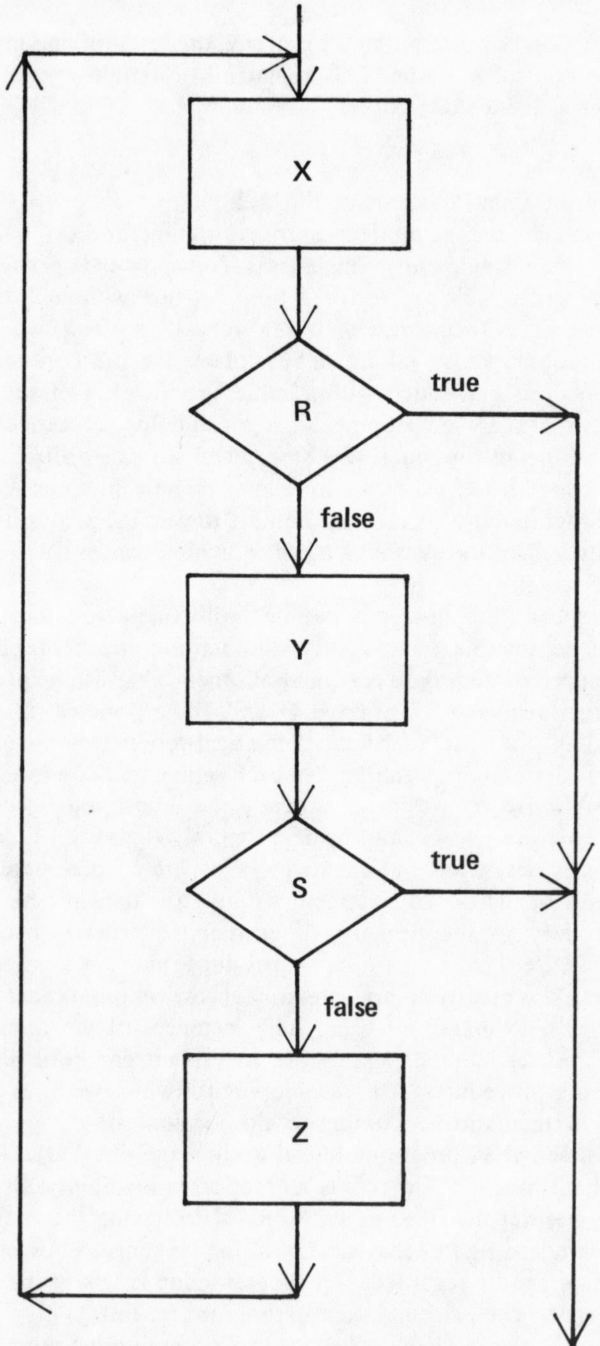

FIG. 1.8 A flowchart not structured with respect to Fig. 1.1

refine a function box into a figure from, say, the set S_1 of one-in/one-out permissible control patterns. This replacing or refining process could produce the sequence of figures:

1–7, 1–6, 1–5, 1–4, 1–3

resulting in the final flowchart of Fig. 1.2.

Here you can see the motivation for restricting the set of permissible figures to being single-entry/single-exit. This property permits us to "plug in" a permissible figure for a function box without introducing new connections with the rest of the flowchart. In effect, when we do such substitutions, we are taking an I/O "black box" and are breaking it into subfunctions embedded within some specific flow-of-control pattern. That is, we are developing an algorithm by successively giving greater structure to functions. We stop when we can realize all of the function boxes (in the evolving flowchart) directly in code. Viewed in this way, programming becomes a refining, dissecting, analyzing type of activity rather than the synthesizing of individual statements to accomplish some specified function.

Besides being "plug-in compatible" with one-in/one-out function boxes, the permissible figures have another important property: We know the appropriate way to reason about them. That is, the permissible control structures were constrained to only three principal forms, each corresponding to a standard mathematical-proof technique. So, in top-down structured programming, to each refinement of a function into a permissible figure we can associate an appropriate correctness question. This means we can ensure program reliability by perfoming explicit correctness checks at each step of program development.

The role of the GO TO statement within structured programming is but a corollary to the primacy of correctness criteria, because the unrestricted use of GO TO's can introduce many program-looping possibilities. This greatly complicates any checks on program correctness we might wish to make. By using only instances of the three control forms, we restrict looping possibilities to explicit conditional iteration (and recursive procedures)—that is, looping for which we have a general pattern of mathematical reasoning to aid our analysis.

Of course, when programming in a language like FORTRAN the complete banishment of GO TO's is a practical impossibility. But we can reasonably restrict their use in FORTRAN to having the programmer build the standard figures that are not in the language. Thus, structured programming can be regarded as a programming language independent methodology whose principal goal is program reliability.

There are methodologies of structured programming other than the one sketched. (In fact, we will later present an approach which uses small programs, called segments, rather than a set of permissible figures as the basic unit for successive refinement.) But, generally speaking, structured programming posits a new technical foundation for programming inspired by considerations of program correctness.

1.3 THE SHAPE OF THINGS TO COME

Since structured programming is largely language independent, we want you to give precedence to concepts over syntax. But since correct working programs are the ultimate goal of structured programming, we wanted to use a "real" programming language for our samples. Consequently we will often use PL/I programs and code fragments to illustrate various ideas. Besides, many of the points we wished to communicate are embodied within illustrative code. One major benefit of disciplined structured programming is that code reading becomes an easy, enjoyable task.

Some purists might quibble with our choice of PL/I. Indeed, in his ACM Turing Award Lecture Dijkstra decried the size and the "sheer baroqueness" of PL/I. He said, "When FORTRAN has been called an infantile disorder, full PL/I, with its growth characteristics of a dangerous tumor, could turn out to be a fatal disease."[9] More kindly, we might say that PL/I's multifariousness accurately reflects the complexity of modern computing environments. We selected PL/I from among those languages with which North American programmers are generally familiar.

PL/I offers at least three important features for presenting top-down structured programming. They are basic control structures, macro substitution features, and a preprocessor.

1. *PL/I has some basic control structures needed for structured programming*. These are given in Fig. 1.1. They are normal sequencing and DO-END statement grouping (Fig. 1.1(a)), the IF-THEN-ELSE compound statement (Fig. 1.1(b)), and the DO-WHILE construct (Fig. 1.1(c)).

2. *PL/I has library and macro substitution features*. The preprocessor %INCLUDE statement permits the in-line substitution of program text at compile time. Thus, the classical time/space efficiency considerations of in-line code versus subroutine call can be relegated to a position subordinate to the program's logical structure. In top-down, segmented structured programming this %INCLUDE feature is vitally important

because it provides a practical mechanism for writing *all* programs as short programs.

3. *PL/I has a preprocessor.* We use it to augment PL/I with some convenient one-in/one-out structured figures. This nicely illustrates how other languages can be adapted via a preprocessor to facilitate structured programming.

In the following chapters we will give a detailed account of major aspects of top-down segmented structured programming. Briefly, the sequence of topics will be: some correctness considerations, structured coding, top-down design and integration, the CPT approach to project organization, and an extended example. Top-down segmented structured programming is but one particular approach to producing reliable software. It is not the only way to go. However, it has been demonstrated to work in a production programming environment.

Chapter 2 is intended to orient your thinking toward program correctness. It focuses upon conditional looping (in the form of the DO-WHILE construct). It also introduces and illustrates the notion of a loop invariant, which, as the term implies, expresses some unchanging relationship between the values of variables modified during execution of the loop. Using this concept, we obtain both a better perspective on the purpose of initializing code and some explicit guidelines for programming conditional iterations correctly.

Chapter 3 delineates structured coding and its relationship to program reliability. It presents the three basic figures (SEQUENCE, IF-THEN-ELSE, DO-WHILE) and indicates that they are indeed sufficient for expressing all program logic. To each basic figure we associate correctness questions which the programmer should pose at each instance of use. In top-down structured programming answering these appropriate questions amounts to determining the functional specifications for program subcomponents. A simple, detailed example illustrates this coding and subspecifying process.

In practice the three basic figures are usually augmented with a few additional one-in/one-out figures to give a somewhat more robust set for composing structured programs. In Chapter 3 we propose a particular set of seven single-entry/single-exit flow-of-control forms for structured programming in PL/I. Besides the three basic figures, there is the standard indexed loop, which we call the ITERATIVE-DO, and three forms not explicitly present in PL/I: the SELECT-CASE, which generalizes the IF-THEN-ELSE construct, and two more conditional looping figures, the REPEAT-UNTIL and the LOOP-EXITIF-ENDLOOP. The LOOP-EXITIF-ENDLOOP construct is especially useful; it permits us to express directly a very prevalent programming pattern.

In Appendix A we extend PL/I to include the REPEAT-UNTIL, SELECT-CASE, and LOOP-EXITIF-ENDLOOP structured figures. We accomplish this extension by having each new keyword invoke a preprocessor procedure whose complete code appears in Appendix A. Since top-down structured programming in PL/I crucially uses the preprocessor %INCLUDE statement for segmenting programs, there is little additional program overhead incurred by these convenient language extensions. Appendix B specifies 360/370 assembly language macros for the six one-in/one-out figures (other than SEQUENCE) which we propose for writing structured programs. In Chapter 3 we also illustrate how these same figures can be hand coded in FORTRAN and in COBOL.

Chapter 4 explicates a top-down approach to program design, coding, and integration. This approach employs subroutines and macros (via the preprocessor %INCLUDE) to segment a program into a number of small structured programs. Top-down segmented implementation is compared with the more standard bottom-up strategy. Program testing is then discussed from a top-down perspective. Finally, we treat the important programming technique of recursion.

Chapter 5 examines in some detail IBM's innovative CPT, a highly successful managerial approach to the organization and the operation of software projects. Central to the CPT concept is the separation of programming from clerical activities. This permits the efficient use of highly skilled personnel in actual design and programming. From its inception the CPT approach has embodied a top-down segmented structured programming methodology.

Chapter 6 presents two extended examples of the top-down segmented structured programming approach. The examples are concerned with parallel processes and resource management in a multiprogramming setting. With each logical resource we associate a data structure called a "resource semaphore." We use a resource semaphore to coordinate the queuing and allocation activity attendant to a resource shared by concurrently executing processes (for instance, tasks in PL/I).

The basic data structure is that of a resource semaphore; the routines for accessing these data structures are called REQUEST and RELEASE. We implement these notions in PL/I and give a simple producer/consumer illustration. Next the functional specifications for a hypothetical multiprogrammed, multiprocessing operating system are stated. Then we present (in pseudo-code) a top-down design of this operating system. The design is developed to the point where it can be coded directly in PL/I using request and release operations upon resource semaphores.

An old maxim proclaims "If you're not enjoying it, you're not doing it right." Top-down segmented structured programming is one way to make programming the enjoyable activity it should be.

2. TOWARDS WRITING CORRECT PROGRAMS

Structured programming grew out of attempts to systematically write correct programs. By a "correct program" we mean one that is not only error free but also does exactly what it was intended to do. But how do you know when you have written a correct program? Running with test data and having no errors certainly increases your confidence in a program. But Dijkstra's famous observation applies here: "Program testing can be used to show the presence of bugs, but never to show their absence!"[1] For test data—no matter how large and complex—is usually a very small sample of possible program input. To rigorously show program correctness by testing would require us to run the program on all possible input data. Clearly, that is an absurd undertaking.

However, people do write correct programs. In fact, many who follow a structured programming methodology find that over half their programs work the very first time and continue to work through extensive testing. Such programs are typically only 50 to 400 lines of code. But they are often part of much larger programs. In this connection we quote Harlan Mills:

> There is no foolproof way to ever know that you have found the last error in a program. So the best way to acquire the confidence that a program has no errors is never to find the first one, no matter how much it is tested and used. It is an old myth that programming must be an error-prone, cut-and-try process of frustration and anxiety. But there is a new reality that you can learn to consistently write programs which are error free in their debugging and subsequent use. This new reality is founded in the ideas of structured programming and program correctness, which not only provide a systematic approach to programming but also motivate a high degree of concentration and precision in the coding subprocess.[2]

2.1 A CORRECT PROGRAM

We do not begin at the beginning. Rather, we start with a finished product—some trivial but correct PL/I code—and proceed to a few general programming principles. Later we will go in the other, more interesting direction. But we find it more natural to begin with something well known.

Consider the following sample PL/I program code:

```
J = 0;
SUM = 0;
DO WHILE (J<10);
        J = J + 1;
        SUM = SUM + A(J);
END;
```

This code sums the ten array elements A(1),A(2), . . . A(10) using the variable SUM for the result (and the partial sums).

Let B stand for some relation or test and S stand for one or more program statements. Then the general form of a DO-WHILE in PL/I is

```
DO WHILE (B);
        S;
END;
```

The flowchart in Fig. 2.1 represents the flow of control during execution of the DO-WHILE.
Note that we test B first to decide whether to execute S or not. We don't perform the test B again until after doing the code S. That is, we repeat the DO-WHILE action (evaluate B and, if true, then do S) until we evaluate B and the result is false.

Note in our example that when J is 9, the test J < 10 suceeds. So, J = J + 1 sets J to 10 and we then execute SUM = SUM + A(J) even though the test J < 10 is now false. So, the DO-WHILE does not literally *do* something *while* a test is true. We do not continuously evaluate the test and exit at the very instant it fails.

With this explication of the DO-WHILE—unnecessary for most readers, we're sure—you should agree that our little PL/I program is correct. So, on exit from the code we would have the relation

$$\text{SUM} = \text{A}(1) + \text{A}(2) + \cdots + \text{A}(10) = \sum_{i=1}^{10} \text{A}(i) \text{ true}$$

assuming, say, A(1), • • •, A(10) each had a FIXED BINARY (31) value.

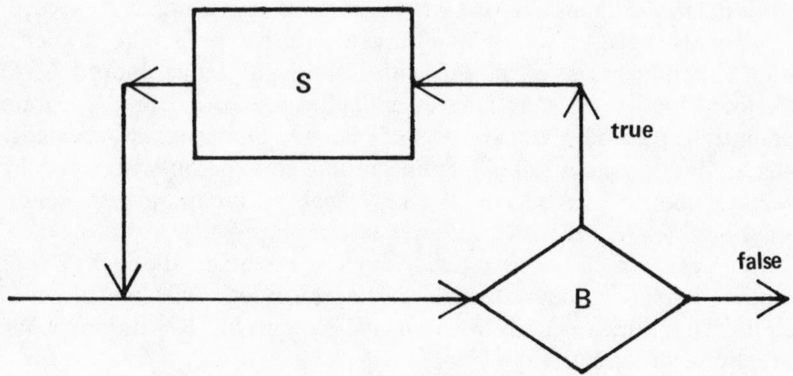

FIG. 2.1 The DO-WHILE flowchart

It is interesting that some initialization code like

```
J = 0;
SUM = 0;
```

is necessary. But we could, for example, replace this code with

```
J = 1;
SUM = A(1);
```

and the program would still be correct. Why is this? And more explicitly, how do you convince yourself that the code is indeed correct? To answer such questions in any meaningful way we must study the DO-WHILE construct further.

2.2 ANALYZING THE DO-WHILE

Programmers code slowly and computers execute quickly; these are basic facts of computer programming. Thus, repeated program execution is the basic justification for programming as an activity. Repetition —either the repeated use of a program or iteration within a program—is fundamental to the cost effectiveness of programming, for you can write some code once and yet have it executed many times. This exploits the relative speeds of the programmer and the computer. Examples of repetition in programming abound; we cite macros, subroutines, program loops, and library routines.

But infinite loops are one of the banes of programming. Accordingly, we also need the ability to terminate iterative computations when a cutoff situation arises. We do this with conditional testing. Indeed, C. A. R. Hoare has stated that "the essential feature of a stored program computer is the ability to execute some portion of a program repeatedly until a condition goes false."[3] Thus, in analyzing the DO-WHILE, we are focusing upon a construct at the very heart of programming—conditional iteration.

There is an interesting result from the mathematical theory of computation concerning the DO-WHILE construct. Dijkstra calls this result "The Fundamental Invariance Theorem for Repetition."[4] We paraphrase this result as follows:

> Let P and B be relations (in the PL/I sense), and let S be a sequence of program statements.
>
> *Assuming* whenever the relation P & B is true and we execute the sequence S we have that P is also true afterwards,
>
> *we can conclude* that if P is true and we execute the code
>
> ```
> DO WHILE(B);
>       S;
> END;
> ```
>
> then the relation P & ¬ B will be true upon exit (if ever) from the DO-WHILE.

To see how intuitively obvious this result is, consider the DO-WHILE flowchart in Fig. 2.2 with the relations filled in where they should hold. We call the relation P a *loop invariant*, since P is true (by assumption) before the DO-WHILE loop, P is also true after each execution of the statement sequence S, and finally P is true upon exit, if ever, from the DO-WHILE loop. (In fact, a stronger relation P & ¬ B is true.) So, the relation P remains true, or invariant, for the execution of the DO-WHILE.

Let's relate this notion of a loop invariant to the sample program of the preceding section. That program used a simple DO-WHILE loop to establish the relation

$$\text{SUM} = \sum_{i=1}^{10} \text{A}(i)$$

at the end of program execution. We take P, the loop invariant, to be the relation

$$\text{SUM} = \sum_{i=1}^{\text{J}} \text{A}(i)$$

and ¬B to be J = 10.

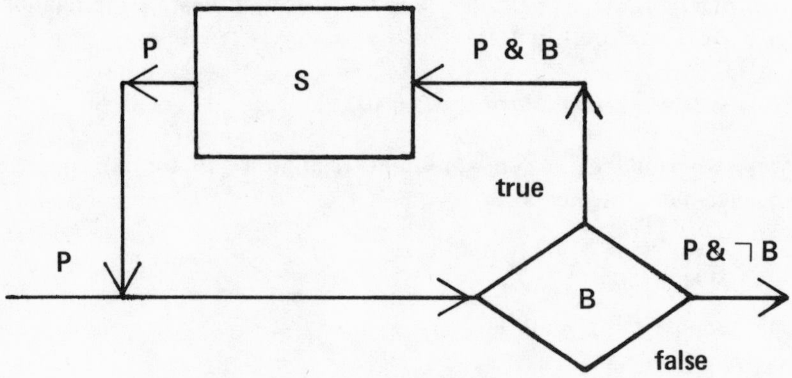

FIG. 2.2 The DO-WHILE invariance theorem

Clearly, the compound relation P & ¬B implies the intended result. Moreover, the initialization code

```
J = 0;
SUM = 0;
```

(vacuously) establishes the relation P, since

$$\begin{aligned} \text{SUM} &= \sum_{i=1}^{J} \text{A}(i) && \text{/* definition of P */} \\ &= \sum_{i=1}^{0} \text{A}(i) && \text{/* when J = 0 */} \\ &= 0 \end{aligned}$$

as does the alternative initialization code

```
J = 1;
SUM = A(1);
```

since here P is

$$\begin{aligned} \text{SUM} &= \sum_{i=1}^{J} \text{A}(i) && \text{/* definition of P */} \\ &= \sum_{i=1}^{1} \text{A}(i) && \text{/* when J = 1 */} \\ &= \text{A}(1) \end{aligned}$$

So, either set of initialization code does establish the relation P.

Now if P & B is true, will P be true after we execute the body of the

DO-WHILE loop? Well, we said $\neg$B is J = 10. So, B must be the relation J$\neg$= 10. Therefore P & B is

$$\text{SUM} = \sum_{i=1}^{J} A(i) \qquad \textit{and} \qquad J \neq 10$$

(*Note*: we could equivalently use the relation J<10 for B.) And the sequence S of statements is

```
J = J + 1;
SUM = SUM + A(J);
```

Let's suppose J = $j_0 \neq 10$ and

$$\text{SUM} = \sum_{i=1}^{j_0} A(i)$$

for some value j_0 between 0 and 9. Then, executing the two statements gives

$$J = j_0 + 1$$

and

$$\begin{aligned} \text{SUM} &= \sum_{i=1}^{j_0} A(i) + A(j_0 + 1) \\ &= \sum_{i=1}^{J} A(i) \qquad \text{which is the relation P} \end{aligned}$$

So, the conditions of the invariance theorem are met. Moreover, executing the statement J = J + 1 sufficiently often guarantees we will eventually exit the DO-WHILE loop with P & $\neg$B being true. This, we have seen, implies our intended result; so, our code is indeed correct.

Using the invariance theorem to show our simple PL/I code correct may seem like using a steamroller to crush a match. But we have an ulterior motive. We remarked that conditional iteration, such as the DO-WHILE construct, was at the core of computing. And the invariance theorem states a fundamental fact about the DO-WHILE. We intended to extract some detailed, practical guidelines for using the DO-WHILE in programming. These guidelines will be very widely applicable because basically they pertain to the use of conditional iteration.

2.3 GUIDELINES FOR USING THE DO-WHILE

Suppose we want the result R. In our previous example R was

$$\text{SUM} = \sum_{i=1}^{10} A(i)$$

We should try to find relations P and B so that the compound relation P & ¬B implies R. For our example we had P as

$$\text{SUM} = \sum_{i=1}^{J} A(i)$$

and B as $J \neq 10$. Then we write PL/I code of the form:

```
Establish P;      /* Initialization */
DO WHILE(B);
        Code which, if executed enough, will change B to ¬B;
        Code which makes P true in light of preceding code;
END;
```

Clearly, P is true before the DO-WHILE (by virtue of initialization); the code inside the loop keeps P true (by design) and also eventually makes ¬B true. So, the DO-WHILE loop will at some time terminate with the relation P & ¬B true. But this implies the desired result R. So, given a result we want to achieve by iteration, the real focus of invention and creation is on finding a loop invariant P and a while-test B such that P & ¬B implies the intended result.

These guidelines give us a truer and deeper perspective on conditional iteration. Some program variables will change their values during the execution of a loop (hence, the name "variables"). But we can best understand the intent of a particular program loop by knowing what the associated loop invariant is. Niklaus Wirth in his book *Systematic Programming* goes so far as to assert that "the lesson that every programmer should learn is that the explicit indication of the relevant invariant for each repetition represents the most valuable element in every program documentation."[5]

All programmers know that an iterated loop requires proper initialization. We can see now that proper initialization is simply establishing the loop invariant P to be true. The code within the loop serves two major purposes:

1. Guarantees that the loop will eventually terminate (i.e., the while-test B will become false).
2. Keeps the loop invariant P true.

So, we enter the loop with the condition P being true and we eventually exit the loop with the stronger condition P & ¬B being true.

Let's illustrate applying these DO-WHILE guidelines to produce a correct program fragment. Suppose we have two integer variables [say, FIXED BINARY (31,0)] DIVIDEND and DIVISOR satisfying the relations

```
DIVIDEND >= 0
DIVISOR >  0
```

and we want to assign values to the program variables QUOTIENT and REMAINDER so that we have the following result R is true:

```
(DIVIDEND = DIVISOR * QUOTIENT + REMAINDER) &
(0 <= REMAINDER) & (REMAINDER < DIVISOR)
```

This compound relation R is the usual definition of what we mean by the quotient and remainder of dividing one integer by another (nonzero) integer. We have expressed R using PL/I syntax. Using PL/I built-in functions, our task is relatively trivial. For we can write

```
QUOTIENT = DIVIDE(DIVIDEND,DIVISOR,31,0);
REMAINDER = MOD(DIVIDEND,DIVISOR);
```

But let's suppose further that we want to find the proper values for QUOTIENT and REMAINDER (i.e., values which satisfy the relation R) using only addition, subtraction, and iteration. We'll do this by following our own DO-WHILE guidelines.

First, we want to find a loop invariant P and a while-test B such that the relation P & ¬B implies the relation R. In fact, one of the best ways to obtain a loop invariant P is to weaken the intended result relation R. Let's do this. We take P to be the relation

```
(DIVIDEND = DIVISOR * QUOTIENT + REMAINDER) &
(0 <= REMAINDER)
```

Of course we want ¬B to be

```
(REMAINDER < DIVISOR)
```

So, then P & ¬B would certainly imply R since P & ¬B *is* R. Therefore, we take the while-test B to be

```
(REMAINDER ¬< DIVISOR)
```

or equivalently

```
(REMAINDER >= DIVISOR)
```

The *second step* is to establish the loop invariant P by initialization. We have been given values for DIVIDEND and DIVISOR (according to the problem statement). So, our initialization must assign values to the variables QUOTIENT and REMAINDER in a way that makes relation P true. We let

```
QUOTIENT = 0;
REMAINDER = DIVIDEND;
```

Then clearly the relation

```
(DIVIDEND = DIVISOR * QUOTIENT + REMAINDER)
```

is true. Also

```
(0 <= REMAINDER)
```

is true because initialization set REMAINDER to the value of DIVIDEND and we were given that

```
DIVIDEND >= 0
```

is true. So, the above initialization does indeed establish P, the loop invariant.

Our partially developed program now has the following form:

```
QUOTIENT = 0;
REMAINDER = DIVIDEND;
DO WHILE( REMAINDER >= DIVISOR );
        Code which if executed enough will eventually make
                ( REMAINDER < DIVISOR ) true;
        Code which makes P true in light of preceding code;
END;
```

The *third step* is to write code which guarantees that the loop will eventually terminate. If we are given that the while-test

```
(REMAINDER >= DIVISOR)
```

is true and we eventually want

```
(REMAINDER < DIVISOR)
```

to be true, then since the DIVISOR value is given and remains unchanged, we must reduce the value of REMAINDER. We select the obvious assignment

```
REMAINDER = REMAINDER - DIVISOR;
```

which, if executed enough, will make the while-test false. That is, we keep subtracting the DIVISOR from REMAINDER until we get

```
(REMAINDER < DIVISOR)
```

being true. And we always will, since we were given that

```
(DIVISOR > 0)
```

was initially true.

The *fourth and final step* is to write code which keeps the loop invariant P true after doing the assignment

```
REMAINDER = REMAINDER - DIVISOR;
```

We know the relation

```
(0 <= REMAINDER)
```

is true afterward, since the assignment is only executed if the while-test

```
(REMAINDER >= DIVISOR)
```

is true. So, we need only write code which keeps the relation

```
(DIVIDEND = DIVISOR * QUOTIENT + REMAINDER)
```

true after the assignment to REMAINDER.

Let's suppose we have association of values with variables shown in Fig. 2.3, and let's suppose the relation P is true. That is,

$$dd = dv * q + r \quad and \quad r \geqslant 0$$

For example, we might have $dd = 7$, $dv = 2$, $q = 2$ and $r = 3$ when finding the result of dividing 7 by 2. Let's further suppose that the while-test (REMAINDER >= DIVISOR) is true. That is, $r \geqslant dv$. After we execute the assignment to REMAINDER, we would have a new value, say that given in Fig. 2.4. Clearly, we must now assign a new value to QUOTIENT to keep the loop invariant true. We use the algebraic identity

$$\begin{aligned} dd &= dv * q + r \\ &= dv * (q + 1) + (r - dv) \end{aligned}$$

to infer that we should do the assignment

```
QUOTIENT = QUOTIENT + 1;
```

to keep the relation P true. So, our final code is

Variable	Value
DIVIDEND	dd
DIVISOR	dv
QUOTIENT	q
REMAINDER	r

FIG. 2.3 General form of variables and their values for finding true quotient and remainder

Variable	Value
REMAINDER	r–dv

FIG. 2.4 General snapshot of REMAINDER after assignment

```
QUOTIENT = 0;
REMAINDER = DIVIDEND;
DO WHILE( REMAINDER >= DIVISOR );
        REMAINDER = REMAINDER - DIVISOR;
        QUOTIENT = QUOTIENT + 1;
END;
```

We *know* this code is correct because we developed it directly from our DO-WHILE guidelines which, in turn, we obtained from the DO-WHILE invariance theorem.

We treated this simple example in some detail to emphasize a particular style of thinking. The invariance theorem provides a secure basis for our DO-WHILE guidelines. Accordingly, these guidelines express something fundamental about using conditional iteration in programming. And conditional iteration is the very heart of computing. We have seen that initialization code is not some afterthought, but basically it establishes some loop-invariant relation. And two major goals determine the purpose of code within a program loop, namely:

1. Guaranteeing that the iteration will eventually halt.
2. Maintaining the truth of some loop-invariant relation.

Moreover, the loop exit condition (the while-test) and the loop-invariant relation are directly linked to the intended result (of using the program loop).

We conclude this section by succinctly repeating the DO-WHILE guidelines: Given a desired result R expressed as a relation, find relations P and B such that P & ¬B implies R. Then write code with the general form

```
Establish P;     /* Initialization */
DO WHILE( B );
        Code which, if executed enough, eventually makes ¬B
            true;
        Code which keeps P true;
END;
```

2.4 FURTHER EXAMPLES OF LOOP INVARIANTS

This section gives some sample code containing loops and specifies the relevant loop invariants. We hope this small exercise in code reading will orient you toward correctness considerations. That is, we want you to convince yourself that careful reasoning about programs is a better guide to correctness than extensive testing. Here, this simply means checking the code from the perspective of the DO-WHILE guidelines rather than hand-simulating with sample data.

EXAMPLE 2.1. A function procedure which for a vector A (i.e., a one-dimensional array) of FLOAT values returns the maximum value of A's elements

Loop invariant:

$$M = MAX(A_{lbound}, A_{lbound+1}, \ldots, A_{ELT})$$

Clearly, when ELT is the upper bound of the array A, we will have M as the maximum of A's elements and we can then return M as the function result.

(In this example we use the PL/I built-in array manipulation functions LBOUND and HBOUND.)

```
VECTOR_MAX: PROC(A) RETURNS (FLOAT);
                         DCL   A(*)   FLOAT;
                         DCL   ELT   FIXED BIN,
                                 M  FLOAT;
                           ELT = LBOUND(A,1);
                           M = A(ELT);
                           DO WHILE( ELT < HBOUND(A,1) );
                              ELT = ELT + 1;
                              IF A(ELT) > M  THEN
                                     M = A(ELT);
                           END;
                           RETURN( M );
                  END VECTOR_MAX;
```

Note that we could insert alternative code with the *iterative*-DO replacing the DO-WHILE. For instance, we might use

```
M = A( LBOUND(A,1) );
DO ELT = LBOUND(A,1) + 1 TO HBOUND(A,1);
       M = MAX( M , A(ELT) );
END;
```

As we remarked, conditional iteration is at the very heart of programming. For this reason we studied the DO-WHILE construct in detail and developed some programming guidelines from it. The DO-WHILE served as a prototype for a central programming notion. In a sense, the ITERATIVE-DO is a frequently occurring special subcase of conditional iteration. Usually with the ITERATIVE-DO we march through some code with successive values of a control variable. So, we standardly have loop termination guaranteed and the exit condition given. This means we can realize the ITERATIVE-DO by using the DO-WHILE construct.

For example, the ITERATIVE-DO loop

```
DO VAR = START TO FINISH BY INCREMENT;
        statements;
END;
```

is equivalent to the DO-WHILE code

```
s = START; f = FINISH; i = INCREMENT;
VAR = s;
DO WHILE( (i >= 0 & VAR <= f) | (i< 0 & VAR >= f) );
        statements;
        VAR = VAR + i;
END;
```

Where *s,f,i* are variables with the proper attributes and do not appear elsewhere in the program. With this equivalence understood, we can consider relevant loop invariants for ITERATIVE-DO constructs.

EXAMPLE 2.2. A function procedure to do polynomial evaluation using Horner's method

The general polynomial

$$P(X) = C_N X^N + C_{N-1} X^{N-1} + \cdots + C_1 X + C_0 = \sum_{j=0}^{N} C_j X^j$$

is to be evaluated. The function POLY will be passed an array C(*) of floating point coefficients and a particular value for X. The code makes use of the identity

$$P(x) = (\ldots(C_N x + C_{N-1})x + C_{N-2})x + \ldots + C_1)x + C_0$$

which requires only N multiplications and N additions.

```
POLY: PROC(C,X) RETURNS(FLOAT);
          DCL  C(*) FLOAT,        /* COEFFICIENTS */
               X    FLOAT;
          DCL VALUE FLOAT,
               ( I , N ) FIXED BIN;
```

```
        N = HBOUND( C, 1 );
        VALUE = C( N );
        DO I = N-1 TO 0 BY -1;
           VALUE = VALUE * X + C( I );
        END;
        RETURN( VALUE );
    END POLY;
```

Here we assume the coefficient array has a lower bound of zero. The reader should check that the *loop invariant*:

$$\text{VALUE} = \sum_{j=\text{I}+1}^{\text{N}} \text{C}(j) * \text{X} ** (j - (\text{I}+1))$$

is true after the initialization

```
VALUE = C( N );
I = N - 1;
```

and is kept true by the assignments

```
VALUE = VALUE * X + C( I );
I = I - 1;
```

in the above order. Note that on exit from the ITERATIVE-DO the value of the variable I is −1 and with the loop invariant being true we have that VALUE = P(X).

EXAMPLE 2.3: Linear search of a table; set DATA to found value or to null string
Suppose we have the following table:

```
DCL  1 TABLE(N),
       2 KEY  CHAR(5),
       2 DATA  CHAR(50);
```

which has been properly initialized. We use the variables

```
DCL   KEY   CHAR(5),          /* TO BE LOOKED UP  */
      DATA   CHAR(50),        /* RESULT OF SEARCH */
      I  FIXED BIN;           /* LOOP INDEX */
```

and assume KEY has been assigned a value for which TABLE is to be searched.

```
I = 1;
DO WHILE( I <= N & KEY ¬= TABLE.KEY(I) );
      I = I + 1;
END;
```

```
IF I <= N
        THEN DATA = TABLE.DATA(I);
        ELSE DATA = '';
```

Here the first three lines of code could be replacd by

```
DO I = 1 TO N WHILE( KEY ¬= TABLE.KEY(I) );
```

and in either case we have the

loop invariant: KEY ¬= TABLE.KEY(j) for $1 \leqq j \leqq$ I − 1

So, when we exit the loop, the while-test is false. This means either I = N + 1 and the KEY is not in the TABLE or

```
KEY = TABLE.KEY(I)
```

and this is the first occurrence of the KEY.

EXAMPLE 2.4: Bisection search of an ordered table (increasing order); set DATA to found value or to null string (also set MATCH to table index of found value or to zero)

We have the declarations:

```
DCL 1 TABLE(N),
      2 KEY FIXED BIN,
      2 DATA CHAR(50);
DCL KEY FIXED BIN,
    DATA CHAR(50),
    (LOW,MID,HIGH,MATCH) FIXED BIN;
```

and we again assume that TABLE has been initialized and KEY has a value to be looked up.

```
MATCH = 0;
LOW = 1;
HIGH = N;
DO WHILE( LOW <= HIGH & MATCH = 0 );
        MID = (LOW + HIGH) / 2;
        IF KEY = TABLE.KEY(MID)
           THEN MATCH = MID;
           ELSE IF KEY < TABLE.KEY(MID)
              THEN HIGH = MID - 1;
              ELSE LOW = MID + 1;
END;
IF MATCH > 0
        THEN DATA = TABLE.DATA(MATCH);
        ELSE DATA = '';
```

Here we have

loop invariant: TABLE is sorted *and* TABLE.KEY (LOW : HIGH) is the part of the table remaining to be examined for an occurrence of KEY *and* TABLE.KEY(1:LOW – 1) and TABLE.KEY(HIGH + 1:N) do not contain KEY

To verify the above code it is perhaps best to obviate concern over the vagaries of PL/I's fixed-point division operator by replacing the first statement in the loop body with

```
MID = DIVIDE( LOW + HIGH , 2 , 15 , 0 );
```

at some loss in reading clarity. Note that on exit from the DO-WHILE loop the while-test is false. That is, either LOW > HIGH or MATCH ≠ 0. In conjunction with the loop invariant this means either KEY is not in the table or KEY appears at TABLE.KEY(MATCH) *and* LOW ≦ MATCH ≦ HIGH (in fact, MATCH is the MID point). So, the loop invariant and the while-test being false imply the intended result. The reader should check that the remaining features of the DO-WHILE guidelines are satisfied.

Specifically, the guidelines require that initializing code establishes the loop invariant, the truth of the loop invariant is preserved by execution of the loop body, and executing the loop body iteratively eventually makes the while-test false.

EXAMPLE 2.5: leftmost (prefix) order tree search; return pointer to found node or null pointer

We want a function procedure which takes a pointer to a tree and a KEY, then does a leftmost search of the tree for the KEY and returns the appropriate pointer value.

To make the tree to be searched very general, we use PL/I's REFER option in a self-defining based structure. In this way the number of subnodes can vary with each node in the tree. For example, the procedure in which the tree is built might contain the declaration.

```
DCL   1 NODE BASED( NEW_NODE ),
        2 KEY CHAR(5),
        2 DATA CHAR(50),
        2 #SUBNODES FIXED BIN,
        2 SUBNODES( #BRANCHES REFER( #SUBNODES ) ) PTR;
DCL   #BRANCHES FIXED BIN;
```

So, each node of the tree will have a 5-character key or name, a 50-character data value, an indicator of the number of subnodes (i.e., the value of #SUBNODES), and an array of pointers to the respective subnodes.

To form a new node with, say, 7 subnodes we would write

```
#BRANCHES = 7;
ALLOCATE NODE;
```

which when executed uses 7 as the array bound for SUBNODES and assigns 7 to #SUBNODES. All subsequent references to this NODE now pointed to by NEW_NODE (including the statement FREE NODE;) use the value of #SUBNODES to determine the size of the SUBNODES array. For this reason the structure NODE is said to be self-defining. The structure of a tree NODE is represented in Fig. 2.5.

Suppose a tree built up of such nodes is pointed to by the pointer variable TREE and the variable NAME has a 5-character value. Then we want a function procedure SEARCH such that the call SEARCH(TREE,NAME) returns a pointer to the first (in a leftmost ordering of the tree) NODE whose KEY equals NAME if there is such a node in the tree. If NAME is not in the tree, then SEARCH should return the null pointer.

Our tree search program is:

```
SEARCH:
    PROC(ROOT,KEY) RETURNS(PTR) RECURSIVE;
        DCL ROOT PTR,
            KEY CHAR(5);
        DCL 1 NODE BASED(ROOT),
              2 KEY   CHAR(5),
              2 DATA  CHAR(50),
              2 #SUBNODES  FIXED BIN,
              2 SUBNODES( DUMMY REFER( #SUBNODES ) ) PTR;
        DCL MATCH PTR,
            I FIXED BIN,
            DUMMY FIXED BIN STATIC;
          MATCH = NULL;
          IF ROOT ¬= NULL THEN
            IF KEY = NODE.KEY
              THEN MATCH = ROOT;
              ELSE DO I = 1 TO   #SUBNODES
                                 WHILE( MATCH = NULL);
                  MATCH = SEARCH( SUBNODES(I) , KEY );
                  END;
          RETURN( MATCH );
    END SEARCH;
```

In giving this example, we do not expect that all readers are familiar with either the REFER option or even with RECURSIVE procedures. Rather, we just want to show a simple loop invariant for some very general code; at the same time we offer a nice illustration of the utility of these features.

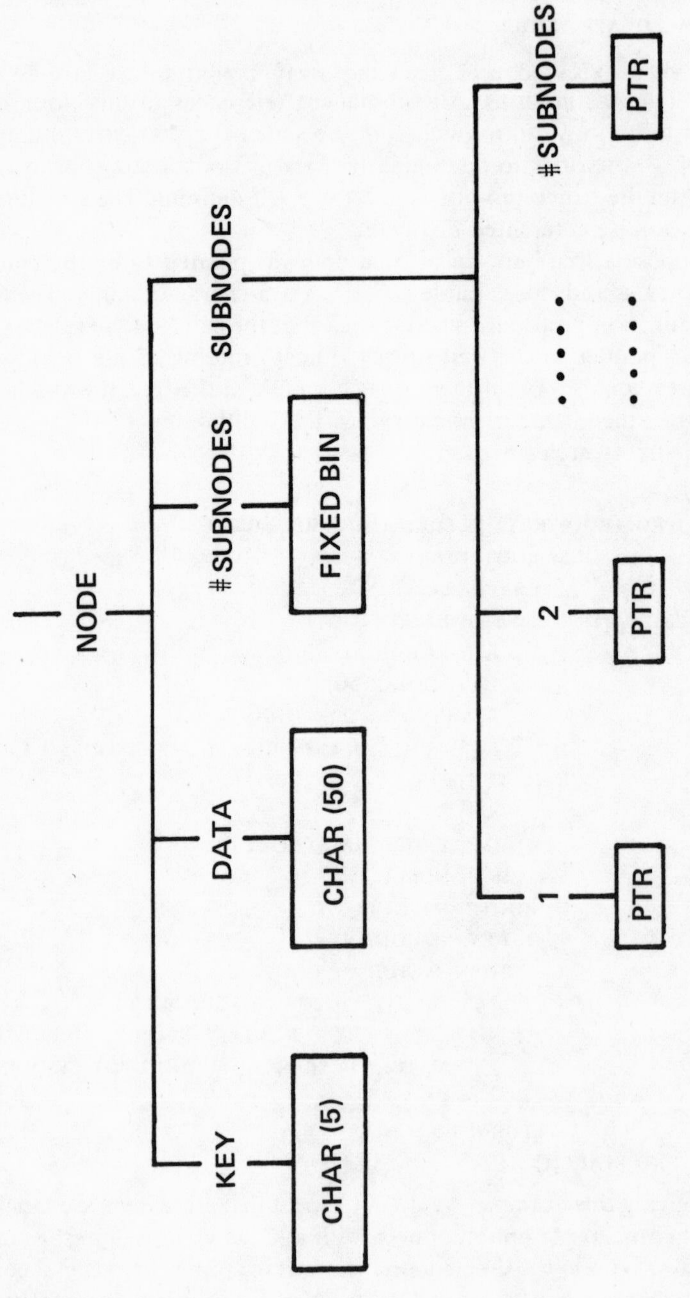

FIG. 2.5 Structure of a node for the tree to be searched

For the loop in the SEARCH procedure we have

loop invariant: subtree pointed to by SUBNODES(j) does not contain a node with the proper KEY value for $1 \leqq j \leqq \text{I} - 1$.

Since recursion is used, more than just the DO-WHILE guidelines must be satisfied for guaranteeing code correctness. For recursion is yet another way of doing iterative computations. In this case we should also check that

1. When called with a NULL pointer as its first argument, SEARCH terminates and returns a NULL pointer value (this is immediate from the code).
2. Assuming SEARCH terminates with the proper result for all trees of depth k, we should verify that SEARCH then will terminate properly for trees of depth $k + 1$.

Notice that whether we are reasoning about the DO-WHILE construct or about RECURSIVE procedures, we must do a form of inductive reasoning about our programs. One major advantage of clear, functional code is that we can understand it better and hence we can more easily reason about it. We want this perspective on program correctness to influence the way we construct programs as well as the way we analyze them.

3. PROGRAM CORRECTNESS AND STRUCTURED PROGRAMS

Experience confirms that almost any sensible set of programming conventions, when adopted by a software group, will improve the eventual product. Some standards and criteria—even if somewhat arbitrary—are better than none. Top-down structured programming is a specific methodology for producing extremely reliable software. It has had some dramatic real-world successes.

This methodology developed out of reflections upon the computing process and, in fact, has a mathematical basis. Accordingly, structured programming is much more than an arbitrary set of conventions that improve programmer performance. It does indeed work, but why it works is neither an accident nor an obscure mystery. And writing structured programs is certainly not some arcane art accessible only to the anointed.

As a prelude and a partial justification for the methodology, this chapter presents some elementary notions, facts, and techniques. It introduces the concept of a function to explain more precisely what is meant by a program being correct. It also considers some basic programming flow-of-control features such as the DO-WHILE. Then we can clearly specify what we mean by a "structured program." We indicate that one can write a structured program in any computer language; we illustrate this assertion by building various structured flow-of-control figures in FORTRAN and in COBOL.

3.1 FUNCTIONS AND PROGRAM CORRECTNESS

A programming project properly starts with specifications. These specifications detail the kind of input data the program must process and the type of output desired. Viewed more generally, the specifications define a function, as shown in Fig. 3.1. In fact, we often refer to them as a program's functional specifications. They designate what a program should do, not how a program is to realize the correspondence between input and output. Functional specifications tell us, in effect, for any given input element what the corresponding output element should be. Here we take input and output in a very general sense. An input element is not just a particular argument value but also particular values for any accessible data (for example, global variables, the data base). Similarly, an output element is the total result of meeting the functional specifications for a particular input element. An output element thus could consist of more than just a value returned. For instance, changes in global variables and the data base might be part of a specified output. In summary, "input" refers to *what a function "knows"* and "output" refers to *what a function does*—its total effect.

To understand more fully what a program's functional specifications must be we turn to the mathematical notion of a "function." Mathematicians define a function to be a set of ordered pairs, say

$$F = \{(x_1,y_1), (x_2,y_2), \ldots\}$$

such that if (x,y) is in F and (x',y') is in F and $x = x'$, then $y = y'$. When (x,y) is in F, we usually write $F(x) = y$. For example, we might define a function COACH by

COACH = {(Redskins, Allen), (Cowboys, Landry), (Dolphins, Shula), . . . }

For COACH to be a true function we require, for instance, that every pair in COACH with "Redskins" as a first component has "Allen" as its second component. Then COACH is a simple table look-up function.

We call the set of first members of a function the *domain* and the set of second members the *range*.

$$\text{domain of } F = \{x_1,x_2, \ldots\}$$
$$\text{range of } F = \{y_1,y_2, \ldots\}$$

In our example,

domain of COACH = {Redskins, Cowboys, Dolphins,. . . }
range of COACH = {Allen, Landry, Shula,. . . }

Clearly, the domain of a function is the set of possible inputs (in our general sense) and the range is the set of possible outputs. To specify a particular function, we must give more than just the domain and the

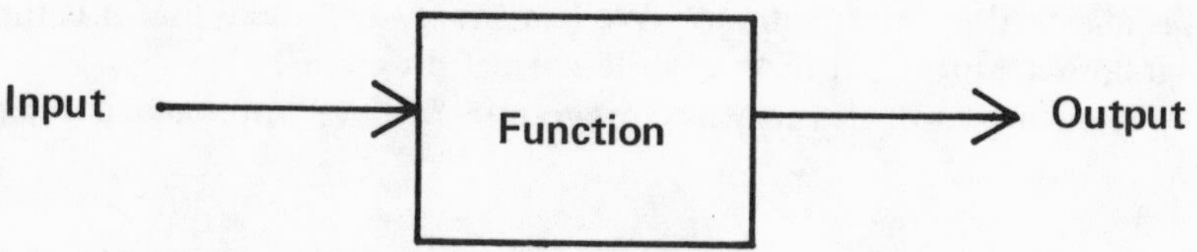

FIG. 3.1 Program specifications as a function

range; we must also give the correspondence between input elements and output elements. If we were slavishly to follow the mathematical definition of a function, we would list each possible input element paired with its appropriate output element. This is feasible when the domain is small, as in the example function COACH. However, most interesting functions have a very large domain. So, as an alternative to such a listing, mathematicians give a *rule of correspondence* between domain elements and range elements.

For example, we might write

domain of SQUARE = positive integers
range of SQUARE contained in the positive integers
rule : SQUARE $(x) = x^2$
for any positive integer x

instead of

SQUARE = {(1,1), (2,4), (3,9), (4,16), . . . }

to define a function SQUARE.

A computer program is a realization of a function. When we need a program written to do something, we should first give functional specifications for the desired program. And functional specifications for a program—since they are, in effect, defining a function—must contain at a minimum the domain, the range, and a rule of correspondence. The same also applies to the specification of subroutines, modules, and so on.

It is the programmer's task to start with the specifications of some function F and then to construct a program P which realizes the specifications. We know every program computes some function. That is, each program has a domain of inputs (perhaps empty), a range of outputs (perhaps empty or useless), and a rule of correspondence in the sense that we always get the same output each time we give the same input. Since each program implements some function, let's denote the function that program P realizes by $[P]$. Given specifications of a function F, we say program P is a *correct program* for F if the function

[*P*] is identical to the function *F*. We can simply say, then, that it is the programmer's principal task to write correct programs.

There are two classic ways programmers have approached their task:

1. *Bottom-up:* starting with simple functions (programs) and building up more complex functions until finally constructing *F*.
2. *Top-down:* starting with *F*'s specifications and repeatedly breaking down functions into simpler functions until reaching easily coded functions.

The bottom-up approach is essentially a synthesizing activity, while the focus when proceeding top-down is upon analysis.

Top-down structured programming specifies the ways you can analyze or break down a function. These "ways" quite naturally are those we best understand. For these we can give detailed guidelines to use during the programming process, as we have done with the DO-WHILE. In the next section we consider some basic ways for breaking a function into simpler functions.

3.2 THE THREE BASIC FIGURES

In designing a program from its functional specifications, programmers sometimes symbolize an algorithm by a flowchart. The flowchart presents a graphic recipe for computing some function. If done correctly, the flowcharted function *is* the very same function given by the program's specifications.

The neat, boxed format for flowcharts often misleads and deceives the programmer. Flow lines crossing and boxes with multiple entries or multiple exits can cook up a spaghetti bowl of control logic. Programs embodying such involuted logic are exceedingly difficult to understand and to check out. They are virtually impossible to modify correctly.

The phrase "top-down structured programming," as used in this book, refers to a particular methodology for program design and construction. At every stage of the program creation process, it gives definite guidelines to answer "What should I do next?" and "Is the program I'm writing correct so far?" The entire programming process becomes more systematic and more manageable simply by making these questions and their answers explicit.

Such benefits obviously cost something. The "cost" of top-down structured programming is a restriction on how programmers may control the execution of statements. In other words, we make programs and their flowcharts more intellectually manageable by limiting the ways they can be composed. Specifically, we confine the flow-of-control through a program to combinations of only three types:

1. Executing statements sequentially.
2. Selecting the next statement based on a test.
3. Conditional iteration.

You construct a structured program by repeatedly using only these three basic forms of composition.

Notably, this excludes the GO TO or explicit transfer of control from the programmer's repertoire (except as needed to implement the three basic types). At first encounter the banishing of such a fundamental computing operation seems strange. After all, branching instructions are an integral part of every machine and assembly language. However, there are several solid reasons for advocating GO TO-less programming. We cite the following:

- Unrestricted use of the GO TO encourages jumping around within programs, making them difficult to read and difficult to follow.
- The GO TO is unnecessary as a programming language construct in the sense that any flow-chartable control logic can be realized without using the GO TO and using only the three basic types. (We indicate this in Section 3.5.)
- The GO TO refers explicitly to a program text via its label (or destination); accordingly, it militates against functional thinking (i.e., domain, range, rule of correspondence) and thus against reasoning about a program's correctness.
- Many who have started programming without the GO TO (and often with some structured programming methodology) have noticed a marked improvement in their thinking, their productivity, and their programs.

Let's now give a particular flowchart for each of the three flow-of-control types, starting with the SEQUENCE flowchart shown in Fig. 3.2.

These three basic flowchart figures can be expressed directly in PL/I code. As we will see, this enables us to merge the design process with the coding process. Clearly, the PL/I programs produced in this way will have no GO TO's. Thus it is easy to read such programs sequentially—from top to bottom—without jumping around. This fol-

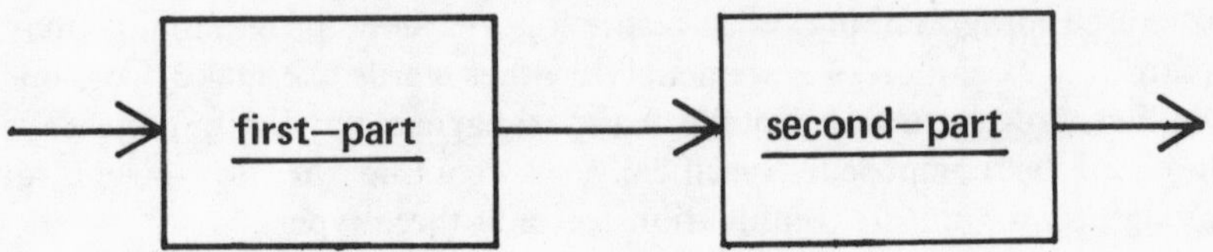

FIG. 3.2 The SEQUENCE figure

lows from the single-entry/single-exit property of the basic figures. The programmer can better understand the relationship between his PL/I program text and the computation invoked.

Note the function boxes FIRST-PART, SECOND-PART, THEN-PART, ELSE-PART, and DO-PART in the basic flowcharts. If we were to take some function *F* and recast it into an IF-THEN-ELSE flowchart (Fig. 3.3), then we would have broken (analyzed, elaborated, factored, refined) *F* into two subfunctions corresponding to the THEN-PART and the ELSE-PART of the figure. To do *F* now, we would use one or the other subfunction, depending on the result of the IF-TEST.

Similar remarks apply to refining a function *F* into a SEQUENCE or a DO-WHILE figure (Fig. 3.4).

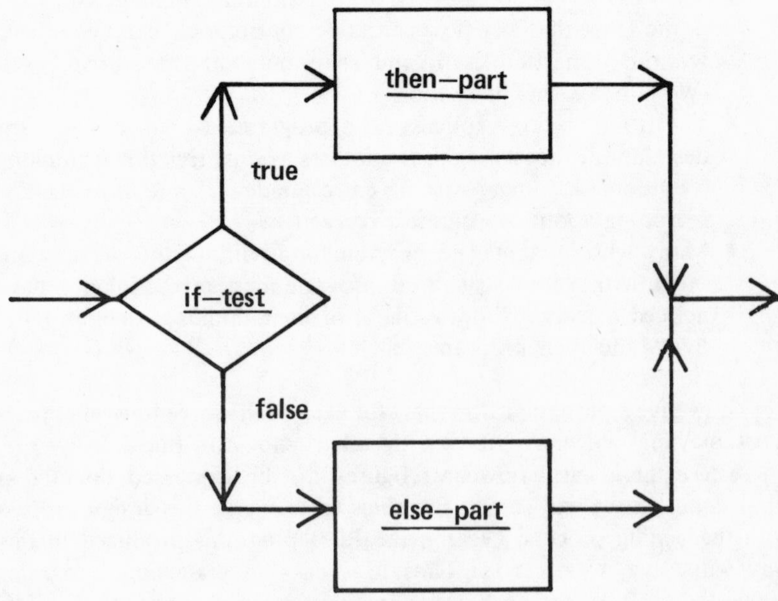

FIG. 3.3 The IF-THEN-ELSE figure

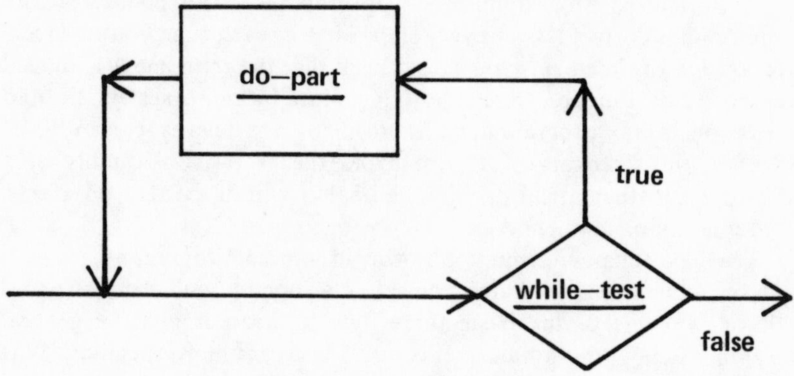

FIG. 3.4 The DO-WHILE figure

For now, we define a *structured program* to be any program whose flowchart we can get by the repeated use of only the three basic flowchart figures. *Top-down structured programming* is a methodology for producing structured programs. It starts with the original functional specifications and, proceeding in a step-by-step fashion, repeatedly refines a function into subfunctions. At every step you select some function and refine it into one of the three basic figures. The refinement process continues until actual programming language statements can express all remaining subfunctions. Refinement is an expansion process: It fills in details and goes from functional specifications toward program code.

"What should I do next?" We can now give a preliminary answer to this question. Select a function *F* for further development. Elaborate *F* either (1) by coding *F* directly into PL/I statements, or (2) by replacing *F* with a refinement using one of the three basic figures. You start this process with the program's functional specifications and repeat it until only PL/I code remains.

3.3 CORRECTNESS GUIDELINES: QUESTIONS AND ANSWERS

Whenever you code some function, you always informally convince yourself that the code you wrote actually is the same function-in-question. Every programmer does this. But since programmers spend almost half their time debugging, they evidently find themselves too persuasive. The pertinent question, "Is my program correct so far?" needs recasting to be useful.

In structured programming you informally—but explicitly—verify the program's correctness at every step. That is, each time you replace a function by a refinement, you must check that the refinement is indeed the very same function. Such verifying must be more systematic and more explicit than programmers, left to their own devices, currently do. However, this checking must also avoid the excessive formality of a full-fledged mathematical proof. The goal is writing correct programs, not doing minor mathematics.

We have characterized top-down structured programming as an analysis activity. At every step you refine a function either directly into code or into one of the basic three figures. Accordingly, the general question, "Is my program correct so far?" becomes more specific: "Was my last refinement correct?"

We can obtain useful guidelines to refinement correctness by associating detailed questions (or a checklist) with each basic figure. When you refine a function into a basic figure, you are basically realizing a given function in terms of subfunctions. So, we will express refinement correctness as a relation between these subfunctions and the given function.

For example, suppose *F* is a given function and we refine *F* into the SEQUENCE shown in Fig. 3.5.

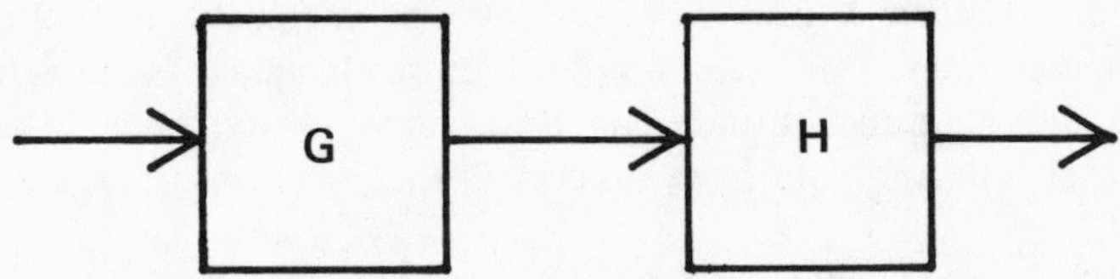

FIG. 3.5 SEQUENCE refinement of *F*

Then we should ask ourselves, "Does *G* followed by *H* do *F*?" This is the standard SEQUENCE correctness question; we should ask and answer it each time we do a SEQUENCE type of refinement. Figure 3.6 illustrates such simple function refinement.

<u>function name:</u> COMPUTE-NET-PAY

<u>domain:</u> HOURLY_WAGE, HOURS_WORKED, DEDUCTIONS

<u>range:</u> NET_PAY

<u>rule-of-correspondence:</u>

NET_PAY = HOURLY_WAGE * HOURS_WORKED − DEDUCTIONS

FIG. 3.6 Specifications of COMPUTE-NET-PAY function

Suppose we decide to refine the function of COMPUTE-NET-PAY first by a SEQUENCE figure and then into code. We create a new variable GROSS-PAY to link the first part of the sequence with the second part. We get

```
GROSS_PAY = HOURLY_WAGE * HOURS_WORKED;
NET_PAY   = GROSS_PAY     - DEDUCTIONS;
```

Now we pose the correctness question:

> "Does the assignment
> GROSS_PAY = HOURLY_WAGE * HOURS_WORKED;
> followed by the assignment
> NET_PAY = GROSS_PAY − DEDUCTIONS;
> do the function COMPUTE-NET-PAY?"

A quick check of the specifications for the function COMPUTE-NET-PAY should compel you to answer "yes." So, the SEQUENCE refinement, which introduced a new intermediate variable, is correct. We must also declare the variable GROSS_PAY if this use is its first occurrence.

This example is quite trivial. But whenever you do a SEQUENCE refinement of a given function, you should ask and answer the SEQUENCE correctness question:

> "Does the first-part of the sequence followed by the second-part do the given function?"

If the answer is immediate, fine—you don't have to spend much thought at this part of the developing program. But the way to write correct programs is to check for correctness at every step of the program development. SEQUENCE refinements are often where interfaces occur in large programs. An important SEQUENCE decision is often what the form of interface information between the first-part and the second-part should be. In our trivial example we interfaced the two parts via the variable GROSS_PAY.

When we refine a function *F* into the SEQUENCE of "*G* followed by *H*," the principal creative choice is in what the function *G* should be. For once we have picked a function *G* this will determine what the function *H* is, if the SEQUENCE refinement is to be correct.

Similarly, when we do an IF-THEN-ELSE refinement of a function *F*, say into

```
IF  B
    THEN  G;
    ELSE  H;
```

the choice of the test B fully determines what the functions G and H will be. So, our essential decision when doing an IF-THEN-ELSE refinement is how to partition the function *F*.

The IF-THEN-ELSE correctness question is straightforward:

> "When B is true, does G do *F*, *and* when B is false, does H do *F*?"

Let's consider the function given in Fig. 3.7.

<u>function-name</u>: ABSOLUTE-VALUE
<u>domain</u>: X
<u>range</u>: Z
<u>rule-of-correspondence</u>: Z = |X|
(i.e., Z equals the magnitude of X expressed as a nonnegative value)

FIG. 3.7 Specifications of ABSOLUTE-VALUE function

If we do an IF-THEN-ELSE refinement into the code,

```
IF   X >= 0
  THEN   Z = X;
  ELSE   Z = -X;
```

then we should ask ourselves the correctness question:

> "When $X \geq 0$ does the assignment [Z = X;] realize the ABSOLUTE-VALUE function, *and* when X < 0 does the assignment [Z = −X;] realize the ABSOLUTE-VALUE function?"

Clearly the answers are "yes." So, our IF-THEN-ELSE refinement of the ABSOLUTE-VALUE function is indeed correct. Note that the test ($X \geq 0$) determined what the then-part and the else-part assignments should be. In most cases, when we refine a function, we are not yet at the PL/I code level. But the correctness questions still apply.

Thus far we have restricted top-down structured programming to successively refining functions into basic figures. To ensure program correctness, we have associated a simple correctness question with the SEQUENCE and the IF-THEN-ELSE figure. After refining a function into one of these figures, you should ask yourself the associated correctness question. For uniformity we require correctness questions associated with the DO-WHILE figure.

In Chapter 2 we analyzed the DO-WHILE figure in considerable detail and obtained some specific programming guidelines. We now rephrase these as five DO-WHILE correctness questions. Let P denote the loop invariant and let B stand for the while-test. Our five questions are:

1. What is P?
2. Is P true before executing the DO-WHILE?
3. Does P & ¬B imply the desired output result (generally obtained from the rule-of-correspondence)?
4. If B and P are true and we execute the loop body once, will P still be true afterward?
5. If we execute the loop body enough times, will the test B eventually be false (i.e., will we eventually exit the loop)?

As we have seen, an affirmative answer to questions 2, 3, 4, and 5 guarantees a correct DO-WHILE refinement. And the solution to 1 is the creative part, the essence of the DO-WHILE construct.

Note that if we do not use recursive procedures in building a structured program from the basic figures, then the only looping in our program comes from the DO-WHILE figure. And if every time we refine a function into a DO-WHILE we can with certainty answer "yes" to question 5, then we are systematically guaranteeing that our program will *never* get into an infinite loop.

The specific correctness questions and the termination question for the DO-WHILE provide step-by-step guidelines for writing correct programs which always halt. By restricting yourself to only single-entry/single-exit flow-of-control forms and by answering the associated correctness questions, you must think more deeply during program creation. This in itself is good. But the end product—well structured, correct, easier-to-read programs—more than compensates you for the "cost" of extra, explicit, directed thinking.

Top-down structured programming answers important questions concerning the programming process. "What should I do next?" Pick a function. If you cannot code it directly, then select one of the basic flow-of-control forms: SEQUENCE, IF-THEN-ELSE, or DO-WHILE. Refine the function into the selected form. "Is the program correct so far?" With each refinement ask and answer the associated correctness questions. If the answers are "yes," then the program is indeed correct so far. A "no" answer means the proposed refinement should be thrown out. "Will the program ever get into a infinite loop?" Not if we guarantee that the WHILE-TEST will eventually be false for every DO-WHILE we write.

Undeniably, you must invest extra thought and effort to repeatedly pose such questions. But considerations of correctness properly belong in the design and coding phases. For the goal of programming is to write correct programs—not to finally finish debugging. Surprisingly, this is a realistic and practical goal.

3.4 TOP-DOWN STRUCTURED PROGRAMMING: A FIRST GLIMPSE

Top-down structured programming is more than a general approach that makes some good programming practices explicit; it is a systematic methodology, so much so that we can define top-down structured programming itself by means of a pseudo-program. To be sure, such a pseudo-program can only be executed by programmers. But we then have a step-by-step discipline for the programming process—a sort of "how to" write correct programs.

We define top-down structured programming by the following pseudo-program:

```
/* TOP-DOWN STRUCTURED PROGRAMMING */
   "Get initial program specifications as a function";
   DO WHILE ("a function remains to be refined");
         "Select a function, call it F, which remains to be refined";
         IF "you can code F directly in PL/I" THEN
            DO;
               "Code F into a sequence of PL/I statements";
               "Check that these statements are really equivalent to F";
               /* THIS CHECK SHOULD BE IMMEDIATE */
            END;
         ELSE
            DO;
               "Refine F using one of the 3 basic figures";
               "Answer the appropriate correctness questions";
               IF "all your answers are OK" THEN
                     "Replace F by the refinement you did";
            END;
   END;
```

This pseudo-program succinctly captures the fundamental ideas: Each programming step is just an explicit choice from several alternatives. Later, we will give additional criteria for making refinement selections or design decisions. We will also extend the selection range of figures to include, for instance, the ITERATIVE-DO. But the modus operandi will remain intact.

Clearly, this methodology merges the design and the coding process.

It is also clear that the "outputs" of this pseudo-program will differ greatly according to the individual programmers who execute it. Some programs will be clearer and more efficient than others. For there are a number of design and coding decisions involved in constructing a program. This methodology makes such decisions explicit. And it restricts the choices to intellectually manageable ones where we can check correctness at every step. So, although the "outputs" will differ with the programmers, all of the "outputs" should be correct, structured programs. Such a process guarantees structured programs by restricting the flow-of-control choices. And it guarantees program correctness as it proceeds, not as an afterthought following completion of the code.

Let's now apply this top-down structured programming process to constructing a correct program. We have selected a simplified line editor to illustrate in some detail this step-by-step-refinement method of programming. The problem is as follows: Write a PL/I program fragment to process a sequence of characters from some logical record. The program produces an output line and the line's length. Each input character is:

1. An *end-of-line character,* meaning exit the code with the output line

   LINE(1),LINE(2), . . . ,LINE(LENGTH)

   consisting of the first LENGTH entries in the single character array LINE( ).
2. A *delete-line character,* meaning ignore the sequence of characters processed to this point and reset LENGTH to zero.
3. A *regular character* to be placed directly into the output line being stored in the array LINE( ).

We assume that the array LINE( ), which acts as a buffer, is declared large enough for any logical record. So, if we keep putting characters into LINE( ), we won't overflow, exceeding the array's upper bound. And if we reach the end of the finite logical record, which contains the input character sequence, then we assume the transmission of an end-of-line character.

The problem specification refers to some information external to the desired code, namely: the array LINE( ), the LENGTH variable for the current line length, the end-of-line character, and the delete-line character. We precisely reflect this (interface) information by assuming the code we write is within the scope of the following declaration:

```
DECLARE

        DELETE_LINE_CHAR
              CHARACTER(1)
              INITIAL('#'),

        END_OF_LINE_CHAR
              CHARACTER(1)
              INITIAL('/'),

        LENGTH
              FIXED BINARY,

        LINE (line-width)
              CHARACTER(1)
;
```

Here, we again assume *line-width* is large enough for the logical record containing the input data. For illustration purposes, we take '#' as the delete-line character and '/' as the end-of-line character.

For example, the sequence of characters between quote marks

"A QUICK BROWN#FOX JUMPED OVER THE #LAZY DOGS/"

taken as input should, upon output, result in LINE( ) and LENGTH having the values

```
LINE(1) = 'L'
LINE(2) = 'A'
LINE(3) = 'Z'
LINE(4) = 'Y'
LINE(5) = ' '
LINE(6) = 'D'
LINE(7) = 'O'
LINE(8) = 'G'
LINE(9) = 'S'
LENGTH = 9
```

We can say nothing—and can assume nothing—about array elements LINE(INDEX) where INDEX > LENGTH. The initial program specifications are now complete and (hopefully) clear.

The structured programming process starts when we "get initial program specifications as a function." We can write the specification given in Fig. 3.8.

function name: *process-character-sequence*
domain:
(i) input: a sequence of characters from a logical record; each character is
(1) an end-of-line character, or
(2) a delete-line character, or
(3) a regular character for the array LINE( )
(ii)global data: the declared variables DELETE_LINE_CHAR, END_OF_LINE_CHAR, LENGTH and the single character array LINE( ) which is declared large enough to hold any logical record.
range: a line, whose length is LENGTH, consisting of the first LENGTH entries in the array LINE( ), i.e., LINE(1),LINE(2), . . . ,LINE(LENGTH)
rule-of-correspondence:
The output line is the longest sequence of regular input characters (i.e., type (3) input) which immediately precede the first END_OF_LINE_CHAR. (Recall: we assume at least one such character at the end of the logical record.)

FIG. 3.8 Functional specifications for *process-character-sequence*

What do we do next? Answer: Refine the function *process-character-sequence* using one of the three basic figures. Such a choice reflects a conscious design decision for the program we are writing. We consider whether we now want to refine the function into (1) a sequence of actions, (2) a test and conditional actions, or (3) the repetition of some action. We should, in general, investigate the ramifications of each choice for the ease of answering the appropriate correctness questions, the ease of doing further refinements, the "naturalness" of the refinement, and so on.

When our task is to process a sequence of data items, we usually refine this into conditional iteration. That is, we often process the input sequence item by item until we are done. Clearly, we need some way of getting the next character from the input sequence. But the exact nature of the input record and the format of the data have not been specified.

So, we will assume that we have a function procedure GET_A_CHAR which returns a single character of type 1, 2, or 3 each time we call it. That is, we have

```
GET_A_CHAR: PROCEDURE RETURNS (CHARACTER(1));
                  Body of procedure;
                  END GET_A_CHAR;
```

with the specifications, as illustrated in Fig. 3.9.

<u>function name</u>: GET_A_CHAR, a PL/I function procedure
<u>domain</u>: a sequence of characters from a logical record;
each character is
(1) an end-of-line, or
(2) a delete-line, or
(3) a regular
character. The last character in the sequence (i.e., the end of the logical record) is an end-of-line character.
<u>range</u>: the function returns a character of type (1), (2), or (3) with each call
<u>rule-of-correspondence</u>: GET_A_CHAR returns the next character in the input sequence (i.e., the first character on the first call, the second character on the second call, . . .)

FIG. 3.9 Functional specifications for GET_A_CHAR

Note the specifications for GET_A_CHAR are incomplete because we have not explicitly detailed either the logical input record or the data format. At some later point, when we decide upon such specifics, we can appropriately augment GET_A_CHAR's specifications. That is, in general we obtain both the program and the data representations by the refinement process. We introduced the procedure GET_A_CHAR to hide and to isolate the effect of later data representation decisions from our developing program for the function *process-character-sequence*.

We have decided to refine the function *process-character-sequence* into a DO-WHILE figure. So, we must determine an appropriate loop-invariant. Now a function's rule of correspondence expresses the desired output result from a given input. We usually obtain an apt loop-invariant by weakening the desired result. Let's analyze the desired result.

The *input* is a finite sequence of characters

$C_1, C_2, \ldots, C_N$

Each character is one of the three types: (1) end-of-line, (2) delete-line, or (3) regular. The last character, C_N, is an end-of-line character since it represents the end of the logical record containing the input sequence.

For the output: If C_i is the first end-of-line character in the sequence (and we know there is at least one, C_N), then the output in the array LINE must be the longest sequence of regular characters immediately preceding C_i. So, we would have the subsequence of regular characters

$$C_{i-k}, \ldots, C_{i-1}$$

Stored in the array LINE as

LINE(1), . . . ,LINE(k)

with the variable LENGTH having k as its value; moreover, either C_{i-k} is C_1, the very first character in the sequence, or C_{i-k-1}, the immediately preceding character, is a delete-line character.

We rephrase this desired result without using subscripts by first letting the new variable CHAR stand for the currently scanned input character. Then our desired end result is:

> LINE(1), . . . ,LINE(LENGTH)
> is the longest sequence of regular
> characters immediately preceding CHAR
> *and*
> CHAR is the first end-of-line character
> in the input sequence.

For CHAR to be the first end-of-line character we need only write and execute the code

```
CHAR = GET_A_CHAR;
DO WHILE (CHAR ¬= END_OF_LINE_CHAR);
        CHAR = GET_A_CHAR;
END;
```

This forms the skeleton of our DO-WHILE refinement. Obviously we take the loop invariant to be

> "LINE(1), . . . ,LINE(LENGTH) is the
> longest sequence of regular characters
> (in the input sequence) immediately
> preceding the current value of CHAR"

Let's call this loop invariant *P*. To establish *P* by initialization we simply do the assignment

```
LENGTH = 0;
```

which makes *P* vacuously true. So, our DO-WHILE refinement of the function *process-character-sequence* becomes

```
LENGTH = 0;
CHAR = GET_A_CHAR;
DO WHILE (CHAR ¬= END_OF_LINE_CHAR);
        process-CHAR;
        CHAR = GET_A_CHAR;
END;
```

This introduces the new function *process*-CHAR. We get the functional specifications for *process*-CHAR from asking and answering the DO-WHILE correctness questions.

We know now what the loop invariant *P* is. And *P* is (vacuously) true by initialization before execution enters the DO-WHILE loop. If we execute

```
CHAR = GET_A_CHAR;
```

enough times, the loop will certainly terminate since there is at least one END_OF_LINE_CHAR in the input sequence. By our choice of the loop invariant, the relation

P and (CHAR = END_OF_LINE_CHAR)

implies our intended result. This covers four of the five DO-WHILE questions.

Finally, we need to know (1) if we assume *P* is true, and (2) we assume

(CHAR ¬= END_OF_LINE_CHAR)

is true, and (3) if we then execute the loop body

```
        process-CHAR;
        CHAR = GET_A_CHAR;
```

will the loop invariant *P* still be true? If we can answer "yes," then we know our DO-WHILE refinement of *process-character-sequence* is correct. But to answer this last question, we must know the specifications of the function *process*-CHAR, which we have yet to define. So, we simply make the specifications for *process*-CHAR satisfy the correctness criteria. That is, we often use the correctness question associated with a refinement to determine the specifications of the new functions the refinement introduced. Answering the correctness question becomes, in effect, specifying completely the subfunctions of the refinement. For example, we have the specifications given in Fig. 3.10.

---

function name: *process*-CHAR
domain:
(i) input: the single character variable CHAR;
CHAR's value is either a delete-line character or some regular character
(ii)global data: the declared variables DELETE_LINE_CHAR, LENGTH and the single character array LINE
range: same as the domain global data, i.e., a line, whose length is LENGTH, being LINE(1), . . . ,LINE(LENGTH)
rule-of-correspondence: Assuming the loop invariant *P* is true before executing *process*-CHAR, we want *P* to also be true after executing the code

```
process-CHAR;
CHAR = GET_A_CHAR;
```

FIG. 3.10 Functional specifications for *process*-CHAR

We now must refine the function *process*-CHAR. In the specifications we note that the input variable CHAR is either a delete-line character or some regular character. This suggests we should refine *process*-CHAR into an IF-THEN-ELSE figure as follows:

```
IF      CHAR = DELETE_LINE_CHAR        THEN
        Delete-Line-Action;
ELSE
        Regular-Action;
```

We still must determine the appropriate "*Action*" in the two cases. To do this we ask the IF-THEN-ELSE correctness question:

"If CHAR is a DELETE_LINE_CHAR, does the
Delete-Line-Action do the *process*-CHAR function,
and if CHAR is a regular character does the
Regular-Action do the *process*-CHAR function?"

To answer this question we must fill in what the *Delete-Line-Action* and the *Regular-Action* are. And we want to do this in such a way that we can answer "yes."

Recall that we want the loop invariant

"LINE(1), . . . ,LINE(LENGTH) is the

longest sequence of regular characters
(in the input sequence) immediately
preceding the current value of CHAR"

to be true after executing the code

```
process-CHAR;

CHAR = GET_A_CHAR;
```

assuming the loop-invariant (and CHAR ≠ END_OF_LINE_CHAR) true before the code. So, when CHAR is the DELETE_LINE_CHAR we do

```
Delete-Line-Action;
CHAR = GET_A_CHAR;
```

but then a delete-line character must immediately precede the current value of CHAR in the input sequence. Our "*Delete-Line-Action*" then is simply the assignment

```
LENGTH = 0;
```

This was necessary in order to make the loop invariant true, and it has the obvious effect of deleting the line.

Similarly, whenever CHAR is a regular character, we will execute

```
Regular-Action;
CHAR = GET_A_CHAR;
```

So, to keep the loop invariant true, our "*Regular-Action*" must be to add the regular character to the end of LINE. We do this with the PL/I code

```
LENGTH = LENGTH + 1;
LINE(LENGTH) = CHAR;
```

Our IF-THEN-ELSE refinement of *process*-CHAR is

```
IF      CHAR = DELETE_LINE_CHAR         THEN
        LENGTH = 0;
ELSE
    DO;
        LENGTH = LENGTH + 1;
        LINE(LENGTH) = CHAR;
    END;
```

which is all in PL/I code.

And by the way we constructed the code for *Delete-Line-Action* and *Regular-Action,* we know our IF-THEN-ELSE refinement of *process*-CHAR is indeed correct.

But now we are finished. For, starting with the function *process-character-sequence,* we have applied our top-down structured programming methodology until we have expressed everything in PL/I code.

The program fragment we finally produced is

```
DECLARE CHAR CHARACTER(1);
   LENGTH = 0;
   CHAR = GET_A_CHAR;
   DO WHILE (CHAR ¬= END_OF_LINE_CHAR);
         IF CHAR = DELETE_LINE_CHAR THEN
               LENGTH = 0;
         ELSE
               DO;
                  LENGTH = LENGTH + 1;
                  LINE(LENGTH) = CHAR;
               END;
         CHAR = GET_A_CHAR;
   END;
```

And we know this code is correct provided that the procedure GET_A_CHAR (whenever it is written) meets the specifications we gave it.

In the remainder of this book we won't go into such detail when developing program code. However, we wanted to show explicitly the step-by-step thought processes a programmer should go through. He should (1) pick a function, (2) refine it using a basic figure, (3) ask the appropriate correctness questions, and (4) answer them. If the answers are immediate, fine; he won't have to spend any time there. If not, then this is certainly the proper point at which to invest time in extra thinking about the program's design. The refinement will often introduce new functions and new data items (like the variable CHAR in our sample program). Answering the correctness questions will often impose specifications on the new functions. And the new data items will usually appear in the specifications of these new functions (and their subsequent refinements). That is, the new data items are for the communication of the new functions. In top-down structured programming we refine both the program and the data representations together. Consider the function procedure GET_A_CHAR of our sample program. If we were provided with more specific details about the logical record which contains the input character sequence, then we could appropriately augment the functional specifications for GET_A_CHAR. And if we were given enough details, we could even develop (using the structured programming process, of course) the PL/I code for GET_A_CHAR.

Too frequently, in real-life programming, a program's functional specifications don't remain fixed. And when we have to modify our program to reflect these changes, systematic design can assist and guide us. We can pinpoint how changes in the specifications propagate downward in the program. We thus obtain new specifications for some of the refinement functions. This might necessitate code changes or even a redesign from some point. But such an approach guarantees we will locate all portions of the program which must be altered. And the degree of alteration is generally directly proportional to the degree of change in the original program specifications.

For example, suppose for our example program we now give a specific limit on the size of a line. And also we can no longer assume that we have declared the array LINE large enough for any logical record. So, before adding a character to LINE, we must first check that this would not exceed the given LINE_LIMIT. If we would go over this limit, then we should treat this as an end-of-line situation. However, we don't want to lose the character which sent us over the limit. So, in those cases where we exit because we went over the line limit, we will have the variable CHAR buffered ahead. In the other case, we will not.

Being sometimes buffered ahead and sometimes not has implications for when we call GET_A_CHAR. Consider the following revision of our example program:

```
DECLARE OVER_LINE_LIMIT
                        BIT(1) INITIAL('0'B);
   LENGTH = 0;
   IF ¬ OVER_LINE_LIMIT THEN
         CHAR = GET_A_CHAR;
   OVER_LINE_LIMIT = '0'B;
   DO WHILE (CHAR ¬ = END_OF_LINE_CHAR
                        & ¬ OVER_LINE_LIMIT);
         IF CHAR = DELETE_LINE_CHAR THEN
            DO;
               LENGTH = 0;
               CHAR = GET_A_CHAR;
            END;
         ELSE
            DO;
               IF LENGTH < LINE_LIMIT THEN
                  DO;
                    LENGTH = LENGTH + 1;
                    LINE(LENGTH) = CHAR;
                    CHAR = GET_A_CHAR;
                  END;
```

```
                ELSE
                    OVER_LINE_LIMIT = '1'B;
            END;
    END;
```

Another change in the specifications might be to include a DELETE_LAST_CHAR character as a fourth type of input. It should cause the last character in LINE to be dropped (say, by "LENGTH = LENGTH − 1;") provided that LENGTH > 0; otherwise, it should be a no-op. We leave it as an exercise for you to modify the example program suitably.

In this section we illustrated in detail how you might apply the top-down structured programming process. By using this methodology, we

- Made the program design process a sequence of explicit decisions
- Actually carried out the design within PL/I code (by using function names)
- Ensured program correctness as we went along (by producing specifications for any new functions we introduced)
- Decided some details of data representation as we were doing the step-by-step refinements.

We developed our example program in a top-down step-by-step fashion. And at every step we knew what we should do next. First, we picked a function. Next, we decided on a basic flow-of-control form. Then, we refined the function into the basic form. After that, we asked the appropriate correctness (and termination) questions. Answering these questions also answered the question, "Is the program correct so far?" And the proper answers usually determined the functional specifications for new functions yet to be refined. We repeated this process until we had only PL/I code.

3.5 THE BASIC FIGURES ARE SUFFICIENT

Up to this point, we have restricted structured programming to the use of only the SEQUENCE, IF-THEN-ELSE, and DO-WHILE figures for program flow-of-control. We have obtained some explicit programming and correctness guidelines by analyzing these three basic figures. Their easy-to-understand control logic greatly simplified our analysis. Surprisingly, we never need to use complex control logic. In fact, just these three basic control forms suffice for any programming we might ever wish to do!

Böhm and Jacopini have shown, in effect, that with only structured programs you could represent any flow-chartable program.[1] This result shows the basic figures SEQUENCE, IF-THEN-ELSE, and DO-WHILE are sufficient to express any program logic, however intricate.

Consequently, the GO TO is an unnecessary programming language feature. But their method of eliminating GO TO's is not a practical programming technique. It involves creating new boolean variables —one for each decision or function box in the original flowchart—in order to simulate a program instruction pointer. A single DO-WHILE loops until the instruction pointer indicates program exit. The *do-part* is a nesting of IF-THEN-ELSE constructs to determine the current instruction, to execute that instruction, and to update the instruction pointer (via the new boolean variables).

Let's illustrate Böhm and Jacopini's general method for showing that the figures SEQUENCE, IF-THEN-ELSE, and DO-WHILE are sufficient. We select the simple nonstructured program flowchart shown in Fig. 3.11.

We first introduce new boolean variables (i.e., declared BIT(1) attribute). They are LOC_P, LOC_Q, LOC_F and EXIT, and they will act as location indicators. Our Böhm-Jacopini-like construction of an equivalent structured program consists of just a single DO-WHILE program which simply interpretively executes the original flowchart.

With TRUE (= '1'B) and FALSE (= '0'B) being BIT(1) constants we have

```
LOC_P = TRUE;
LOC_Q, LOC_F, EXIT = FALSE;
DO WHILE(¬ EXIT);
   IF LOC_P
      THEN DO;
               IF   P
                   THEN    EXIT = TRUE;
                   ELSE    LOC_Q = TRUE;
               LOC_P = FALSE;
           END;
      ELSE  IF   LOC_Q
                 THEN DO;
                         IF   Q
                             THEN   EXIT = TRUE;
                             ELSE   LOC_F = TRUE;
                         LOC_Q = FALSE;
                      END;
```

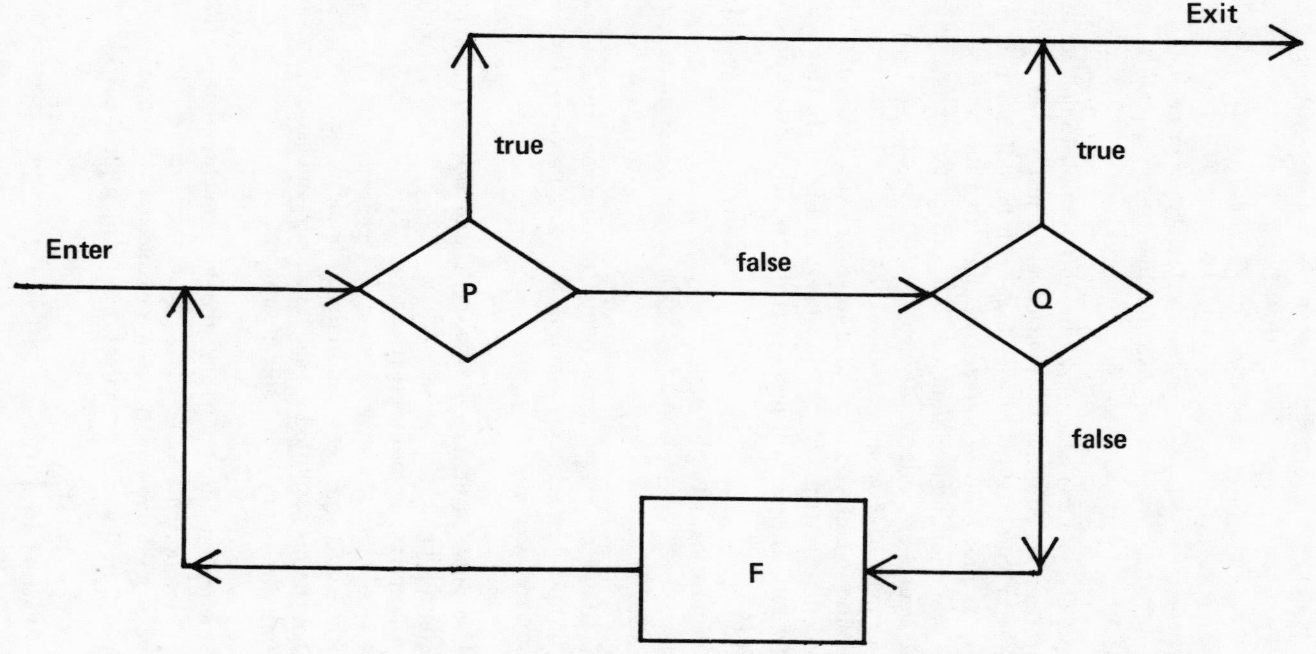

FIG. 3.11 Simple nonstructured flowchart requiring extra variables to structure it

```
                ELSE IF  LOC_F
                         THEN DO;
                              F;
                              LOC_P = TRUE;
                              LOC_F = FALSE;
                           END;
   END;
```

Hopefully, you can generalize from this example to the fact that any flowchart can be equivalently realized using just SEQUENCE, IF-THEN-ELSE, and DO-WHILE control logic along with introducing new boolean variables. As previously remarked, we illustrated this method not as a practical programming technique but as a convincing demonstration that the basic figures are indeed sufficient.

You might have wondered about the need to introduce the extra variables. But in fact, you do need at least one extra variable to structure the function represented by the flowchart in Fig. 3.11. This is a more difficult result, and we will just assert it here. This assertion does not apply to code like

```
DO WHILE (¬P & ¬Q);
        F;
END;
```

since the above code uses a compound relation, namely "¬P & ¬Q," instead of the given relations P and Q. So, more precisely, the "rules of the game" are:

1. Use only SEQUENCE, IF-THEN-ELSE, and DO-WHILE for program control logic.
2. Any IF-TEST or WHILE-TEST can only be
   P, ¬P, Q, ¬Q, V, ¬V
   where V is some newly introduced boolean variable.
3. Statements permitted are the function *F* and assignments of TRUE or FALSE to any new boolean variables.

Then our assertion is that, to realize the same function that the flowchart in Fig. 3.11 represents and to follow the above game rules, you must introduce at least one new boolean variable.

Instead, in this case we might have written the code

```
EXIT = FALSE;
DO WHILE (¬ EXIT);
       IF P
```

```
                THEN  EXIT = TRUE;
                ELSE  IF Q
                          THEN  EXIT = TRUE;
                          ELSE  F;
         END;
```

In Section 3.9 we suggest such structuring of initially unstructured logic as a nice diversionary exercise.

We conclude that the basic figures SEQUENCE, IF-THEN-ELSE, and DO-WHILE are indeed sufficient to realize the control logic for any function we can program. However, we might have to introduce some new boolean variables when writing structured programs.

The Böhm and Jacopini result—the sufficiency of the three basic figures—is analogous to a fundamental result in boolean algebra. Any boolean-valued function of boolean variables can be expressed in terms of the three basic logic operations—AND, OR, and NOT. This means that any logic circuit can be built using combinations of just these three types of gates.

By convention, diagrams are usually restricted to using just AND, OR, and NOT as building blocks since they are cheap, easily understood, and sufficient. There are several other logic functions. For example, NAND and NOR are each sufficient by themselves, and XOR is a standard machine instruction. But it is not recommended to use these other logic functions in circuit diagrams. Such idiosyncratic behavior would lessen a diagram's comprehensibility, and hence the actual circuit would be more difficult to maintain or to modify.

Similarly, adopting a programming convention which restricts flow-of-control composition rules to an easily understood, sufficient, and livable set tends to produce programs that are more comprehensible, more easily maintained, and more easily modified. In the next section we suggest some additional flow-of-control forms which, together with the basic three, make for a very "livable" set. Obviously the ITERATIVE-DO is one such construct.

In fact, from the De Morgan laws it follows that just NOT and either AND or OR are a sufficient set of boolean operations. As an interesting aside, if we modify Böhm and Jacopini's ground rules, then we can analogously compress the sufficient set of control forms. Mills[2] has defined a *proper program* as one whose flowchart has precisely one entry and one exit line, and for each node in the flowchart, there is a path from the entry line through the node to the exit line. Essentially, Böhm and Jacopini have shown that every proper program can be effectively translated into an equivalent program which uses only the SEQUENCE, IF-THEN-ELSE, and DO-WHILE flow-of-control forms. Their transformation allows you to introduce new boolean variables. The nodes in the new program flowchart can be copies of nodes in the original flowchart, or assignments of TRUE or FALSE to new variables, or tests of such variables.

However, if we were also to allow compound tests and the assignment of boolean expressions to the new boolean variables, then we could realize the IF-THEN-ELSE figure using SEQUENCE and DO-WHILE. For the code

```
IF  B
        THEN  s1;
        ELSE  s2;
```

where B is a boolean expression and s1 and s2 are statements, we introduce the new variables B_VAL and ONCE, and we write

```
B_VAL    = B;
ONCE     = TRUE;
DO WHILE(B_VAL & ONCE);
        ONCE = FALSE;
        s1;
END;
DO WHILE(¬ B_VAL & ONCE);
        ONCE = FALSE;
        s2;
END;
```

And if we allow recursive flowcharts, then we can realize the DO-WHILE construct with SEQUENCE and IF-THEN-ELSE as follows. For

```
DO WHILE( B );
        s1;
END;
```

we write

```
CALL WHILE_SIMULATE;
```

where

```
WHILE_SIMULATE: PROC RECURSIVE;
                IF  B  THEN
                    DO;
                        s1;
                        CALL WHILE_SIMULATE;
                    END;
            END WHILE_SIMULATE;
```

But just as specifying circuit diagrams using only, say, NAND would be counterproductive, so would programming with a minimal set of control forms. The logic operations AND, OR, and NOT are a satisfactory basis—a sufficient set that is easy to work with and not too large. Similarly, SEQUENCE, IF-THEN-ELSE, and DO-WHILE are a sufficient basis. Experience confirms that these three (plus a few related control forms presented in the next section) are also a satisfactory basis for constructing programs.

3.6 OTHER STRUCTURED FIGURES

Doing structured programming in PL/I is facilitated by having language constructs corresponding to each of the three basic figures. In programming languages, such as FORTRAN or assembly language, which do not have explicit syntax for the basic figures, there are several ways to accommodate structured programming. First, you can regard realizing, say, the DO-WHILE flow-of-control as a further refinement. So, you build a DO-WHILE out of what is available in your language (e.g., the GO TO). Notice that using GO TO's to synthesize structured figures is a far cry from their unrestricted use. We give some examples in Sections 3.7 and 3.8 of how one might code structured figures in FORTRAN and in COBOL, respectively. A second approach is to extend your programming language to include the desired figures. Here a preprocessor is a natural choice—either macros for assembly language or compile-time facilities such as PL/I's. Appendix B sketches a syntax and an implementation strategy for 360/370 Assembly Language macros for structured figures. And Appendix A gives actual PL/I preprocessor code for realizing some further structured figures which we discuss in this section.

We know the three basic figures are sufficient in themselves. But we have seen that the ITERATIVE-DO is natural to use when running over an index. Section 2.4 treated the ITERATIVE-DO in terms of the DO-WHILE. There are several permissible formats and parameters for the ITERATIVE-DO. Two common forms are:

```
DO variable = exp-1 TO exp-2 BY exp-3;
      statements;
END;
```

and

```
DO variable = exp-1 TO exp-2 BY exp-3 WHILE(test);
      statements;
END;
```

The PL/I Language Reference Manual[3] details the DO statement in its full generality. The above two forms are convenient additions to the set of permissible flow-of-control structures. A wise convention when using these forms is to forbid any statement in the loop to modify the control *variable*. Then if the index increment *exp-3* is not zero, we are guaranteed that the ITERATIVE-DO terminates. Moreover, we know what is true upon loop exit. For example, in the second form above, if we had

```
DO ENTRY = 1 TO TABLE_SIZE WHILE( TABLE(ENTRY) ¬= KEY );
END;
```

then on exit we know that

```
( ENTRY = TABLE_SIZE + 1 ) |
( 1 <= ENTRY & ENTRY <= TABLE_SIZE &
  TABLE(ENTRY) = KEY )
```

is true. This in conjuction with a loop invariant such as

TABLE(j) ¬= KEY for $1 \leq j \leq$ ENTRY − 1

show how natural it is to use the ITERATIVE-DO to correctly code functions which rely on indexing.

The DO-WHILE figure is a particular realization of conditional iteration; the ITERATIVE-DO is a special case of conditional iteration which we don't need—if we have the DO-WHILE—but which is a natural programming construct compatible with structured programming. For the ITERATIVE-DO figure is also single-entry/single-exit and hence proper for functional refinement.

Structured programming is built upon three flow-of-control forms: sequencing, conditional iteration, and selecting from alternative paths. We need the figures SEQUENCE, IF-THEN-ELSE, and DO-WHILE as specific instances of the basic forms. The important thing was that we had a figure for each of the flow-of-control forms and that each figure was of the single-entry/single-exit type. Our choice was somewhat biased by their explicit presence in PL/I.

Recall that in top-down structured programming, at every step you select a function G and a figure H and then refine G into the form H; then you check that the refinement is indeed correct. We've added the ITERATIVE-DO as another figure to refine functions into. We will now give three more such figures which we built into PL/I using the compile-time preprocessor. This will make the set of figures for refining more robust but still "natural" and straightforward to use. These figures, like the ITERATIVE-DO, occur often in practice and are present in some programming languages. We call these new figures REPEAT-UNTIL, LOOP-EXITIF-ENDLOOP, and SELECT-CASE. The first two perform conditional iteration; the SELECT-CASE is a generalization of the IF-THEN-ELSE for selecting alternative execution paths.

The REPEAT-UNTIL is very similar to the DO-WHILE figure. The two differences are that the REPEAT-UNTIL has the exit test after each execution of the enclosed statements (which therefore is executed at least once), and exit takes place when the test evaluates to TRUE.

The REPEAT-UNTIL has the flowchart given in Fig. 3.12, which we write in PL/I as:

```
REPEAT;
   G;
UNTIL( B );
```

where the function G stands for one or more PL/I statements (including other REPEAT-UNTIL figures) and B is an expression which evaluates to true or false. Clearly, we could hand code a REPEAT-UNTIL figure with a DO-WHILE and a boolean variable. For example,

```
TEST = FALSE;
DO WHILE( ¬ TEST );
      G;
      TEST = B;
END;
```

But it is convenient not to have to build each nonbasic figure anew with each use, and the implementation of REPEAT-UNTIL using preprocessor procedures (given in Appendix A) is quite instructive.

The LOOP-EXITIF-ENDLOOP is a general conditional iteration figure which includes the DO-WHILE and the REPEAT-UNTIL figures as special cases. One form of it has the flowchart in Fig. 3.13, which we can write in PL/I (using the preprocessor code of Appendix A) as

```
LOOP;
      G;
EXITIF( B );
      H;
ENDLOOP;
```

where the functions G and H eventually become one or more PL/I statements and B is a boolean-valued expression. Note that when G is the null statement, we get the same functional effect (with extra execution of the null statement) as the code

```
DO WHILE( ¬B );
      H;
END;
```

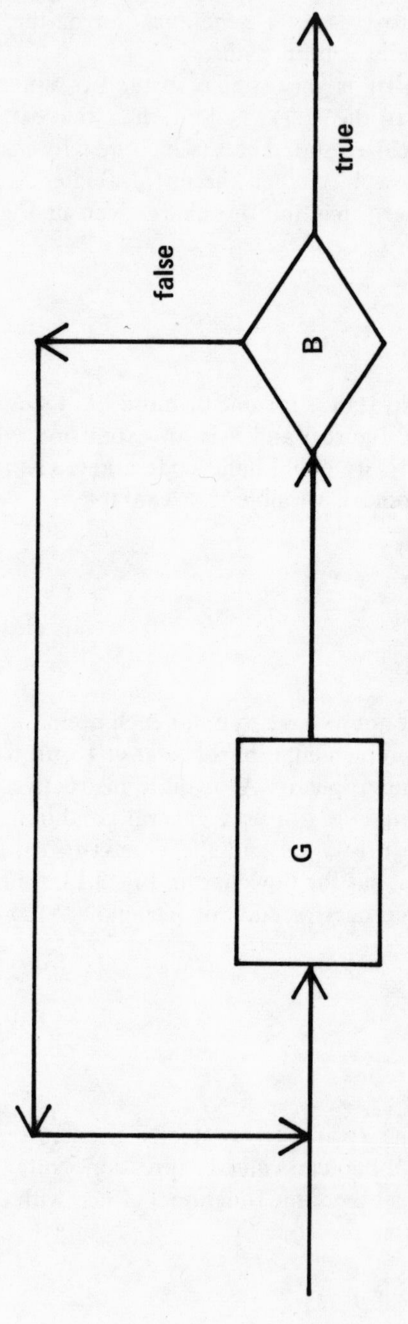

FIG. 3.12 The REPEAT-UNTIL figure

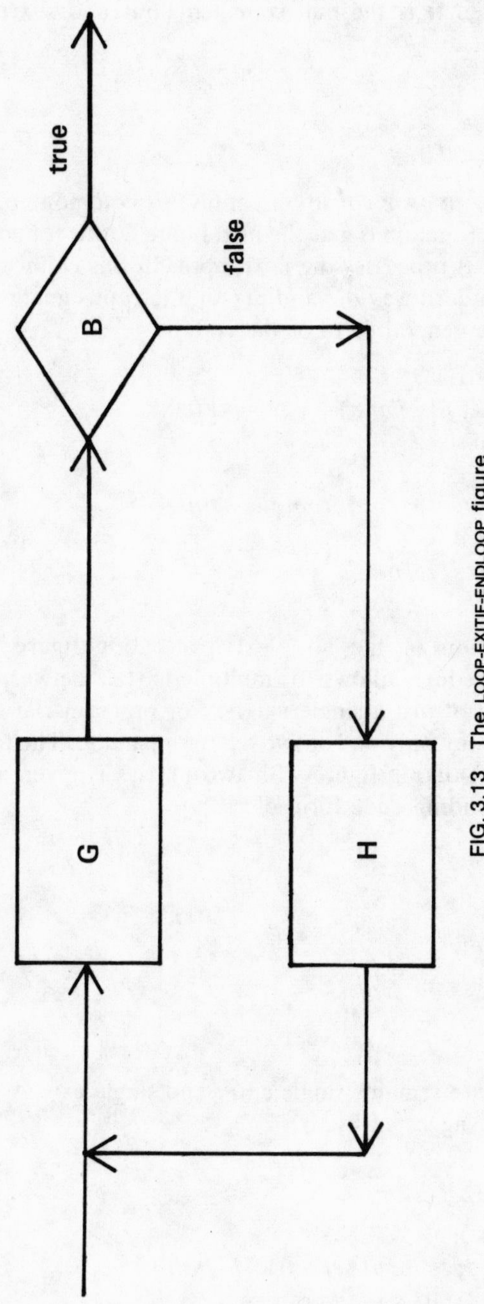

FIG. 3.13 The LOOP-EXITIF-ENDLOOP figure

and similarly when H is the null statement, our LOOP-EXITIF-ENDLOOP code is equivalent to

```
REPEAT;
      G;
UNTIL( B );
```

The LOOP-EXITIF-ENDLOOP construct captures a common computational pattern where the function G gets the next input, B tests for completion of the iteration, and H processes the next input. In this connection we can recommend a standard way of handling an interrupt signaling the end of an input file. The general form of the code is

```
DCL EOF BIT(1);
ON ENDFILE( file-name )   EOF = TRUE;
EOF = FALSE;
LOOP;
      Get-next-record from file-name;
EXITIF( EOF );
      Process-record;
ENDLOOP;
```

The implementation of the LOOP-EXITIF-ENDLOOP figure using PL/I preprocessor procedures allows for multiple EXITIFS between LOOP; and ENDLOOP; instead of just a single EXITIF. For program clarity, however, we recommend using only one or two EXITIFS in a loop. The flowchart for the LOOP-EXITIF-ENDLOOP figure with two EXITIFS is given as Fig. 3.14, with the corresponding code form of

```
LOOP;
      F;
EXITIF( P );
      G;
EXITIF( Q );
      H;
ENDLOOP;
```

Note that the figure remains single entry and single exit. A possible use of two EXITIFS is suggested by:

```
LOOP;
      Get-input;
EXITIF( EOF );
      Analyze-input-set-VALID-indicator;
EXITIF( ¬ VALID );
      Process-valid-input;
ENDLOOP;
```

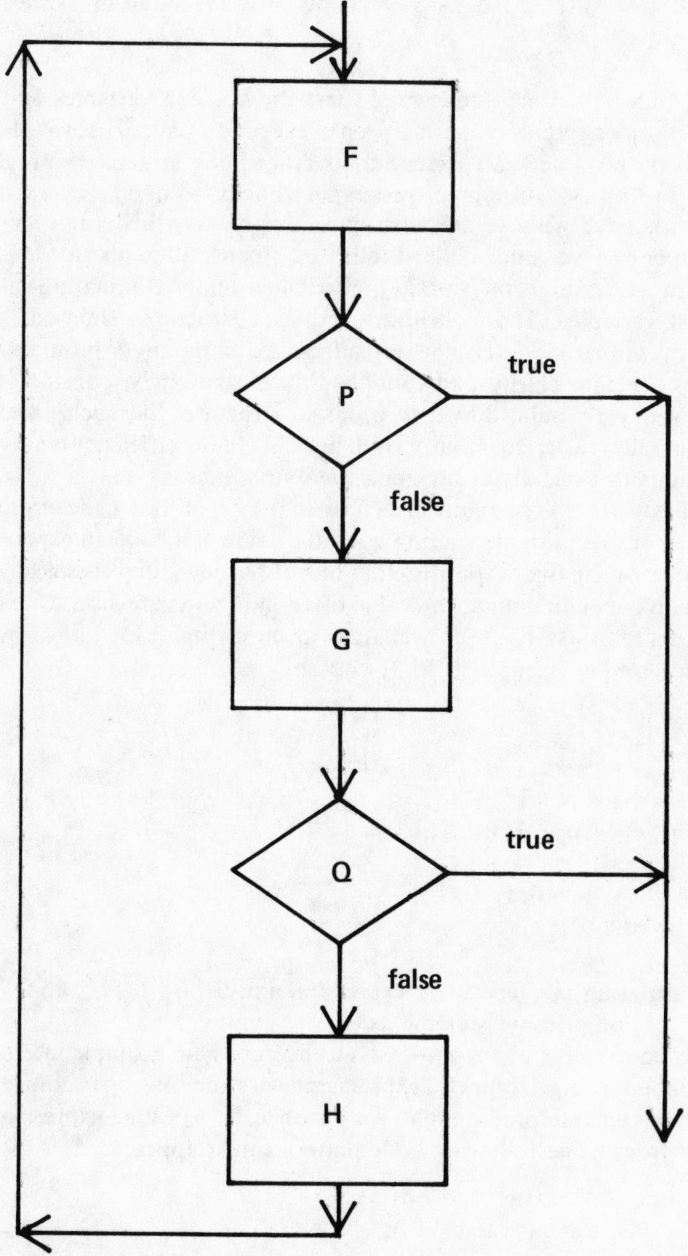

FIG. 3.14 The LOOP-EXITIF-ENDLOOP figure with two EXITIFS

On exit from the above loop we know that the boolean expression

```
( EOF | ¬ VALID )
```

is true. The subsequent code might test the boolean variables EOF and VALID in order to determine the proper execution path. The use of such indicators introduces an execution overhead for structured programming. In theory, structured programs should be less efficient than programs coded without any restraints; in practice, this is not so. It is being penny-wise and dollar-foolish to focus attempts to improve program (execution or storage) efficiency upon eliminating a few boolean variables. The algorithms and data structures embodied in a program primarily determine its efficiency. Structured programming stresses program clarity and functionality. Accordingly, considerations of efficiency are subordinate to program structure. But such programs are generally easier to modify and thus facilitate efficiency-motivated alterations in basic algorithms and data structures.

The IF-THEN-ELSE figure specifies that one of two code groups is selected for execution depending upon the value of a boolean expression. The SELECT-CASE figure specifies that one of N code groups is selected for execution depending upon the value of an interger expression. One form of the SELECT-CASE figure flowchart is given in Fig. 3.15.
We express this example in PL/I code by

```
SELECT( exp );
        CASE( 1 ):   G1;
        CASE( 2 ):   G2;
        CASE( 3 ):   G3;
        CASE( 4 ):   G4;
        DEFAULT:     Gd;
ENDSELECT;
```

where *exp* is an integer-valued expression and G_1, G_2, G_3, G_4, and G_d are groups of one or more statements.

As an example of SELECT-CASE's utility, consider a simple interpreter for code involving arithmetic expressions with the four operators +, −, *, and /. (Our interpreter might, for instance, be handling expressions in postfix form.) The following code pattern might appear:

```
DCL  OP  CHAR( 4 )  INIT('+-*/'),
        RATOR  CHAR( 1 );

        Get-current-RATOR;
```

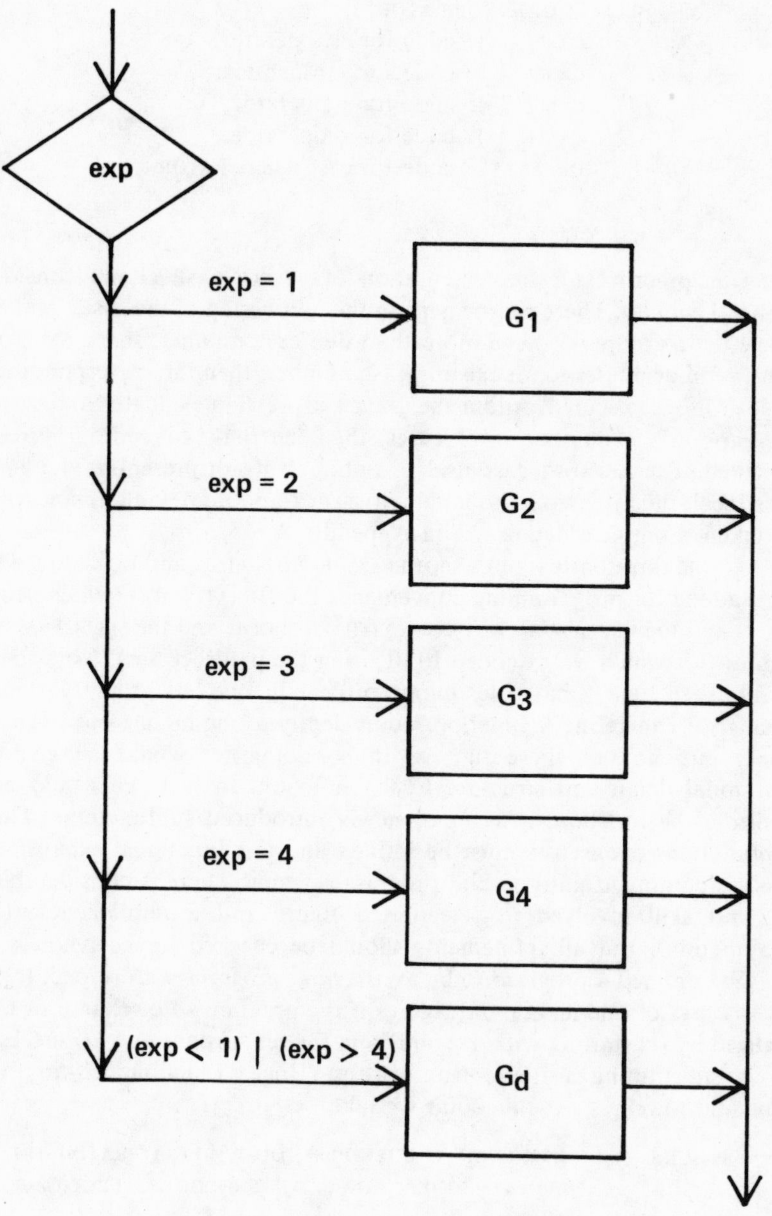

FIG. 3.15 An instance of the SELECT-CASE figure

```
SELECT( INDEX(OP,RATOR) );
        CASE( 1 ): code for + operator;
        CASE( 2 ): code for - operator;
        CASE( 3 ): code for * operator;
        CASE( 4 ): code for / operator;
        DEFAULT:   code for case where RATOR is
                        not +, -, *, or /;
ENDSELECT;
```

Our preprocessor implementation of SELECT-CASE allows considerable flexibility. There can be gaps in the numbering of the cases, and a single code group can have more than one case number. If the SELECT expression evaluates to an existing case number, then the corresponding code group is executed. And if the SELECT expression evaluates to one of the gaps in the numbering of cases, then the DEFAULT code group is executed. The DEFAULT case itself is optional; if not present as the last case label, then it is taken to label ENDSELECT and no default action will be taken. Complete details are in Appendix A.

To the three basic figures SEQUENCE, IF-THEN-ELSE, and DO WHILE we have added for programming convenience the ITERATIVE-DO (which is in PL/I) and the REPEAT-UNTIL, LOOP-EXITIF-ENDLOOP, and the SELECT-CASE figures (for which we extended PL/I using the preprocessor). Note that all of these figures have the important one-in/one-out property. This means we can refine a function (equivalently a one-in/one-out "black box") into any of these figures. In so doing we would be giving additional detail and structure to the function. In fact, we would be realizing the function in terms of newly introduced subfunctions. The subfunctions themselves must be refined and this functional expansion process continued until a valid program remains. There is considerable art and skill involved in selecting a figure and a refinement into subfunctions. But all refinements should be checked for correctness.

We defined a program to be a *structured program* with respect to a set FIGURES of one-in/one-out figures if the program's flowchart can be realized by (1) starting with a figure from the set FIGURES and (2) successively substituting a figure from FIGURES for a function box in the evolving flowchart. At this point we take

FIGURES = { SEQUENCE, IF-THEN-ELSE, DO-WHILE, ITERATIVE-DO, REPEAT-UNTIL, LOOP-EXITIF-ENDLOOP, SELECT-CASE }

3.7 STRUCTURED FLOW-OF-CONTROL IN FORTRAN

FORTRAN does not have language constructs which correspond to the IF-THEN-ELSE or the DO-WHILE figures, as does PL/I. Nor does

FORTRAN contain a REPEAT-UNTIL, a SELECT-CASE, or a LOOP-EXITIF-ENDLOOP construct. Accordingly, to write structured programs in FORTRAN we need either to extend FORTRAN with a macro preprocessor (as we do for PL/I in Appendix A) or to build a structured figure out of FORTRAN statements each time we need one.

In this section we show how you might do the second of these alternatives. That is, we give some FORTRAN programming conventions for realizing the structured figures. Obviously, we will use the GO TO statement and statement labels as basic building blocks for synthesizing these figures. This does not mean that you should use the GO TO indiscriminately in FORTRAN. Rather, structured programming in FORTRAN should use the GO TO only for realizing a structured figure.

Like almost all programming languages, FORTRAN has sequencing (but not DO-END or BEGIN-END statement grouping) and an ITERATIVE-DO form. We must construct the other structured flow-of-control figures by using FORTRAN code, particularly the logical IF and GO TO statements. In what follows, we will first give the flowchart of a structured figure (Fig. 3.16) and then we will present a FORTRAN realization of that figure (Fig. 3.17). We let E stand for a logical expression and we let F, G, F_1, F_2, . . . denote functions (which will eventually be FORTRAN code), and we use the numeric labels 10,20, . . . for illustrative purposes.

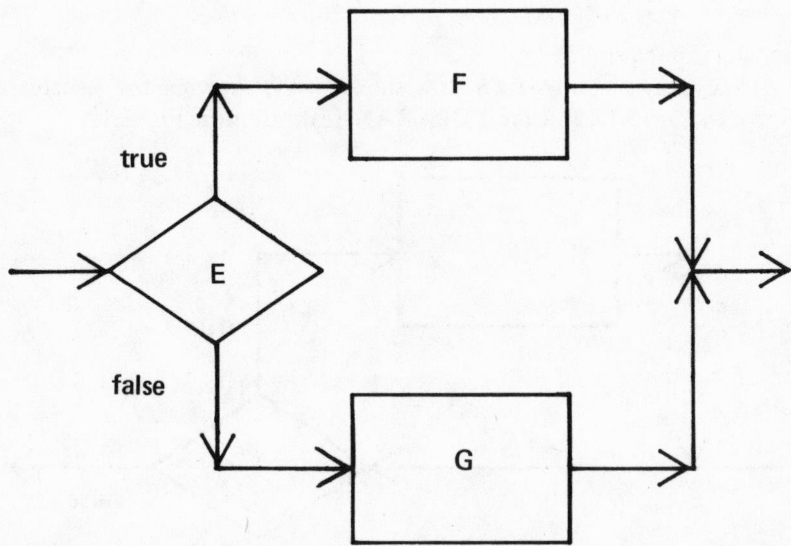

FIG. 3.16 The IF-THEN-ELSE figure

```
         IF (.NOT. (E))   GO TO 10
             F
             GO TO 20
   10    CONTINUE
             G
   20    CONTINUE
```

FIG. 3.17 FORTRAN realization of IF-THEN-ELSE

Of course, if the ELSE clause is not used (i.e., you have a simple IF-THEN), you can write

```
         IF (.NOT. (E))   GO TO 10
             F
   10    CONTINUE
```

or, if F is a single executable statement, you can use

```
         IF ( E ) F
```

In practice, you can gain some minor efficiency by simplifying the logical expression (.NOT. (E)) wherever possible. For example, the logical expression

```
         ( .NOT. ( J .LT. K ))
```

simplifies to

```
         ( J .GE. K )
```

and gains in clarity.

We treat the DO-WHILE in a similar way, showing the structured figure in Fig. 3.18 and the FORTRAN realization in Fig. 3.19.

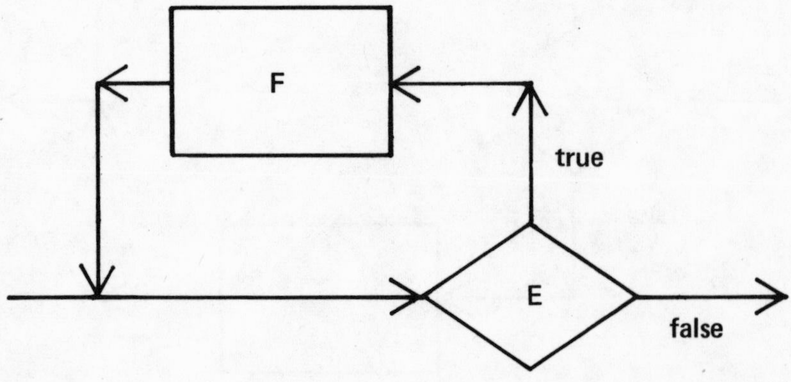

FIG. 3.18 The DO-WHILE figure

```
C       DOWHILE
   10          CONTINUE
               IF ( .NOT. ( E ) )  GO TO 20
                     F
                     GO TO 10
   20          CONTINUE
C       END-DOWHILE
```

FIG. 3.19 FORTRAN realization of DO-WHILE

The REPEAT-UNTIL is easier to code in FORTRAN than the DO-WHILE. The figure is given in Fig. 3.20 and the realization in Fig. 3.21.

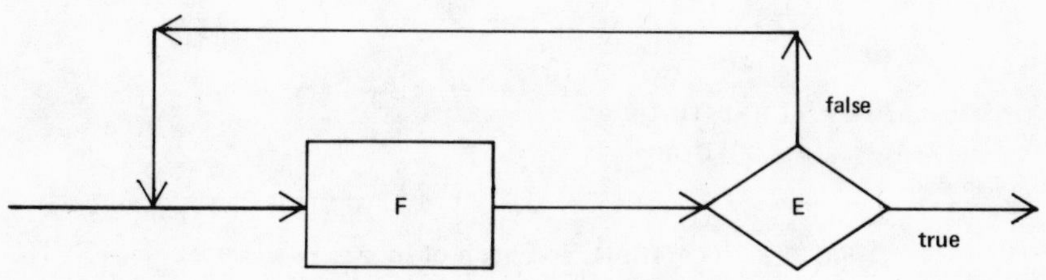

FIG. 3.20 The REPEAT-UNTIL figure

```
C       REPEAT
   10          CONTINUE
                     F
               IF ( .NOT. ( E ) ) GO TO 10
C       UNTIL ( E ) IS TRUE
```

FIG. 3.21 FORTRAN realization of REPEAT-UNTIL

As we remarked in Section 3.6, the LOOP-EXITIF-ENDLOOP (Fig. 3.22), in effect, combines the DO-WHILE and the REPEAT-UNTIL figures. The FORTRAN realization is shown in Fig. 3.23.

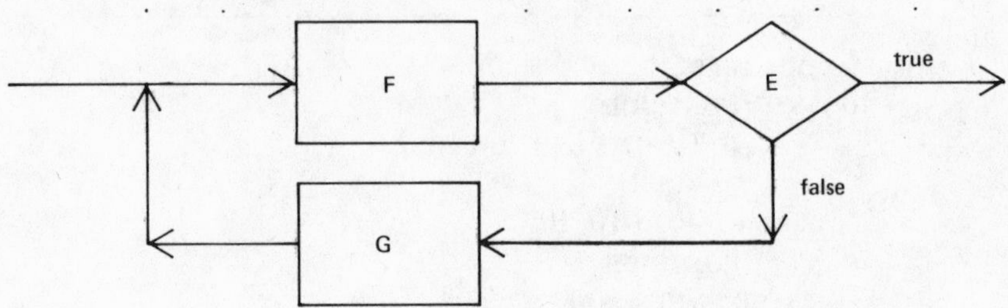

FIG. 3.22 The LOOP-EXITIF-ENDLOOP figure (with one exit)

```
C      LOOP
   10        CONTINUE
                  F
C      EXIT IF ( E ) IS TRUE
             IF ( E ) GO TO 20
                  G
                  GO TO 10
   20        CONTINUE
C      END-OF-LOOP
```

FIG. 3.23 FORTRAN realization of LOOP-EXITIF-ENDLOOP

The last figure for us to handcraft in FORTRAN is the SELECT-CASE. We could use a nested sequence of IF-THEN-ELSE figures for synthesizing a SELECT-CASE figure (Fig. 3.24). But here (as in the PL/I preprocessor generated code for SELECT-CASE) the preferred implementation uses a computed GO TO statement (Fig. 3.25) where *exp* is an integer-valued expression in FORTRAN.

We have hand-coded the structured figures not already in FORTRAN. You can employ similar coding patterns to realize the structured figures in another programming language. When doing structured programming in a language like FORTRAN, you have essentially one extra level of refinement required (over a language like PL/I).

So, the concept of a structured program and the process of structured programming are language independent. But it is certainly easier to use a programming language already containing structured flow-of-control constructs.

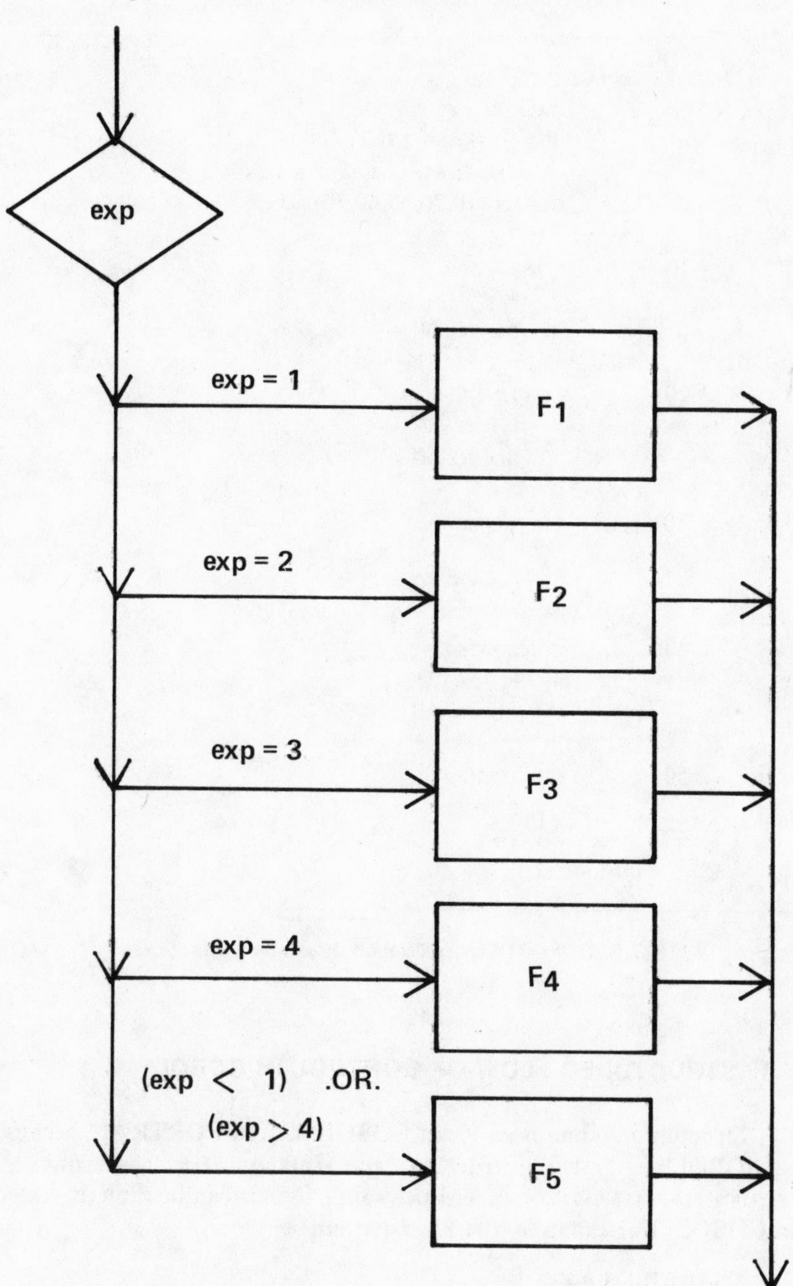

FIG. 3.24 An example of the SELECT-CASE figure

```
C     SELECT
            KASE = exp
            IF (      (KASE .LT. 1)
     +          .OR. (KASE .GT. 4) ) KASE = 5
            GO TO (10,20,30,40,50),KASE
C     CASE-1
   10       CONTINUE
                F1
                GO TO 60
C     CASE-2
   20       CONTINUE
                F2
                GO TO 60
C     CASE-3
   30       CONTINUE
                F3
                GO TO 60
C     CASE-4
   40       CONTINUE
                F4
                GO TO 60
C     DEFAULT
   50       CONTINUE
                F5
   60       CONTINUE
C     END-SELECT
```

FIG. 3.25 FORTRAN realization of example SELECT-CASE

3.8 STRUCTURED FLOW-OF-CONTROL IN COBOL

Structured coding is easier in COBOL than in FORTRAN because of COBOL's IF-ELSE construct and the PERFORM verb. The SEQUENCE, IF-THEN-ELSE, ITERATIVE-DO, and DO-WHILE figures can be directly coded in COBOL. For example, the PL/I pattern

```
DO WHILE( b );
      group;
END;
```

could be rendered in COBOL as

```
PERFORM DO-PART UNTIL(NOT b).
```

where we have

```
DO-PART.
        group.
```

as a separate paragraph. Here *b* stands for a test condition which evaluates to either true or false and *group* denotes one or more program statements. Since the basic three figures plus the ITERATIVE-DO are, in effect, present, GO TO-free structured COBOL programming is feasible.

Note, however, that COBOL's IF-THEN-ELSE figures cannot be nested as generally as in PL/I because COBOL has no DO-END statement grouping construct. In COBOL, only the last statement in a sequence of statements (within one sentence) may be a conditional statement. Hence GO TO and/or PERFORM statements are occasionally needed to simulate some of PL/I's nested conditional statement combinations in COBOL. For example, the PL/I code

```
IF pred1 THEN DO;
        stmt1;
        IF pred2
              THEN stmt2;
              ELSE stmt3;
        stmt4;
        END;
```

may be coded in COBOL as

```
IF pred1 THEN
      PERFORM THEN-PART.
```

where

```
THEN-PART.
        stmt1.
        IF pred2
              THEN stmt2
              ELSE stmt3.
        stmt4.
```

is a separate paragraph.

In this section we will first give a PL/I code pattern and then an equivalent COBOL realization for each of the remaining structured figures, REPEAT-UNTIL, SELECT-CASE, and LOOP-EXITIF-ENDLOOP. Of course, GO TO's will be required to hand code these latter figures.

The REPEAT-UNTIL pattern

```
REPEAT;
        group;
UNTIL(b);
```

can be coded in COBOL as

```
        PERFORM REPEAT.
        PERFORM REPEAT UNTIL(b).
```

with the separate paragraph

```
REPEAT.
        group.
```

or, if *group* is but a few lines, the pattern can be kept in-line by the paragraph

```
REPEAT.
        group.
        IF (NOT b) THEN GO TO REPEAT.
```

Here and in what follows the paragraph names are for illustrative purposes only.

The SELECT-CASE pattern

```
SELECT(integer-expr);
        CASE(1):     group-1;
        CASE(2):     group-2;
        CASE(3):     group-3;
        DEFAULT:     group-0;
ENDSELECT;
```

can be synthesized by

```
        PERFORM SELECT-BEGIN THRU SELECT-END.
```

with the separate code

```
SELECT-BEGIN.
        COMPUTE PICK = integer-expr.
        GO TO CASE-1,
                CASE-2,
                CASE-3
            DEPENDING ON PICK.
        GO TO DEFAULT.
```

```
CASE-1.
        group-1.
        GO TO SELECT-END.
CASE-2.
        group-2.
        GO TO SELECT-END.
CASE-3.
        group-3.
        GO TO SELECT-END.
DEFAULT.
        group-0.
SELECT-END.
        EXIT.
```

Note that if PICK has a value other than 1, 2, or 3, the "GO TO DEFAULT." statement will be executed. This computed GO TO realization of SELECT-CASE in COBOL does not permit gaps and duplications in the case numbering, unlike our PL/I preprocessor version in Appendix A.

The LOOP-EXITIF-ENDLOOP pattern (with a single EXITIF)

```
LOOP;
        group-1;
EXITIF(b);
        group-2;
ENDLOOP;
```

when translated into COBOL becomes

```
        PERFORM LOOP THRU LOOP-END.
```

with the subsequent code

```
LOOP.
            group-1.
        IF  b THEN GO TO LOOP-END.
            group-2.
            GO TO LOOP.
LOOP-END.
        EXIT.
```

Finally, we treat a special case of the above pattern wherein the loop is exited because an end-of-file occurs. The PL/I pattern is

```
DCL  EOF  BIT(1);
   ON ENDFILE(file-name)  EOF = TRUE;
   EOF = FALSE;
```

```
LOOP;
    group-1;
    GET or READ from file-name;
EXITIF( EOF );
    group-2;
ENDLOOP;
```

and the corresponding COBOL code invoked by

```
PERFORM LOOP THRU LOOP-END.
```

is

```
LOOP.
            group-1.
            READ file-name
      AT END  GO TO LOOP-END.
            group-2.
            GO TO LOOP.
LOOP-END.
      EXIT.
```

Thus, even with the simulation of some nonbasic figures, structured coding in COBOL is relatively straightforward.

3.9 A DIVERSION: STRUCTURING UNSTRUCTURED CODE

In Section 3.5 we showed that given any flowchart, we can obtain an equivalent one by the repeated use of only the SEQUENCE, IF-THEN-ELSE, and DO-WHILE figures. That is, to represent any computational logic, it suffices for us to use only combinations of the three basic figures. Programs constructed out of the basic figures (and also the ITERATIVE-DO, REPEAT-UNTIL, LOOP-EXITIF-ENDLOOP, and SELECT-CASE, which we can obtain by combinations of the basic three) we call structured.

Obviously, the approach used in Section 3.5 was to indicate a general truth, not to give a practical way to program. But, as we have suggested elsewhere, structured programming does require you to reorient your thinking. We have found certain exercises seem to help people in this reorientation. One such exercise is to take a nonstructured flowchart and rewrite it into an equivalent (and reasonable) structured program (i.e., not using the method in Section 3.5). Further, the sufficiency of just SEQUENCE, IF-THEN-ELSE, and DO-WHILE for expressing all program logic becomes better understood after you do several of these exercises.

Now, for a flowchart and program code to be equivalent, they must in all cases determine the same computations. That is, the order of evaluation of tests and functions must be the same in each. This is a simple concept, but it requires some care in application. For example, consider the nonstructured flowchart in Fig. 3.26, where P, Q, and R are expressions which evaluate to TRUE (= '1' B) or FALSE (= '0' B), and F, G, and H are functions which code will realize.

The logic represented by this flowchart is not structured since we cannot obtain this exact flowchart by combinations of SEQUENCE, IF-THEN-ELSE, and DO-WHILE. To structure this logic we might attempt the PL/I code:

```
IF (P & Q) THEN
        G;
ELSE
        IF (¬P & R) THEN
                H;
        ELSE
                F;
```

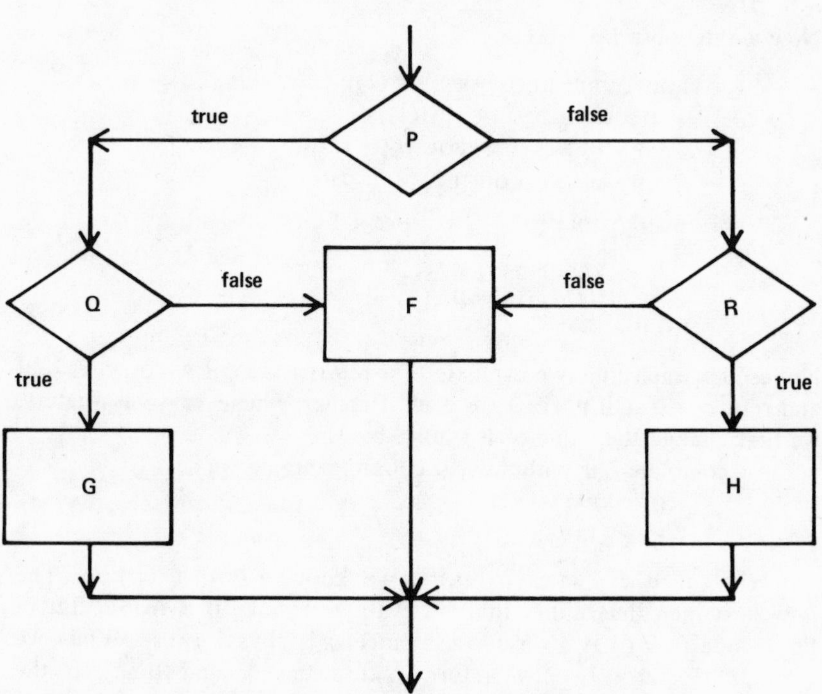

FIG. 3.26 A nonstructured flowchart

The flowchart and the above code depict the same computations in most but not in all cases. For in the PL/I code, if the expression "(P & Q)" evaluates to FALSE, then we evaluate the expression "(¬P & R)". That is, we evaluate P twice in some circumstances, whereas we always evaluate P just once in computations represented by the flowchart. Let's construct a pathological case where these two methods differ. We use the variables

```
DECLARE
    TRUE
        BIT (1)
        INITIAL ('1'B),
    FALSE
        BIT (1)
        INITIAL ('0'B),
    P_COUNT
        FIXED DECIMAL
        INITIAL (0),
    (Q, R)
        BIT (1)
;
```

Now we define P by

```
P:  PROCEDURE  RETURNS  (BIT (1));
        DECLARE  VALUE  BIT(1);
        P_COUNT  =  P_COUNT + 1;
        IF  MOD(P_COUNT,2) = 1  THEN
            VALUE  =  TRUE;
        ELSE
            VALUE  =  FALSE;
        RETURN  (VALUE);
    END  P;
```

Notice that each time we evaluate P, it returns TRUE if P_COUNT is odd and returns FALSE if P_COUNT is even. Further, whenever we evaluate P, we first change the value of P_COUNT by 1.

To complete our pathological counterexample we set

```
Q = FALSE;
R = TRUE;
```

Now, if P evaluates to TRUE, we know P_COUNT is odd. The flowchart then determines that we evaluate F since Q is FALSE. But in PL/I code (P & Q) is always FALSE since Q is always FALSE. When we evaluate (¬P & R) P now returns FALSE this second time, so the expression (¬P & R) is TRUE, FOR R is always TRUE. Therefore, the PL/I code determines that we execute H while the flowchart indicates F.

Similarly, if P first evaluates to FALSE, the flowchart will specify H for execution and the PL/I code will select F instead.

Obviously, the procedure P was contrived. Good programmers would never use such an aberration. However, it does demonstrate that the flowchart and the PL/I code determine, in general, different classes of computations.

Now the code

```
IF  P
   THEN DO;
            IF  Q
                THEN  G;
                ELSE  F;
        END;
   ELSE DO;
            IF  R
                THEN  H;
                ELSE  F;
        END;
```

is indeed equivalent to the flowchart.

But notice that we have two copies of the function F in the above code. If F itself stands for a large section of code, then the above formulation is not very acceptable. To avoid duplication of F, we could replace each instance of F by "CALL F_SUBR" and then declare

```
F_SUBR:  PROCEDURE;
                 F;
         END F_SUBR;
```

Or, alternatively, we could precede the code with

```
DO_F  =  FALSE;
```

replace each of the two F occurrences by

```
DO_F  =  TRUE;
```

and immediately follow the code with

```
IF DO_F THEN F;
```

Either alternative—calling the subroutine F_SUBR or setting the DO_F indicator—produces code which is both equivalent to the original flowchart *and* uses F only once in the code text.

As a second example, consider the nonstructured flowchart in Fig. 3.27.

We will give several PL/I encodings which are equivalent to this

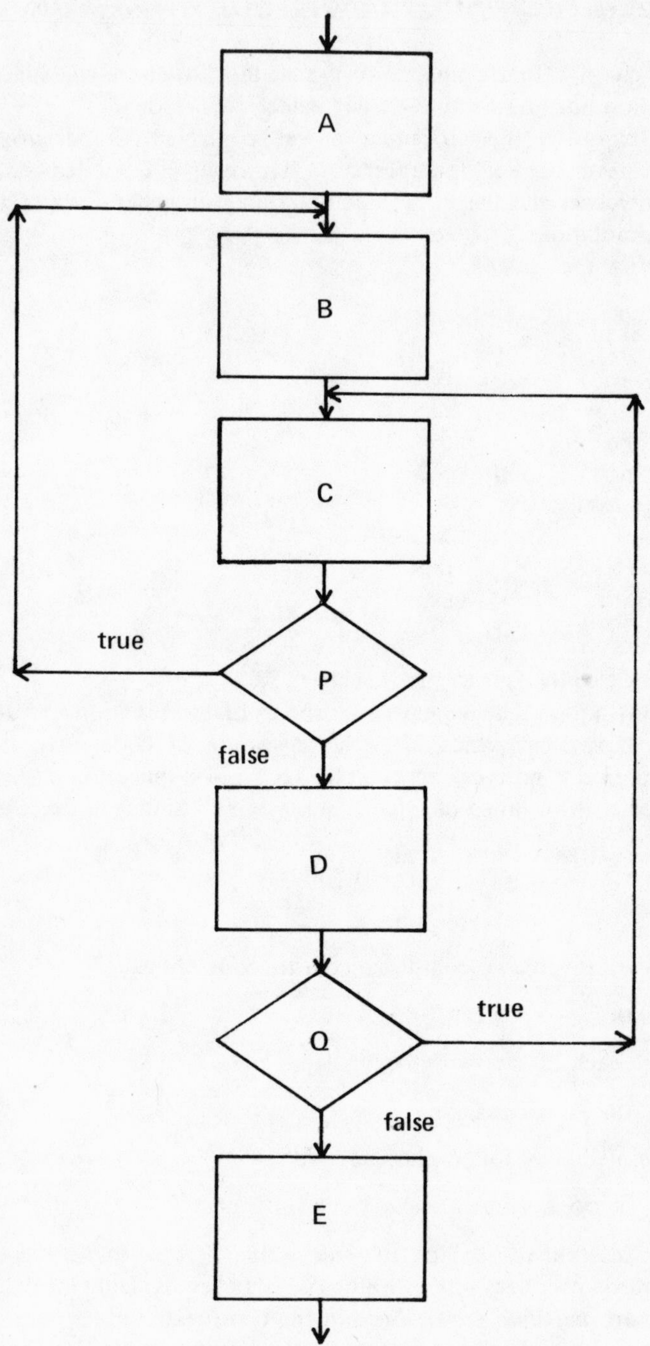

FIG. 3.27 A second nonstructured flowchart

flowchart. Further, each version will have the tests P, Q and the functions A, B, C, D, E only once in its PL/I text.

```
A;
CALL  B_SUBR;
Q_VAL  =  TRUE;
DO WHILE (Q_VAL);
        CALL  C_SUBR;
        DO WHILE (P);
              CALL  B_SUBR;
              CALL  C_SUBR;
        END;
        D;
        Q_VAL  =  Q;
END;
E;
```

where, of course,

```
B_SUBR:  PROCEDURE;                     C_SUBR:  PROCEDURE;
               B;             and                     C;
         END B_SUBR;                             END C_SUBR;
```

and Q_VAL is declared as BIT(1).

The initialization of Q_VAL to TRUE ensures that we execute the DO-PART of the outer DO-WHILE at least once. Thereafter, Q_VAL reflects the value of Q. This is a classic example of why we sometimes want the REPEAT ... UNTIL construct. Here we can use it without introducing a new variable such as Q_VAL. We write

```
A;
CALL  B_SUBR;
REPEAT;
        CALL C_SUBR;
        DO WHILE (P);
              CALL  B_SUBR;
              CALL  C_SUBR;
        END;
        D;
UNTIL (¬Q);
E;
```

We can write an equivalent PL/I program which avoids both duplicating function code and using subroutine calls. We do this by introducing new boolean variables, P_LOOP and Q_LOOP (i.e., they have the BIT(1) attribute).

```
A;
P_LOOP = TRUE;
Q_LOOP = FALSE;
DO WHILE (P_LOOP | Q_LOOP);
        IF ¬ Q_LOOP THEN B;
        C;
        P_LOOP = P;
        Q_LOOP = FALSE;
        IF ¬ P_LOOP THEN
                DO;
                        D;
                        Q_LOOP = Q;
                END;
END;
E;
```

Some might object that the equivalent structured PL/I code is not as clear, not as easy to understand, as the original unstructured flowchart. In reply, there are two points which you should realize. First, converting an unstructured flowchart directly into code by using GO TO'S would also sacrifice some clarity. In general, we lose something when we go from a two-dimensional graphical picture to a sequence of textual statements. The second point is that the exercise *started* with an unstructured flowchart. Naturally expressing equivalent logic in structured code is not the goal of structured programming. Rather, we discipline the logic we use in developing our programs. The result is a very direct correspondence between our structured final code and any flowchart that depicts our program's logic.

4. TOP-DOWN STRUCTURED PROGRAMMING

This chapter presents a particular methodology, called top-down segmented structured programming, for producing structured PL/I programs. First, we describe and illustrate this approach to programming. Next, we contrast top-down coding and integration with the more standard bottom-up strategy. Then, we consider some implications of top-down programming for testing. Finally, we mention recursion as a technique which naturally blends with a top-down approach.

4.1 TOP-DOWN PROGRAMMING

In Section 3.4 we proffered a definition of top-down structured programming. The definition was in terms of a pseudo-PL/I program. It described a step-by-step process of going from a program's functional specifications to a PL/I program. This process, with its "correctness questions," is a programming elaboration of some mathematical results. The goal is correct programs; the means are the three basic figures, which are known to be sufficient, and their associated "correctness questions."

We could extend the pseudo-program definition to include other structured (one-entry/one-exit) figures, such as ITERATIVE-DO, REPEAT-UNTIL, LOOP-EXITIF-ENDLOOP, and SELECT-CASE. We would associate an appropriate correctness question with each new figure. But instead we will assume the reader is now sufficiently aware of correctness considerations to properly examine his use of a nonbasic figure.

In this section we describe a top-down methodology for program design *and* construction. This approach is in the same spirit as that of Section 3.4; instead of proceeding step-by-step at the figure level, we do this stepwise refinement process at the "small" program level. In so doing we will describe an actual recommended programming practice and not some theoretical ideal.

The general idea is that *all* programs should be short. We can read, comprehend, and check short programs for correctness, especially if they are nicely structured and formatted. However, most interesting programs contain many statements. How can a program with many statements be considered a short program? The answer, of course, is to use procedures and macro substitutions; PL/I supports both of these important language features. This points out the principal role of subroutines (and macros) in structured programming: They permit us to abstract and express the essentials of an algorithm and, therefore, to partition a program into meaningful, manageable units.

To enforce the discipline of writing all programs as short programs, Mills introduced the notion of a segment.[1] A *segment* ordinarily is a listing page (or less) of program text (i.e., 50 or fewer lines of code). A segment will typically name other segments to be included (via a preprocessor %INCLUDE *seg-name*; statement) or to be called as function or subroutine procedures. Except for segments consisting of declarations, segments are small structured programs.

In languages like COBOL and FORTRAN, which do not have a general macro substitution facility, we achieve program segmentation with both subroutines and hand-coded simulations of substitutions.

In COBOL we principally use the PERFORM verb to segment our programs, as in

```
PERFORM   SEGMENT-S.
```

where the paragraph SEGMENT-S will appear on a separate listing page. In some cases you can use a COPY statement to segment, but the copied text cannot contain another COPY statement.

Just as we used GO TO's to realize those structured figures not explicitly present in FORTRAN (in Section 3.7), so we will also use GO TO's to synthesize macro substitution. For example, we might have the code fragment

```
C
C  INCLUDE SEGMENT-S
C
              GO TO   1001
   1002       CONTINUE
```

as part of one FORTRAN segment. Then on another listing page we would have

```
C
C  SEGMENT-S
C
 1001      CONTINUE
             Code for segment S
           GO TO   1002
```

With this coding technique we can write nicely segmented FORTRAN programs without sacrificing the freedom to expand any subroutine in-line in order to improve our program's execution time. For clarity purposes, it is best not to generalize (?) this "in-line subroutine" technique to accommodate multiple inclusions of a single FORTRAN code segment.

Since segments are structured programs, they have one entry (at the top of the listing page) and one exit (at the bottom of the page). Structured figures are not broken across segment boundaries. For instance, a code listing page with an IF also contains the matching THEN and ELSE (if there is one) in order to visually highlight their logical relationships. Similarly, an END appears in the same segment as its corresponding DO, BEGIN, or PROC. Each segment of a program thus can be read from top to bottom. If we have the functional specifications for a segment, it is a very feasible task informally to check that segment for correctness.

The segment becomes the basis for top-down programming. Given functional specifications, we first write a program segment which meets these specifications. Since it is unlikely that one page of PL/I code will suffice, our first segment must refer to other segments in order to fit on a single listing page. In introducing new segment names, we must determine their functional specifications. Our first segment (corresponding to the program's high-level flowchart) can be checked for correctness *assuming* the other segments referred to meet their specifications. The process repeats itself until no named but uncoded segments remain.

We can characterize this iterative approach by the following pseudo-code:

```
LOOP;
        Get uncoded functional specifications;
EXITIF ( no uncoded specifications remain );
        Write a segment to meet the specifications;
        Check the correctness of the segment;
ENDLOOP;
```

Here the first *Get* selects the original program specifications. The *Write* instruction, of course, implies a short structured program. Quite likely this instruction will result in new segment names and their attendant specifications. The *Check* is, in effect, an informal proof of the segment program's correctness. The assumptions we may use in our proof are the functional specifications for the newly introduced segment names. *Proof* is too formal a word, but it implies the spirit in which the segment code is checked. Restricting ourselves to a segment discipline makes such detailed code checking (by both author and others) a realistic undertaking. Checking for correctness is important because it is a much more efficient and better method to guarantee program reliability than is program testing.

Subsequent *Get* instructions usually select segment names and their specifications *in execution order*. That is, the next segment to be coded is the next segment encountered in executing the program in its current form. For example, declarations are usually coded and values generated before coding any segments which reference the declared variables. This means that data structures (as program interfaces) are defined in code and that subsequent references are to their coded form.

Coding in execution sequence is a relatively different mode of operation. Generally, programs are designed top-down and coded bottom-up. Execution sequence for a program implies that the first code we write is the program's JCL. For major programs, instead of drawing a system flowchart detailing the program's files, disks, tapes, and so on, you explicitly specify this in the JCL. This has the advantage of being both ultraprecise and checkable for proper syntax.

After the JCL, any initial link edit code, specifying the number of object modules to be used (if known at this point), overlays, and so on should be written. At this stage dummy files, load module stubs, and the like are required. Finally, execution sequence gets us to our main program, which we will write in PL/I source code.

The main PL/I program is now written in segments. Because we are restricted to one listing page per segment, our coding of the main program focuses first on the high-level functions and control logic. Considerations of specific algorithmic or representational details are postponed to later, subordinate segments. In a sense, coding in execution sequence applies the philosophy of structured programming to the actual development of large, complex software.

We can view a program constructed in this way as a tree of segments. The top or root of the tree is the first code segment which depicts the program's overall control logic and functional capabilities. Intermediate segments in the program tree in effect summarize what is done by the segments below. The bottom segments are short structured programs (or declarations) which name no other segments. Thus, the program itself becomes the principal documentation for the program. To understand, to maintain, or to modify a particular code segment, we start at the top of the program tree and read downward until reaching the segment in question. Each segment we encounter along this path can be read from top to bottom, which means that the function and the precise context of any given code segment can be directly determined.

Each segment is a one-in/one-out function box to its parent in the tree. And each code segment expresses in skeleton form the design and function of all segments below it in the program tree. This means, of course, that the bulk of the code is on the lower levels, but the "most important" code appears in the top-level segments.

Consequently, the focus in top-down programming is to resolve the major program design issues early and in actual code. If the program's functional specifications change, then the implications of this change are easier to see. And if these changes occur in the early phase of a programming project (as they tend to do), recoding is generally easier since the bulk of the code remains to be written. Here recoding coincides with redesigning.

Once a segment (or group of segments) has been written, we would like to integrate it into an evolving *executable* system. But typically, the segment names other uncoded segments to be called or included. To stay executable, we insert a program stub for each as yet uncoded segment.

A *program stub* is some very short code which we enter into a library to serve as a place-holder for an uncoded segment. A program stub should at minimum permit any code that references it to continue executing. A stub must therefore meet any interface requirements specified for the uncoded segment.

To aid in execution tracing, a stub will often print a message such as GOT TO THIS STUB. Stubs can be used to do system simulation prior to final implementation. In this case stub code would also consume execution time and storage space in accordance with projections. Later, since a stub satisfies the necessary interfaces, it can be expanded into the segment for which it stands.

Even for a very large project in top-down programming you have an executable system at an early stage. As new segments are added, the system grows in function. Integration is continuous rather than being a separate activity. The most important code (i.e., the highest level segments) becomes the most exercised. New errors tend to be localized within newly added segments, thus facilitating debugging.

In the top-down approach, segments at the same level are usually coded in the order in which they will be executed. We do this because the earlier executed segments usually produce data required by the later segments. Practicality often requires that the data management code of a large system be written at an early stage (e.g., the file maintenance code for an information-retrieval system or the process and resource management code for an operating system). This allows for early testing of the interfaces between a system and its intended users (or their data).

New segments are referenced by either a procedure call or preprocessor %INCLUDE. The trade-off between these two methods is the classic space/time exchange for subroutines/macros. Procedures are an essential programming tool, but library and macro facilities, such as in PL/I, are an important adjunct to procedural programming languages; they permit us to segment our programs at the source code level without the accompanying execution-time overhead of procedures. Moreover, we can now make efficiency considerations, such as in-line code versus subroutine, subordinate to developing the program's logical structure.

The initial top-down design of a program should be done in a pseudo-code that mixes English-language statements with PL/I. In this pseudo-code for design we depict program control logic with the syntax of the structured figures and we express program functions initially in English. This approach to program design has several advantages. It avoids specific macro/subroutine decisions and thus permits unencumbered functional thinking during design. It replaces flowcharts for system documentation with easy-to-read pseudo-programs. Moreover, there is a natural transition from the top-down design of a system expressed in structured pseudo-code to the actual top-down coding process.

To illustrate, many programs exhibit the following top-level structure:

```
Open data files;
        Initializing action;
            LOOP;
               Get data;
            EXITIF( end-of-data );
               Check data;
               IF data valid
                  THEN Process data;
                  ELSE Error action;
            ENDLOOP;
        Concluding action;
Close data files;
```

Here the *Initializing action* would, in effect, establish the appropriate loop invariant, and the *Concluding action* might include the outputting of final results. The *end-of-data* indicator is often set by an end-of-file condition. The *Process data* function could expand into any of the structured figures, such as the SELECT-CASE. And processing often encompasses doing (intermediate) output.

We express the top-down design of a program's basic algorithms and logical data structures in segmented pseudo-code. This approach embodies some features of the "levels of abstraction" design approach. We cite the following correspondences:

1. The data objects (e.g., PLAYING_BOARD and CUSTOMER_ACCOUNT) and the data operations (e.g., MAKE_MOVE and ADD_TRANSACTION) are *abstract* in the sense they are not PL/I primitives.
2. Top-down design using segments imposes a *hierarchical structure* upon the program.
3. Since design segments are generally short structured pseudo-code programs, they typically contain declarations of abstract data objects (e.g., IO_DEVICE or ROW_INDEX) which either may be accessed by lower level segments (i.e., *shared information*) or may be referenced only in the declaring segment (i.e., *private information*).
4. Design segments are, in effect, programs written for *abstract machines*. The machine instructions and operands include the abstract operations and abstract data objects used in the segment. These operations may subsequently become design segments themselves, and eventually (in the coding phase) the data objects will be given a concrete PL/I realization. Abstract machines supporting the same data objects and operations are often realized by common subroutines.
5. Finally, segments provide one means for *isolating or "hiding" information* in order to reduce widespread dependency upon specifics which are likely to undergo future changes. For instance, only a few design segments need know about an I/O display device, which may be realized initially as a TTY and later changed to a CRT. Using design segments in this fashion helps to confine the effects of modifications to a certain level (of abstraction) within the system.

Often the final program code follows directly from the data-representation choices. For example, suppose we wanted to linearly search a sequence of *Type* T data items for an element with property P.

We might program the search in pseudo-code by:

```
     DCL  SEQ  Data-Structure-for-a-Sequence-of-Type-T-Items,
          ELT  Type T,
          FOUND  Boolean INIT(False),
          END_OF_SEQ  Boolean INIT(False);
  ON END(SEQ)  END_OF_SEQ = True;
          ELT = First-Elt(SEQ);
          DO WHILE(¬FOUND & ¬END_OF_SEQ );
               IF ELT has property P
                  THEN  FOUND = True;
                  ELSE  ELT = Next-Elt(SEQ);
          END;
```

The *Type* T could be arithmetic, character, or even a PL/I structure. And the data structure SEQ might be an array, a character string, or a linked list. Once we have selected specific representations for *Type* T and SEQ, then we have largely determined the code for *First-Elt, Next-Elt,* and detecting the end of SEQ.

Moreover, the principal reason for initially designing in pseudo-code rather than in PL/I directly is to discover which data operations the program will perform. In effect, the various data operations (such as test ELT for property P and get the next element of SEQ) define the program's data objects. For the data operations constitute all that we really know about the abstract data objects.

The pseudo-code design process should be continued at least until the program's basic data and algorithmic structures have been determined. Data representation choices can then be informed and oriented toward the top-down coding of efficient data operations. Of course, this requires an extra investment of time in the program's design phase, but it will pay dividends throughout the implementation. Expressing program design explicitly in pseudo-code provides a new standard for design documentation which eases the transition into actual coding.

Top-down structured programming requires more thought and explicit design considerations. But the resulting code is easier to understand and, hence, easier to maintain and modify. This approach addresses the two major programming problems associated with developing large systems—integration and debugging. In top-down programming interfaces are defined *in code* before the referencing code is even written. The addition of segments in execution order to the developing system merges coding with integration as an ongoing process. Debugging activity is usually focused upon newly added segments.

4.2 AN ILLUSTRATION: THE GAME OF LIFE

This section utilizes a top-down structured programming approach to construct a sample program. The example is intended to highlight some important features of this programming methodology. It includes top-down design using segments, error handling, data representation decisions, top-down coding, and I/O considerations.

Our task is to write a PL/I program for John Horton Conway's fascinating Game of Life. The game was introduced to the public in Martin Gardner's "Mathematical Games" section of the October 1970 *Scientific American*.[2] The game's simple rules, sometimes lengthy computations, and interesting patterns were a natural for computerizing. Now many computer graphics installations have a demonstration version of Life.

Life is played on a large, rectangular grid of squares. Note from Fig. 4.1 that each square has eight neighboring squares. (Here we ignore squares on the grid border.)

At every move during a game each grid square is either occupied or empty. Life's genetic laws for birth, survival, and death apply to a square, depending upon its status and that of its neighbors. Basically, a game commences with some configuration of occupied squares and then you observe how the pattern changes in accordance with the genetic laws.

There are only two laws, or rules:

1. IF a square S is occupied,

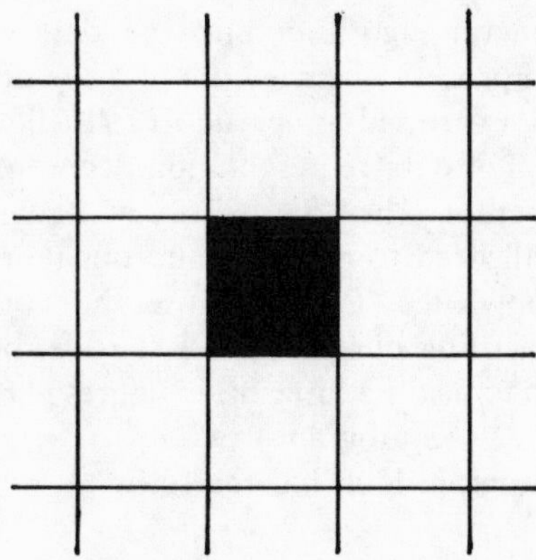

FIG. 4.1 A square (shaded) with its eight neighbors

THEN S remains occupied *if* S has at least two but no more than three occupied neighboring squares;
ELSE S becomes empty.

2. IF a square S is empty,
THEN S becomes occupied *if* S has exactly three occupied neighboring squares;
ELSE S remains empty.

A move in a game consists of *simultaneously* applying these laws to each grid square. For example, Fig. 4.2 shows the fate of a simple pattern.

Now let's give the input/output, or functional specifications, for our proposed Game of Life program. To be concrete, we select a 24-by-24 grid of squares as the playing board.

INPUT. A sequence of game-requests, where a *game-request* is (1) an integer, the number of moves to be performed, followed by (2) some integer pairs, the row and column board positions of the initially occupied squares, terminated by (3) the 0,0 integer pair. (Note: With PL/I's list-directed transmission, no explicit input format need be given.)

OUTPUT. For each game-request print (1) the game-request itself (excepting, of course, the terminating 0,0 pair), indicating any row-column pairs not located on the 24-by-24 board, followed by (2) the successive game moves from the initial configuration (MOVE 0) up to the number of moves requested.

We allow for zero moves being requested (i.e., just printing the initial pattern) and for no row-column pairs preceding a 0,0 terminator (i.e., a pattern of all empty squares).

After getting a program's functional specifications, we should next design both the general algorithm and the data structures for our program. This design process is carried out in a top-down fashion, using structured segments expressed in pseudo-PL/I code. If possible, we should postpone explicit data representation decisions until we actually start coding the program. Then we will know better the various data manipulations we will need to perform, and our representation choices can exploit this knowledge. (We will use the LOOP-EXITIF-ENDLOOP structured figure in writing our pseudo-PL/I code, but for contrast we will restrict ourselves to just the three basic figures plus the ITERATIVE-DO when we actually code the program.)

The principal program loop has the form:

```
LOOP;
        Get a game-request;
EXITIF(end-of-file);
```

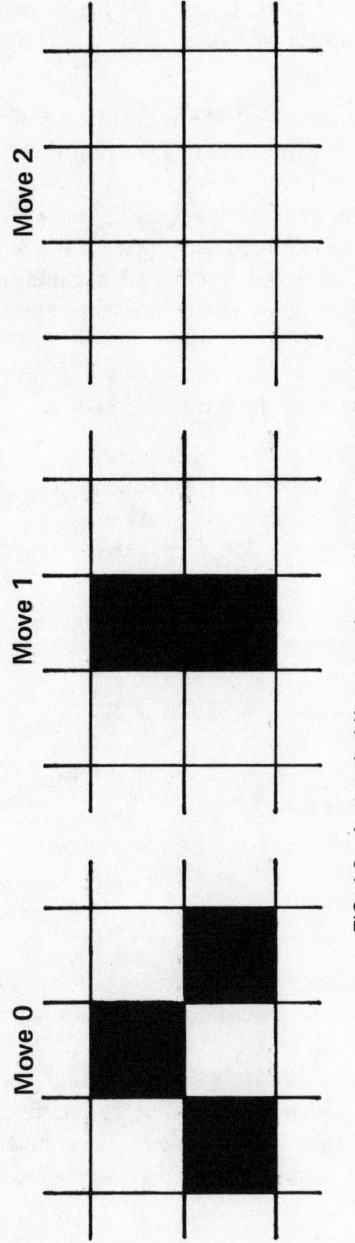

FIG. 4.2 A sample Life game (occupied squares are shaded)

```
            Play the requested game for the requested
                  number of moves;
    ENDLOOP;
```

To illustrate the handling and the reporting of errors we observe that there are really two possible end-of-file conditions:

1. Normal, when we expect another game-request (i.e., on the first GET or on a GET immediately after a 0,0 pair)
2. Abnormal, during the GETting of a game-request (i.e., after we GET the number of moves to do, but before we encounter a 0,0 pair).

This observation leads to the pseudo-code

```
DCL (#MOVES,MOVE#) Integer,
       EOF_1 Boolean INIT(FALSE),
       EOF_2 Boolean INIT(FALSE);
  ON ENDFILE(SYSIN) EOF_1 = TRUE;

  LOOP;
         Get #MOVES;
  EXITIF( EOF_1 );
          Initialize-Board( EOF_2 );
  EXITIF( EOF_2 );
         DO MOVE# = 1 TO #MOVES;
            Make-Move( );
         END;
  ENDLOOP;

  IF EOF_2 THEN Print Error Message;
```

where the *Initialize-Board*(EOF_2); call sets the argument EOF_2 to TRUE if an abnormal end-of-file condition occurs while GETting a game-request.

If we assume the subroutine *Initialize-Board* prints a game-request, then our code still must incorporate a board and the printing of individual moves. Since Life's genetic laws must be simultaneously evaluated, we find it convenient to use two boards, say OLD and NEW. The subroutine call

```
Make-Move( OLD, NEW );
```

will now compute the next move for the OLD board (i.e., the input parameter) and place the resulting pattern on the NEW board (i.e., the output parameter). This gives the following pseudo-code segment:

```
LIFE: PROC OPTIONS(MAIN);

   DCL(#MOVES,MOVE#) Integer,
      (OLD,NEW) Board,
      EOF_1 Boolean INIT(FALSE),
      EOF_2 Boolean INIT(FALSE);

   ON ENDFILE(SYSIN) EOF_1 = TRUE;

   LOOP;
        Get #MOVES;
   EXITIF( EOF_1 );
        Print Header;
        Initialize-Board( NEW, EOF_2 );
   EXITIF( EOF_2 );
        Print-Board( NEW , 0 );
        DO MOVE# = 1 TO #MOVES;
              Swap( OLD, NEW );
              Make-Move( OLD, NEW );
              Print-Board( NEW, MOVE# );
        END;
   ENDLOOP;

   IF EOF_2 THEN Print Error Message;
END LIFE;
```

This top-level segment names four possible additional segments: *Initialize-Board, Print-Board, Swap,* and *Make-Move*. Execution order determines that *Initialize-Board* should be the segment we develop next. The specifications for this segment are simple: the BOARD parameter is the board to be initialized, and the EOF parameter records whether an abnormal end-of-file condition occurred during initialization. Also, the locations of initially occupied squares should be printed. We code this segment straightforwardly:

```
Initialize-Board: PROC( BOARD , EOF );
  DCL      BOARD Board,
           EOF Boolean,
           ( ROW, COL ) Integer;
    ON ENDFILE(SYSIN) BEGIN;
```

```
                        EOF = TRUE;
                        ROW,COL = -1;
                     END;
      Print 'ROW COLUMN' Header;
      Set all BOARD squares vacant;

      LOOP;
         Get (ROW,COL);                /* NEXT SQUARE */
      EXITIF( (ROW=0 & COL=0) | EOF );
         Print Square(ROW,COL);
         IF Square is on the board
          THEN Make BOARD(ROW,COL) Occupied;
          ELSE Print ' NOT ON BOARD' Error Message;
      ENDLOOP;

   END Initialize-Board;
```

The next (in execution order) segment we should write is *Print-Board.* Here the algorithm is just to print (naturally with borders) one row at a time. We will use the character # to denote an occupied square and blank characters for empty squares.

```
   Print-Board: PROC( BOARD, MOVE#);
     DCL BOARD    Board,
         MOVE#    Integer;
     DCL (ROW,COL)   Integer,
         BORDER Character-String INIT( String-Constant ),
         LINE Character-String,
         VB  CHAR( 1 );        /*Vertical Border*/

      Print BORDER;
      DO ROW = 1 TO Max-Row-Index of BOARD;
         Determine VB;
         LINE = '';          /* Set LINE to all blanks     */
                             /* Form next output LINE */
         DO COL = 1 TO Max-Col-Index of BOARD;
            IF BOARD(ROW,COL) Occupied
               THEN Insert '#' into LINE at proper position;
         END; /* COL iteration */

         Print VB || LINE || VB;
      END; /* ROW iteration */
```

```
        Print BORDER;
        Print Subtitle with ('MOVE' , MOVE# );
    END Print-Board;
```

Our next segment candidate is *Swap*. But swapping is an easy operation; however it is directly tied to our eventual choice for representing the data type *Board*. Quite likely, once we make this representation decision, we can replace the

"*Swap*(OLD , NEW);"

statement in our top level segment with in-line code.

So, instead we write some simple structured pseudo-code for *Make-Move*, the last segment name.

```
    Make-Move: PROC( OLD , NEW );
        DCL (OLD,NEW) Board;
        DCL (ROW,COL) Integer;
         DO ROW = 1 TO Max-Row-Index of OLD;
            DO COL = 1 TO Max-Col-Index of OLD;

               Count neighbors of OLD(ROW,COL);
               Set square NEW(ROW,COL) according to the rules;

            END; /* COL iteration */
         END; /* ROW iteration */

    END Make-Move;
```

At this point the program's top-down design is complete. Now we should decide upon a representation for *Board* data types so that we can begin the actual top-down coding. To guide this decision we examine our pseudo-code for the various operations performed on *Board* data items. We find three such operations:

1. Set the ROW,COL square of a *Board* to be either occupied or empty
2. Count the occupied neighboring squares for each *Board* square
3. Swap the *Boards* OLD and NEW.

Based on operations 1 and 2, we let a *Board* be a two-dimensional integer array whose ROW,COL entry has the value 1 (if the ROW,COL square is occupied) or 0 (to signify an empty *Board* square). This representation choice makes operation 2 particularly easy to perform —for any given *Board* square, the sum of the values of all its neighbors is the number of occupied neighboring squares.

We extend the 24-by-24 grid by a border of empty squares so that we do not have to treat a square on the original grid border as a special case whenever we perform operation 2. These considerations lead to:

```
DCL   OLD(0:25,0:25)   FIXED BIN,
      NEW(0:25,0:25)   FIXED BIN;
```

and our dependency upon a particular grid size is reflected in

```
DCL SIZE FIXED BIN INIT(24);
```

which also gives the current maximum row and column index referred to by the design segments *Print-Board* and *Make-Move.*

To perform operation 3 without using a temporary 26-by-26 integer array, we declare the arrays OLD and NEW to be based on the pointers OLD@ and NEW@, respectively. Then with just a third pointer variable, say P, we can code

Swap(OLD, NEW);

in-line by

```
P = OLD@;
OLD@ = NEW@;
NEW@ = P;
```

which is both simple and efficient. Since OLD and NEW are to be based arrays, we now must explicitly allocate them. Also, we should initialize their extra borders (i.e., the 0th and the 25th rows and columns) with empty squares. The code

```
ALLOCATE OLD,NEW;
OLD,NEW = 0;
```

accomplishes these details.

Having made a representation choice for the *Boards* OLD and NEW, and having considered coding ramifications of that decision, we now proceed with our top-down coding using PL/I segments. To start, we will take *Initialize-Board, Print-Board*, and *Make-Move* to be subroutines grouped under the library name PROCS. We permit our top-level code segment to call these procedures (yet to be written) via a

```
%INCLUDE PROCS;
```

statement. Subsequently, we will flesh out these subroutines as PL/I code segments derived from the corresponding pseudo-code design segments. Our top-level code segment is

```
/* THE GAME OF LIFE */
LIFE: PROC OPTIONS(MAIN);

    DCL  (#MOVES,MOVE#) FIXED BIN,
         SIZE FIXED BIN STATIC INIT(24),       /* BOARD SIZE */
         ( OLD@ , NEW@ , P ) PTR,
         OLD(0:25,0:25) FIXED BIN BASED(OLD@),    /* OLD BOARD */
         NEW(0:25,0:25) FIXED BIN BASED(NEW@);  /* NEW BOARD */
    DCL  EOF_1 BIT(1) INIT('0'B),
         EOF_2 BIT(1) INIT('0'B);

    %INCLUDE PROCS;

    ON ENDFILE(SYSIN)   EOF_1 = '1'B;

    /* LIFE PROCEDURE BODY */

    ALLOCATE OLD,NEW;
    OLD , NEW = 0;
    GET LIST( #MOVES );

    DO WHILE( ¬EOF_1 & ¬EOF_2 );           /* PLAY GAMES */

        PUT PAGE EDIT ('NO. MOVES',#MOVES) (A,F(5));

        CALL INITIALIZE_BOARD( NEW , EOF_2 );

        IF EOF_2
            THEN PUT SKIP EDIT (' INITIALIZATION FAILED') (A);
            ELSE DO;

                 CALL PRINT_BOARD(NEW,0);

                 DO MOVE# = 1 TO #MOVES; /* MAKE MOVES */
                      P = OLD@;
                      OLD@ = NEW@;
                      NEW@ = P;
                      CALL MAKE_MOVE(OLD,NEW);
                      CALL PRINT_BOARD(NEW,MOVE#);
                 END; /* MOVE# ITERATION */
```

```
                GET LIST(#MOVES);

            END; /* ELSE CLAUSE */

    END; /* WHILE LOOP */

  END LIFE;
```

Of the three subroutines referenced by this main procedure LIFE, INITIALIZE_BOARD is the first encountered in execution order. It can now be coded directly from its corresponding design segment, which serves, in effect, as its documentation. Of course, we immediately precede each internal procedure, such as INITIALIZE_BOARD, with an appropriate ENTRY attribute declaration.

```
/* INITIALIZE_BOARD PROCEDURE */
DCL INITIALIZE_BOARD ENTRY( (*,*) FIXED BIN , BIT(1) );
INITIALIZE_BOARD: PROC( BOARD, EOF );
      DCL BOARD(*,*) FIXED BIN,
          EOF BIT(1);
      DCL (ROW,COL) FIXED BIN;
      ON ENDFILE(SYSIN) BEGIN;
                             EOF = '1'B;
                             ROW,COL = -1;
                         END;
      PUT SKIP(2) EDIT ('ROW  COLUMN') (A);
      BOARD = 0;
      GET LIST(ROW,COL);
      DO WHILE( (ROW¬=0 | COL¬=0) & ¬EOF );
           PUT SKIP EDIT (ROW,COL) (F(3),F(6));
           IF (1<=ROW & ROW<=SIZE) &
              (1<=COL & COL<=SIZE)
                THEN BOARD(ROW,COL)  = 1;
                ELSE PUT EDIT ('          NOT ON BOARD') (A);
           GET LIST(ROW,COL);
      END;
END INITIALIZE_BOARD;
```

Note that INITIALIZE_BOARD contains the array assignment

```
BOARD = 0;
```

to initialize the squares to being empty. And the main procedure LIFE calls this subroutine with the array NEW as an argument. Thus, as a minor optimization, we could replace the array assignments

```
OLD , NEW = 0;
```

in the code segment LIFE with just

```
OLD = 0;
```

since NEW will be assigned 0 by the INITIALIZE_BOARD subroutine.

The PRINT_BOARD segment should be coded next. Here our principal concern is with producing "nice" output. We would like a board, when printed, to appear nearly square. Now our print line has ten characters per inch (in the horizontal direction), and there are six print lines per inch (in the vertical direction). This means a 26-by-26 configuration of characters (the 24-by-24 grid plus printed borders) would measure 2.6 inches by 4.3 inches.

One simple way to improve upon this 3:5 ratio is to double the horizontal component, giving a 6:5 ratio. In our case, this means using 48 print character positions to represent the status of the 24 squares in a grid row. So, if the ROW,COL entry is occupied (i.e., if BOARD(ROW,COL) = 1), we will place a '#' in the COL+COL position of the output LINE corresponding to ROW. Consequently, we will regard the printed pattern

```
# #
```

as denoting two adjacent occupied grid squares. By this scaling convention, the left end of a LINE (i.e., position 1) can never be a '#'; so, for symmetry, we make each print LINE 49 characters long (i.e., with a blank at the right end also).

To visually reinforce the 2:1 print scaling, we will make every tenth horizontal border element and every fifth vertical border element the particular character '+'. So, a 24-by-24 board will be printed as a 51-by-26 configuration of characters, which is a more nearly square 5.1 inches by 4.3 inches. With our output decisions completed, we can now code the PRINT_BOARD subroutine.

```
/* PRINT_BOARD PROCEDURE */
DCL PRINT_BOARD ENTRY( (*,*) FIXED BIN, FIXED BIN );
PRINT_BOARD: PROC( BOARD, MOVE# );
     DCL  BOARD(*,*) FIXED BIN,
          MOVE#  FIXED BIN;
     DCL  (ROW,COL) FIXED BIN,
          BORDER CHAR( 51 ) STATIC
           INIT('+---------+---------+---------+---------+---------+'),
          LINE  CHAR( 49 ),           /* ROW OF BOARD */
          VB CHAR( 1 );               /* VERTICAL BORDER */
```

```
        PUT PAGE EDIT (BORDER) (A);
        DO ROW = 1 TO SIZE;          /* PRINT ROWS */
           IF MOD(ROW,5) = 0  THEN VB = '+';
                              ELSE VB = '|';
           LINE = '';
           DO COL = 1 TO SIZE;       /* FORM ROWS */
              IF BOARD(ROW,COL) = 1
                 THEN SUBSTR(LINE,COL+COL,1) = '#';
           END; /* COL ITERATION */
           PUT SKIP EDIT (VB,LINE,VB) (3 A);
        END; /* ROW ITERATION */
        PUT EDIT (BORDER) (SKIP,A)
              ('MOVE',MOVE#) (SKIP,X(22),A,F(3));
     END PRINT_BOARD;
```

Only the MAKE_MOVE segment now remains to be coded. We could at this point write a program stub such as:

```
     DCL MAKE_MOVE ENTRY((*,*) FIXED BIN, (*,*) FIXED BIN);
     MAKE_MOVE: PROC( OLD , NEW);
           DCL ( OLD(*,*) , NEW(*,*) ) FIXED BIN;
                PUT SKIP LIST( ' MAKE_MOVE CALLED ' );
     END MAKE_MOVE;
```

which would allow us to compile, execute, and partially test the code we have already completed.

In counting the occupied neighbors of the grid square OLD(ROW,COL), we exploit our representation choices. We just sum the values of the nine pertinent squares—i.e., OLD(ROW,COL) *and* its eight neighbors—within two simple nested loops. Now, if the OLD(ROW,COL) square was occupied, then by the game's laws, in order for the NEW(ROW,COL) square to become occupied, this sum should be either 3 or 4 [i.e., OLD(ROW,COL) has either two or three occupied neighboring squares]. And if the OLD(ROW,COL) square was empty, then this sum must be exactly 3 for a "birth" to take place on the NEW(ROW,COL) square.

We complete our Game of Life program by coding the MAKE_MOVE subroutine.

```
     /* MAKE_MOVE PROCEDURE */
     DCL MAKE_MOVE ENTRY((*,*) FIXED BIN , (*,*) FIXED BIN);
     MAKE_MOVE: PROC( OLD, NEW );
        DCL ( OLD(*,*), NEW(*,*) ) FIXED BIN;
        DCL ( ROW, COL, I, J, COUNT ) FIXED BIN;
```

```
    DO ROW = 1 TO SIZE;
       DO COL = 1 TO SIZE;
          COUNT = 0;
                                /* COUNT NEIGHBORS */
          DO I = (ROW - 1) TO (ROW + 1);
             DO J = (COL - 1) TO (COL + 1);
                COUNT = COUNT + OLD(I,J);
             END; /* J ITERATION */
          END; /* I ITERATION */
          IF   COUNT=3 | ( OLD(ROW,COL)=1 & COUNT=4 )
             THEN NEW(ROW,COL) = 1;
             ELSE NEW(ROW,COL) = 0;
       END; /* COL ITERATION */
    END; /* ROW ITERATION */
 END MAKE_MOVE;
```

There are several ways in which we could improve the execution efficiency of our program. We mention two such optimizations.

1. Currently, for each of the 576 grid squares, we perform nine additions and nine array element accesses. Assuming most of the patterns that the program will process are sparse (i.e., have many more empty than occupied squares), we could use a different board representation so that we do neighbor computations only when necessary. For instance, in the main procedure LIFE we could replace our declaration of the boards OLD and NEW with

```
DCL 1 OLD(0:25,0:25) BASED(OLD@),
          2 STATUS BIT(1),
          2 #NEIGHBORS FIXED BIN;
DCL 1 NEW(0:25,0:25) BASED(NEW@) LIKE OLD;
DCL EMPTY BIT(1) INIT('0'B),
     OCCUPIED BIT(1) INIT('1'B);
```

Then we could recode the subroutine MAKE_MOVE as follows:

```
/* MAKE_MOVE FOR ALTERNATE REPRESENTATION OF BOARDS */
DCL MAKE_MOVE ENTRY( 1 (*,*), 2 BIT(1), 2 FIXED BIN,
                     1 (*,*), 2 BIT(1), 2 FIXED BIN);
MAKE_MOVE: PROC( OLD , NEW );
     DCL 1 OLD(*,*),
              2 STATUS BIT(1),
              2 #NEIGHBORS FIXED BIN;
     DCL 1 NEW(*,*) LIKE OLD;
     DCL ( ROW, COL ) FIXED BIN;
```

```
        NEW.#NEIGHBORS = 0;
        DO ROW = 1 TO SIZE;
           DO COL = 1 TO SIZE;
              IF (OLD(ROW,COL).#NEIGHBORS = 3)
               | ( (OLD(ROW,COL).#NEIGHBORS = 2)
                 &(OLD(ROW,COL).STATUS = OCCUPIED) )
               THEN DO;
                       NEW(ROW,COL).STATUS = OCCUPIED;
                       %INCLUDE UPNGBRS;
                    END;
               ELSE NEW(ROW,COL).STATUS = EMPTY;
           END; /* COL ITERATION */
        END; /* ROW ITERATION */
END MAKE_MOVE;
```

The segment UPNGBRS consists of eight assignments which increase the #NEIGHBORS counter for each neighbor of NEW(ROW,COL). For example, the first such assignment is

```
NEW(ROW - 1,COL - 1).#NEIGHBORS =
                    NEW(ROW - 1,COL - 1).#NEIGHBORS + 1;
```

2. We could expand one or more of the subroutines in-line. For example, we could include the segments PRINT_BOARD and MAKE_MOVE as in-line code in the top-level segment LIFE. The affected code fragment of LIFE would then read:

```
%INCLUDE PRINT_BD;
DO MOVE# = 1 TO #MOVES;    /* MAKE MOVES */
      P = OLD@;
      OLD@ = NEW@;
      NEW@ = P;
      %INCLUDE MAKE_MV;
      %INCLUDE PRINT_BD;
END; /* MOVE# ITERATION */
```

where the texts of PRINT_BD and MAKE_MV are suitably modified versions of the PRINT_BOARD and MAKE_MOVE subroutines, respectively. For instance, the MAKE_MV text would be:

```
DCL ( ROW, COL, I, J, COUNT ) FIXED BIN;
   DO ROW = 1 TO SIZE;
        DO COL = 1 TO SIZE;
           COUNT = 0;
                                /* COUNT NEIGHBORS */
```

```
            DO I = (ROW - 1) TO (ROW + 1);
               DO J = (COL - 1) TO (COL + 1);
                  COUNT = COUNT + OLD(I,J);
               END; /* J ITERATION */
            END; /* I ITERATION */

            IF COUNT=3 | (OLD(ROW,COL)=1 & COUNT=4)
                  THEN   NEW(ROW,COL) = 1;
                  ELSE   NEW(ROW,COL) = 0;
         END; /* COL ITERATION */
      END; /* ROW ITERATION */
```

which, when included in-line, uses PL/I's freedom in the placement of DECLARE statements. (However, PRINT_BD's declarations must be factored out of the segment since they will be inserted in-line twice.) Note that such optimizations preserve the segment structuring of our program.

In passing, we observe that the pseudo-code segments, developed during the design phase, serve as precise (but not too detailed) documentation for the corresponding PL/I code segments. We conclude this illustration of top-down segmented structured programming with some sample program output:

4.3 TOP-DOWN vs. BOTTOM-UP IMPLEMENTATION

In Section 4.1 we described and advocated top-down segmented structured programming. In this approach you start with a program's functional specifications. (Sometimes obtaining a precise statement of the functional requirements for a program is a major undertaking.) Design then proceeds top-down by segments, which are short structured programs written in a PL/I-like pseudo-code. The design segments are usually developed in execution order.

During this process we often declare some very general data types (e.g., PLAYING_BOARD, CUSTOMER_ACCOUNT, PARSE_TREE) and we also specify in pseudo-code some very general data operations (e.g., MAKE_MOVE, UPDATE, FIND_NODE). That is, in the design phase we primarily decide upon a general algorithm and the data it will manipulate. We express these decisions as a structured program written in pseudo-code.

Next, we select particular data structure representations for realizing the general data types used in program design. These representation choices are motivated principally by how easy and how efficient it is actually to code the program's general data operations in PL/I. (Later

```
NO. MOVES    8

ROW  COLUMN
 12    10
 12    11
 12    12
 12    13
 12    14
  0    25      NOT ON BOARD
```

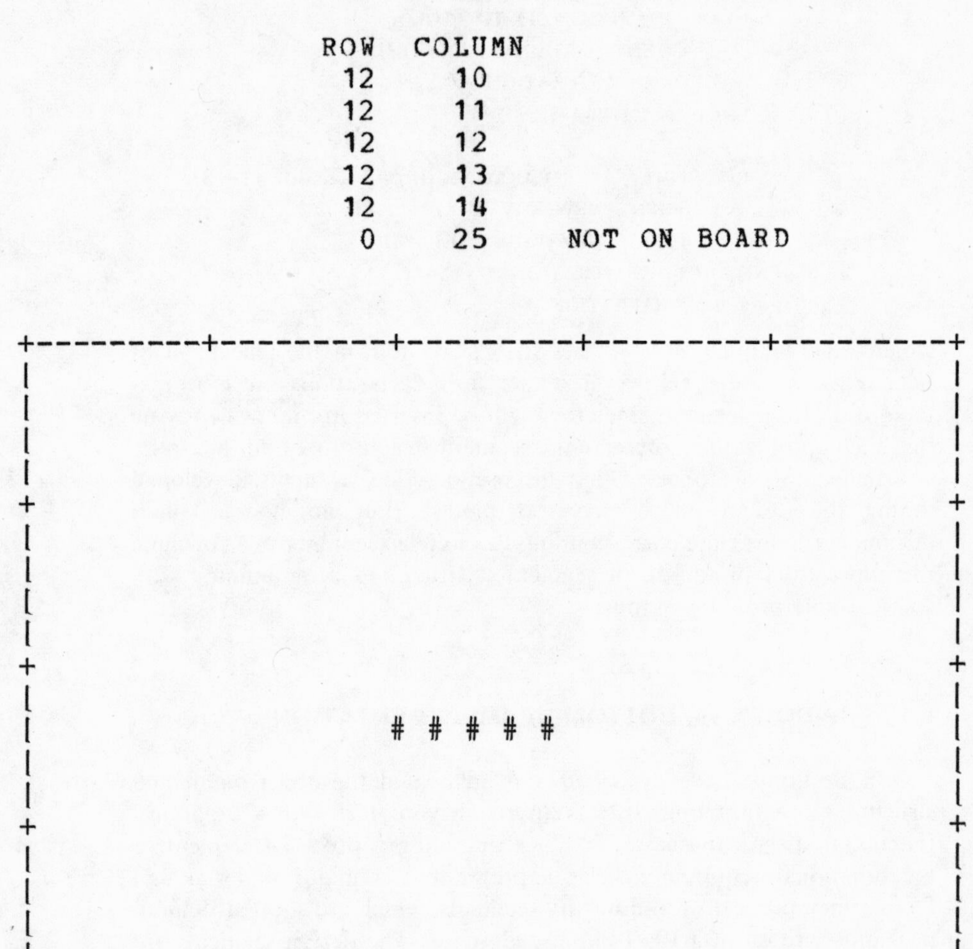

MOVE 0

FIG. 4.3 Sample output of LIFE program

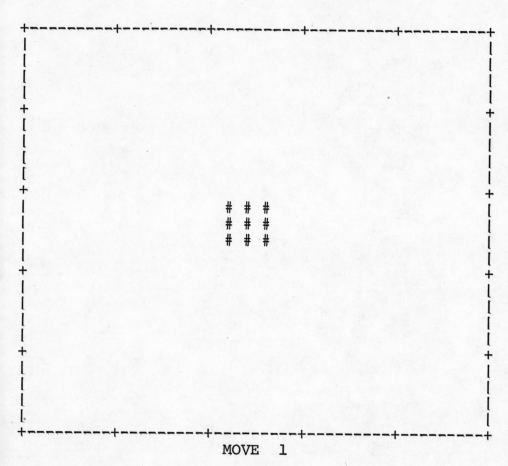

FIG. 4.3 (cont.)

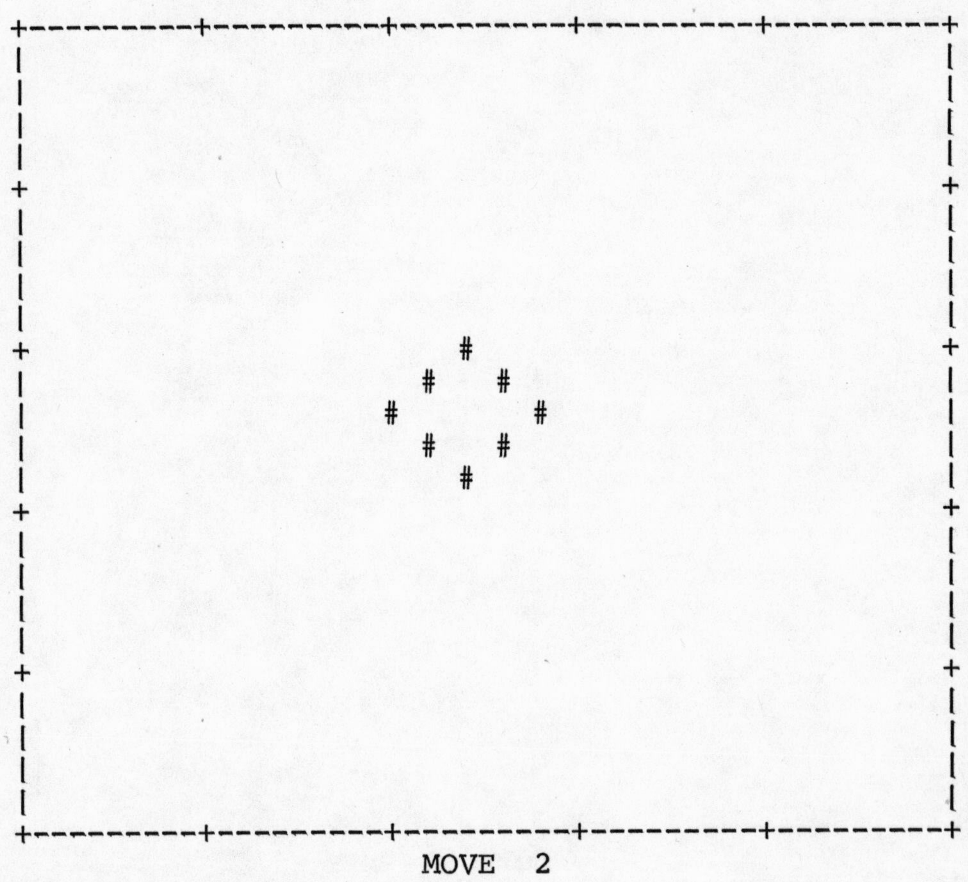

MOVE 2

FIG. 4.3 (cont.)

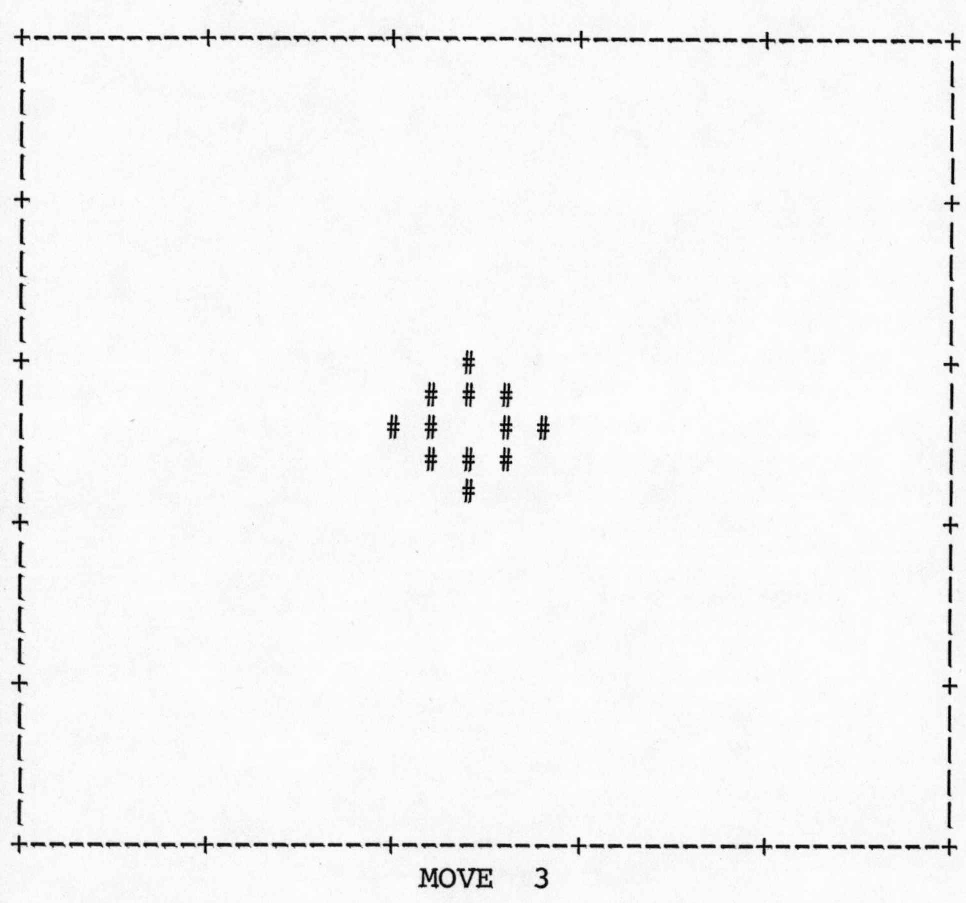

MOVE 3

FIG. 4.3 (cont.)

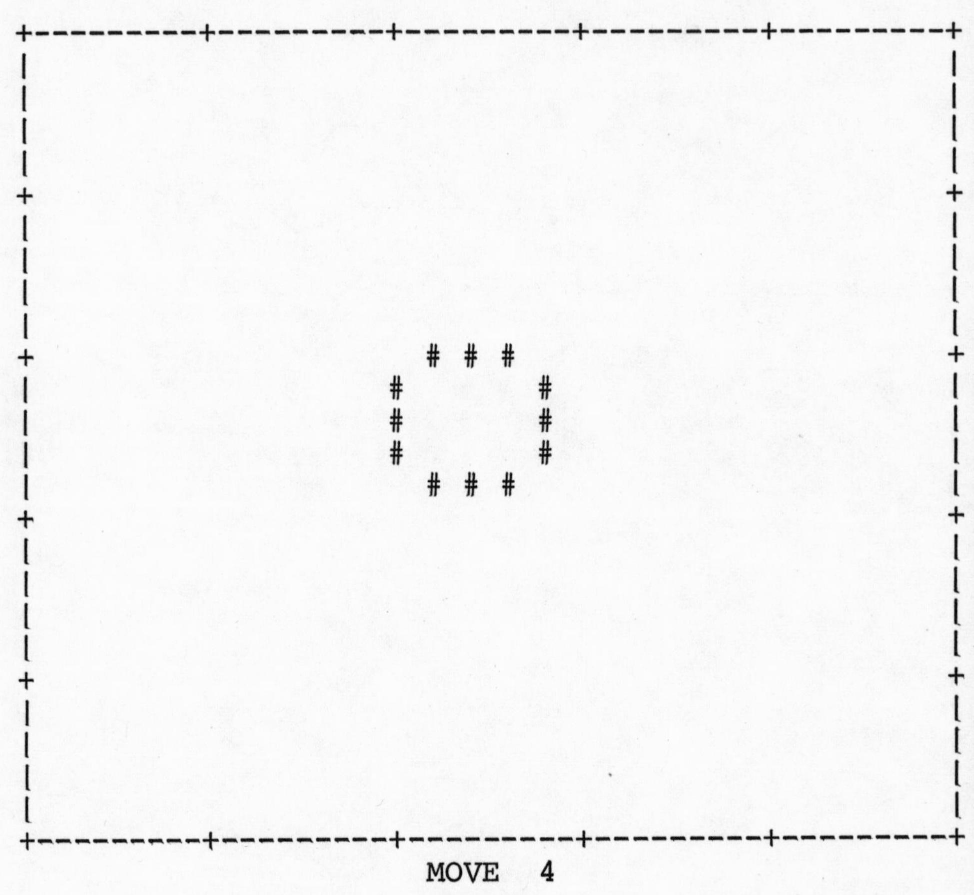

MOVE 4

FIG. 4.3 (cont.)

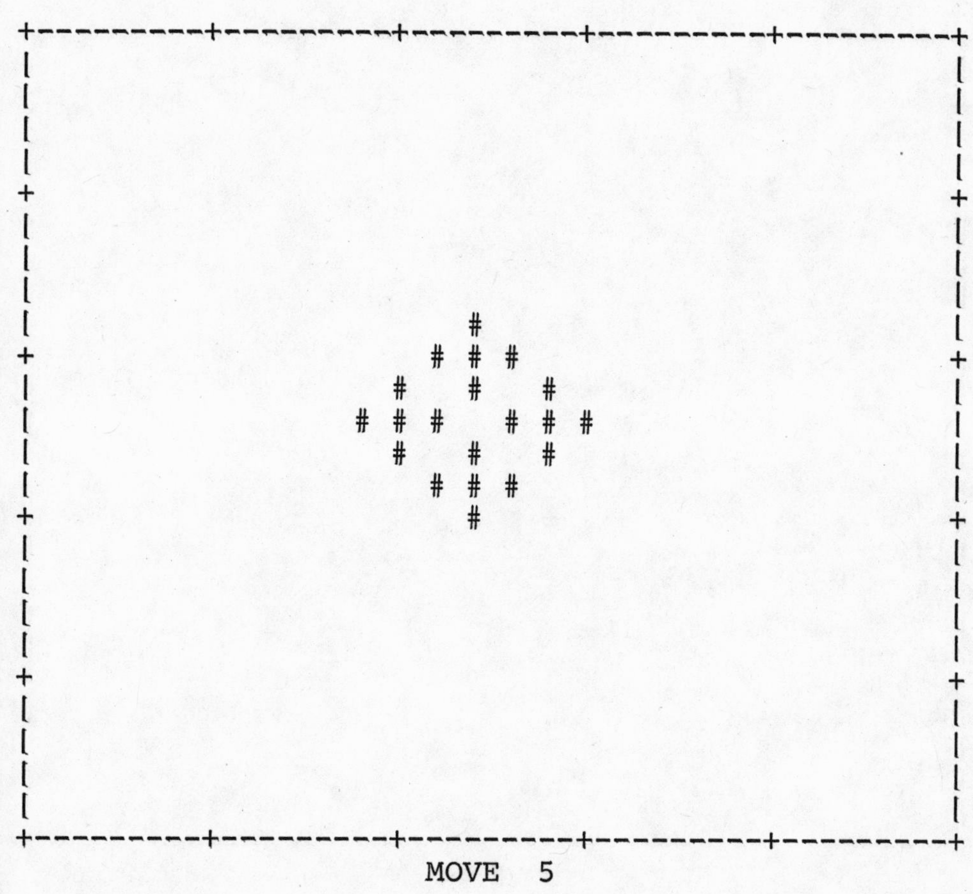

MOVE 5

FIG. 4.3 (cont.)

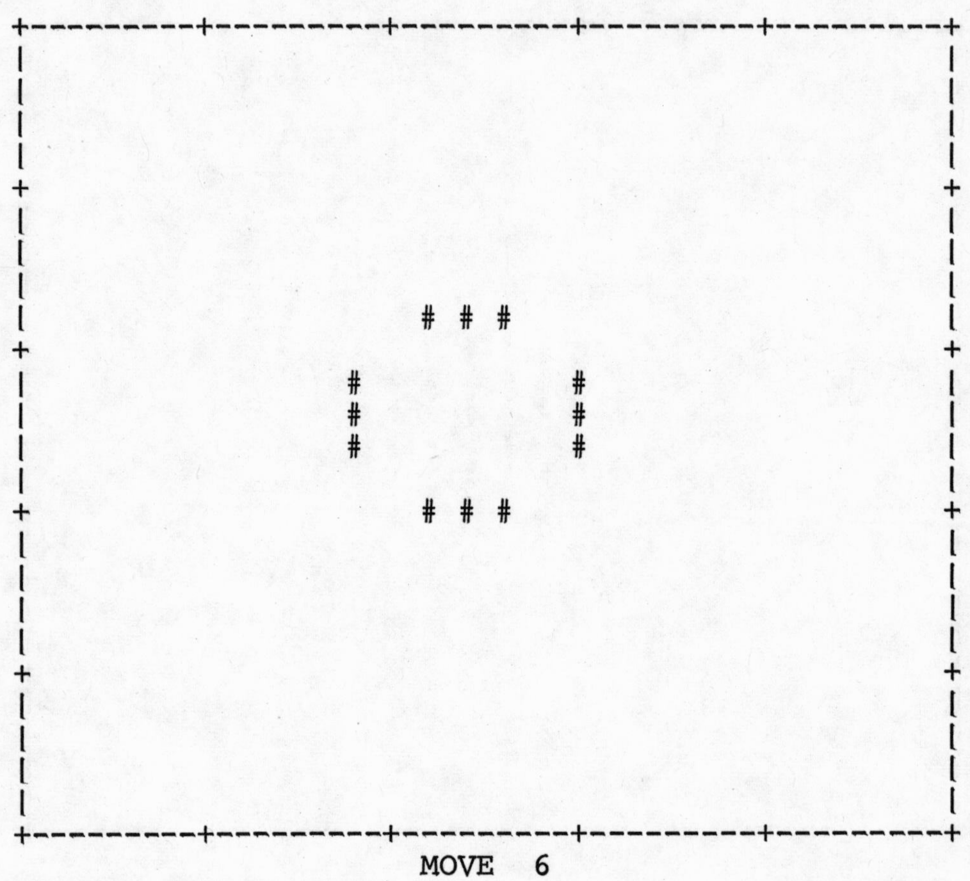

FIG. 4.3 (cont.)

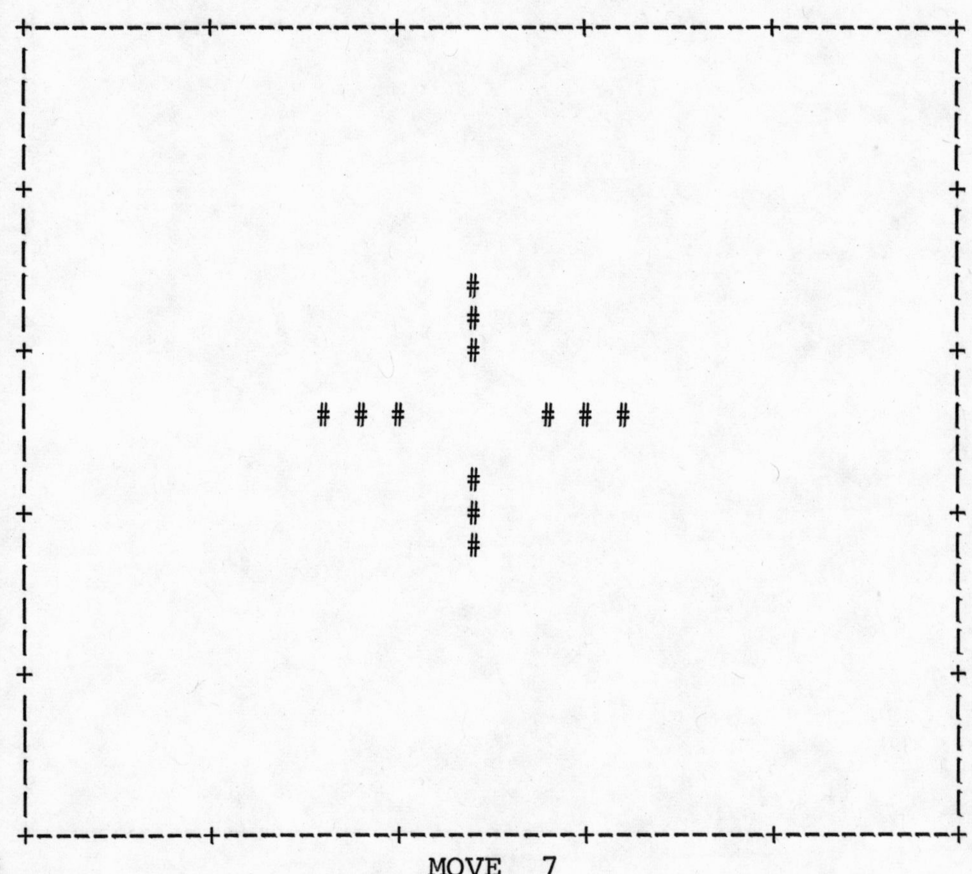

MOVE 7

FIG. 4.3 (cont.)

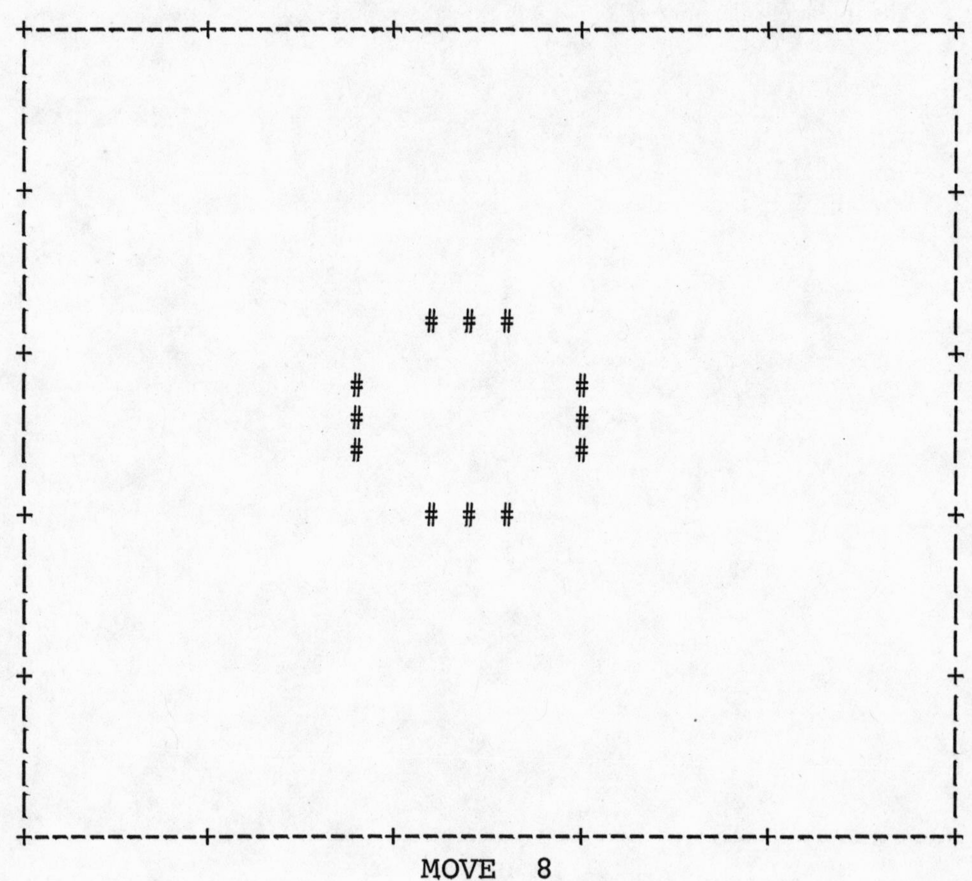

MOVE 8

FIG. 4.3 (cont.)

we decide whether an individual code segment should be included in-line or should be called as a subroutine.)

Many programs are designed in a top-down way (without the use of either segments or pseudo-code). Generally top-down design results in a hierarchical pattern of proposed program components, such as Fig. 4.4. The intended meaning of Fig. 4.4 is that the program component MAIN calls (or includes) in execution order the components INIT, PRINT, and MOVE; further, both PRINT and MOVE call the common subroutine SUBR.

For purposes of illustration, the five named components represent a partitioning of a program into manageable implementation units derived from the design. A named component, such as MOVE, could encompass several design segments and might eventually expand into as many as 400 lines of code. That is, testing and integrating will usually be done in units larger than just a single code segment (i.e., 50 lines or less).

We will compare two distinct approaches to realizing a hierarchically designed program. These approaches—top-down and bottom-up—differ in the way they sequence the implementation activities.

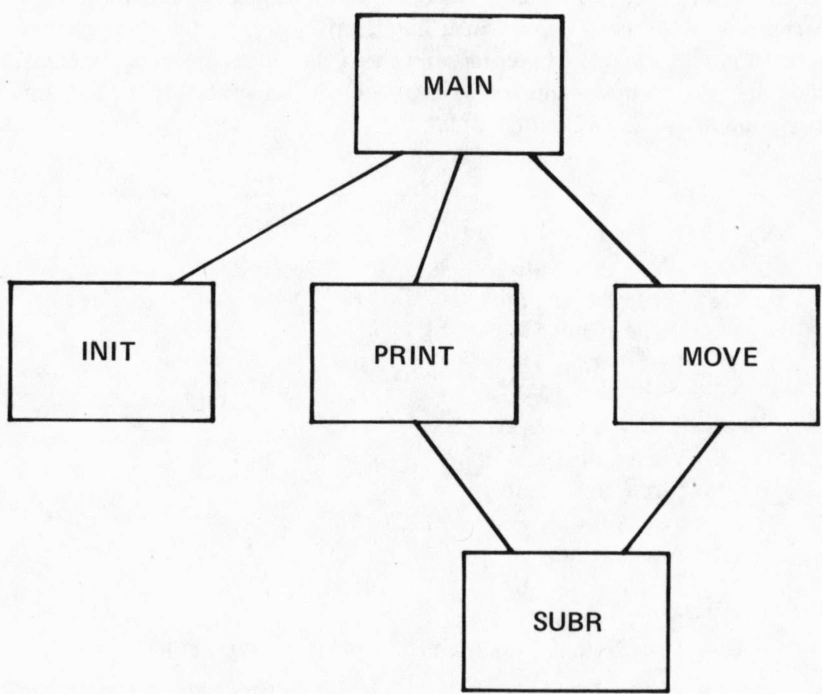

FIG. 4.4 Hierarchy of program components

We have already characterized top-down development with its use of program stubs to achieve an executable and testable system at intermediate points. In a bottom-up development the lowest level program components, such as INIT and SUBR, are coded first and then unit tested. Next, intermediate components in the design hierarchy, such as PRINT and MOVE, are coded and tested together with the completed lower-level components, such as SUBR. This process continues until the top level is finally reached. *Driver programs* are used to provide the necessary execution environment for unit testing of coded components and for integration testing at intermediate points.

Figs. 4.5 and 4.6 depict possible top-down and bottom-up implementation sequences for the program design hierarchy of Fig. 4.4.

Comparing the 14 steps of the two sample implementation sequences, we note that each sequence contains five steps for coding program components, four steps for writing either drivers or stubs, and five testing steps. It is these testing steps which exhibit the essential differences between the two development approaches. Clearly, the most exercised code is the bottom-level routine SUBR in the bottom-up sequence and the top-level procedure MAIN in the top-down implementation. Also, each top-down testing step, including the final system test, adds just a single new component to a developing system, whereas the final bottom-up system test brings together (integrates) four program components for the very first time.

---

1. Write MAIN
2. Write INIT-Stub
3. Write PRINT-Stub
4. Write MOVE-Stub
5. Test (MAIN)
6. Write INIT
7. Test (MAIN , INIT)
8. Write PRINT
9. Write SUBR-Stub
10. Test (MAIN , INIT , PRINT)
11. Write SUBR
12. Test (MAIN , INIT , PRINT , SUBR)
13. Write MOVE
14. Test System (MAIN , INIT , PRINT , MOVE , SUBR)

FIG. 4.5 Possible top-down implementation sequence

1. Write INIT
2. Write INIT-Driver
3. Test (INIT)
4. Write SUBR
5. Write SUBR-Driver
6. Test (SUBR)
7. Write PRINT
8. Write PRINT-Driver
9. Test (PRINT , SUBR)
10. Write MOVE
11. Write MOVE-Driver
12. Test (MOVE , SUBR)
13. Write MAIN
14. Test System (MAIN , INIT , PRINT , MOVE , SUBR)

FIG. 4.6 Possible bottom-up implementation sequence

Bottom-up implementation can commence from many points simultaneously. Thus, it is very amenable to the parallel scheduling of coding, testing and integrating. Fig. 4.7 shows a particular PERT (program evaluation and review technique) chart for the overlapped performance of the activities in the bottom-up implementation sequence of Fig. 4.6. Using a bottom-up approach (and adequate programming personnel), a software project can generate large quantities of code relatively soon after completing the design. However, problems and delays tend to occur during integration.

Bottom-up integration combines a number of individually tested components. Any error detected can be difficult to track down because there are many possible sources. Often an integration error is an interface problem whose solution requires the redefinition of, say, a calling sequence, some data formats, or even the choice of data structure representations. Such changes necessitate some reworking of the components we were attempting to integrate.

A major difficulty with a bottom-up approach to implementation is that component interfaces tend to be defined simultaneously by several programmers. Moreover, coordination of these various definitions can be quite informal, ranging from design documentation through memos and meetings down to simple conversations between programmers. (In any event, such coordination does not use machine-readable code.) Integration testing principally checks the correctness of simultaneous

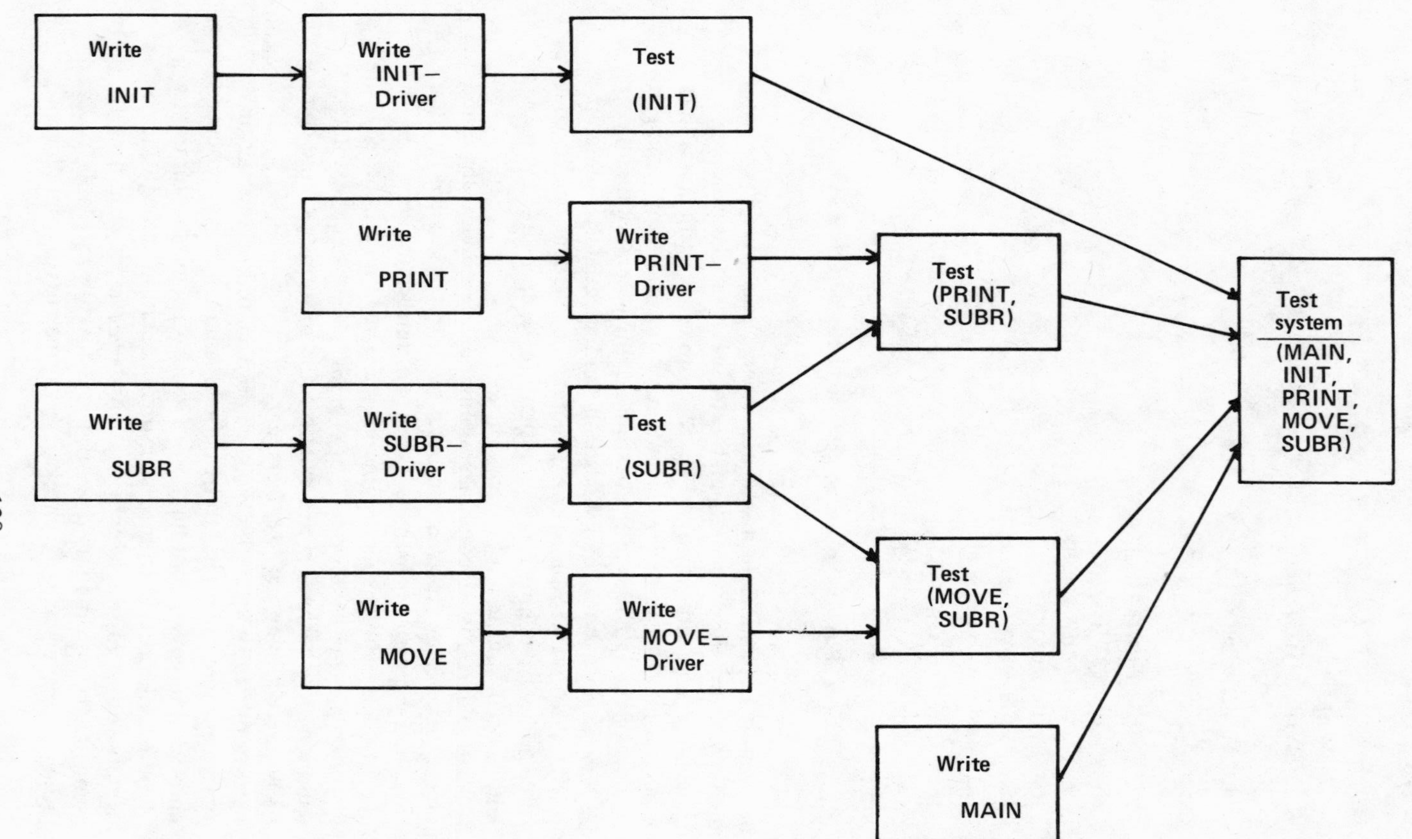

FIG. 4.7 A PERT chart for the bottom-up implementation sequence of Fig. 4.6

interface assumptions. So, the really difficult and time-consuming aspects of bottom-up development happen near the end of a programming project.

Top-down development has no separate integration phase. Rather, starting at the top level, components are coded and then integrated into an executable system which grows in capability with each additional component. This approach alleviates two central problems in software development—debugging and the handling of interfaces.

In top-down programming we declare and generate data before writing any code which references the data. We also use program stubs in order to test the control logic of upper-level components before coding lower-level ones. Thus, subroutine stubs must satisfy the calling sequences which allow the evolving system to stay executable. This means that all program interfaces (both data base definitions and calling sequences) are specified completely in code *before* we code the program components which need to know them.

Top-down testing is typically performed each time we add a program component to the developing system (see Fig. 4.5). Should an error be detected during testing, we can usually localize it to the newly added code since we had previously checked out the system with a stub for the new component. Incidentally, we expand stubs into full-bodied code segments, as we did with MAKE_MOVE in Section 4.2, but driver programs (for bottom-up testing) are customarily discarded after use.

Clearly, implementation using a top-down approach has but a single starting point with parallel coding possibilities emerging as the lower-level components are developed. This implies that the management of a top-down programming effort should be somewhat different from the traditional project organization based on a bottom-up approach. Chapter 5 discusses IBM's highly successful Chief Programmer Team, which is organized around a few skilled professionals employing a top-down segmented structured programming methodology.

4.4 TESTING

This section is concerned with the role that testing plays in the development of reliable software. In the past testing has been the prime method of achieving software reliability. However, experience demonstrates that techniques such as structured coding, top-down design and integration, informal and formal proofs of correctness, Chief Programmer Team organizations, and code reading are considerably more effective in producing reliable software. Testing should play a more limited role. Testing cannot be used to prove the correctness of a program, but it does serve as an additional check on software reliability. Our treatment is based on *Program Testing and Diagnosis Technology* by John Goodenough and Sterling Eanes.[3] They define testing as "the process of collecting and interpreting evidence relating to the reliability of software." As we shall see, there are many limitations on the extent to which we can collect and properly interpret such evidence.

In general, our goal in software testing is to try to eliminate unexpected conditions and sources of failure. Thus our tests must be organized so that a particular source of error is eliminated as completely as possible. In other words, the significance of passing a test should be that the probability of particular kinds of errors remaining in the software is now less than P. We thus turn to the different sources of software errors. Note that we are not concerned with simple compiler detectable errors, such as syntax errors, but with the more subtle errors, such as ambiguous specifications or errors in program logic.

In previous sections we have viewed the software development process as proceeding from a given problem to a specification of a function that solves the problem, to a high-level pseudo-code design for the function's implementation, and finally to the top-down structured coding, integration, and testing of the resulting program. Each of these activities is subject to its own particular types of error. Hence, for each of these activities, you must use different testing techniques, depending on the type of error you are trying to eliminate.

Two important sources of specification errors are failure to understand the full implications of the problem and failure to write an accurate specification.

An incomplete understanding of the problem usually results in inappropriate and inadequate solutions. Sometimes a prototype system is needed to investigate the various aspects of the problem. With the top-down structured approach to programming, you can more easily construct and modify prototypes as required. In general, errors of the first type may be detected by random tests of the system. Such tests should concentrate on the most difficult and least understood parts of the problem analysis.

Inaccurate specifications are quite possibly the most important source of software errors. An accurate specification must be complete, consistent, unambiguous, and precise. It must give (1) the effects the program (or module [subprogram] of a program) will have on its environment, (2) the environmental relationships the program (module) must preserve, and (3) the assumptions the program (module) can make about its environment.

You may test for an incorrect specification and/or failure of a module to satisfy its specification as follows. If a module errs in its effects on its environment, it sometimes produces the wrong answers. In this case test the results. If a module fails to keep environmental relationships invariant, eventually some other module may fail. One way to check for this error is to test the relationship just prior to exit from the module. You can also check for errors in a module's assumptions about its environment by testing the assumptions just after entry to the module. Ambiguity and incompleteness of a specification are probably best discovered by having someone other than the specifications writer or implementor construct the tests.

Errors in the high-level design can result from failure to understand the full implications of the proposed solution and hence its inadequacies or inability to always satisfy the problem requirements. Tests for this type of error are similar to tests for an inadequate understanding of the problem (i.e., random tests of the system).

Construction or implementation errors prevent a specification from being satisfied. Three primary types of construction errors are missing paths, inappropriate path selection, and inappropriate action under a given condition.

Consider the conditional statement

```
IF P THEN S1; ELSE S2;
```

If either the THEN clause or the ELSE clause is omitted (assuming the specifications require both to be present), we have a missing path error. If predicate P does not agree with the specification, we have an inappropriate path selection error. If statement S1 performs the wrong action, we have an incorrect action under the given condition P. The first two types of error usually result from making assumptions inconsistent with the specification. The probability of detecting such errors through testing depends on the extent to which the domain of the incorrect predicate differs from the correct domain. The third type of error usually results from a major blunder and is more easily detected. Note that the technique of exercising all paths in the code is effective only for this third type of error. Experience has shown that top-down structured programming is particularly effective in eliminating construction errors.

Testing plays an important role in analyzing the performance and resource utilization of a system. In general, programmers are unable to accurately predict the resource utilization of their programs. Hence performance testing is necessary. Thus you should program so that performance-improvement modifications may be easily and reliably made, instead of trying to maximize performance immediately. Note that performance testing sometimes detects other errors as well.

Having discussed some of the types of errors which can occur, we turn now to testing strategy. As stated previously, the tests should be organized so that passing a test means that the probability of certain types of error remaining in the software is lessened. Tests should also be organized to effectively eliminate the most probable sources of error. The most important and most heavily used parts of a system should be the most thoroughly tested. Lastly, the type of error you are testing for determines the testing technique you should use. Note that test data should always be in machine-readable form for easy repetition.

In the past three types of testing were traditionally performed: unit testing, integration testing, and regression testing. Unit testing is performed on a completed module with the primary goal of detecting construction errors, of assuring that the module satisfies its specifications. Unit tests usually concentrate on the module's effects on its environment and occasionally on the module's assumptions about its environment. Two forms of unit testing are prevalent, differing in the extent to which the tester knows the internal structure of the module. In black box (minimum internal knowledge) testing, the tester, who should be someone other than the implementor, hypothesizes from the specifications the minimum necessary internal structure, hence determining which inputs are equivalent for testing purposes. On the other hand, when the tester has complete knowledge of the internal structure, he can more easily determine which test inputs are equivalent and at least assure that all control paths are exercised.

Integration and regression testing are performed when the module is integrated with its higher-level environment. Assuming the module was thoroughly unit tested, these tests are directed toward detecting errors in the specifications and high-level design. Integration testing concentrates on exercising the newly added module, whereas regression testing exercises the other modules of the system to see if they have been adversely affected by the new module.

In the previous section we discussed top-down versus bottom-up implementation. The choice of implementation order determines the testing strategy. Bottom-up testing requires the construction of driver programs to simulate the environment for unit testing. Integration and regression testing often occur as by-products of a higher-level unit test. Bottom-up testing suffers from several problems. The driver programs can take a lot of effort to develop and are an additional source of errors. Furthermore, they usually cannot be expanded into the higher-level modules and thus must be discarded after testing. With bottom-up testing the higher-level specifications and design are tested last and least thoroughly. Yet it is these software errors which tend to be most serious and most difficult to correct.

In top-down implementation and testing the unit, integration, and regression testing of modules progresses gradually as the lower levels of the modules are developed. For example, the unit tests of a module M are initially very simple, since all the lower-level modules are represented by stubs. As these stubs are replaced by the functional modules, the unit tests of M are expanded to test M's newly increased functional capabilities. Integration testing occurs much earlier, so that errors in the high-level specifications and design are detected sooner and corrected more easily. Since the upper levels are constantly being exercised, they receive a thorough testing. Furthermore, functional stubs, rather than being discarded, can often be expanded into full functional modules. IBM's Chief Programmer Team approach (see Chapter 5) suggests that the top-down approach is a more efficient and reliable testing strategy.

We point out that the development of tests is similar to the development of programs. In testing, you have a problem to solve—to detect certain types of errors. You must therefore specify and design an appropriate test plan and code the test data. Each of these activities is also subject to error, so that testing is really a check on both the software and the tests themselves.

One valuable testing technique that we recommend is the ASSERT statement, which asserts that a relation or predicate should be true at the point where the statement occurs. Each time an ASSERT statement is executed, its predicate is tested. If the predicate is true, the statement is equivalent to a null statement. But if the predicate is false, an interrupt or error exit occurs. The ASSERT statement is particularly useful for testing:

1. (On entry to a module) the assumptions a module makes about its environment.
2. (Just prior to exit from a module) that a module has not violated supposedly invariant environmental relations.
3. Loop invariants (see Chapter 2).
4. Any other assumptions or invariant relations.

ASSERT statements ease the task of locating the cause of a detected error, since they make the program fail sooner than it might have otherwise. Without ASSERT statements the program might destroy the information needed to locate the error source.

We use the following form of ASSERT statement with PL/I:

IF ¬(*predicate*) THEN SIGNAL CONDITION($ASSERT);

The standard system action when the *predicate* fails is to print an error message and continue with the next statement. You can specify your own failure action with an ON statement such as

```
ON CONDITION($ASSERT) BEGIN;
                        action;
                        END;
```

For convenience we use the PL/I preprocessor to define a preprocessor function ASSERT(*predicate*) which takes a *predicate* and replaces the function call by the IF-THEN statement given above. Thus you can write an ASSERT statement as:

```
ASSERT(predicate);
```

Because too many assertions can consume a lot of execution time, we would like to have the ASSERT function optionally delete an assertion by generating either an IF-THEN statement or a comment. Thus, if the global preprocessor variable ASSERTION is set to 1, ASSERT generates IF-THEN statements. If ASSERTION is 0, ASSERT generates the comment

```
/* ASSERT(predicate) */ ;
```

The PL/I code for ASSERT is

```
        %DCL ASSERTION FIXED;
        %DEACTIVATE ASSERTION;

        %DCL ASSERT ENTRY(CHAR) RETURNS(CHAR);

%ASSERT: PROC(PRED) RETURNS(CHAR);

        DCL PRED CHAR;
        DCL CODE CHAR;

        IF ASSERTION = 1
           THEN CODE = 'IF ¬(' || PRED ||
                       ') THEN SIGNAL CONDITION($ASSERT)';
           ELSE  CODE = '/* ASSERT(' || PRED || ') */';

        RETURN(CODE);
        %END ASSERT;

        %ASSERTION = 1; /* OR 0 */
```

Thus you need only to include the above code at the start of your PL/I program to be able to use ASSERT statements.

We can extend this idea of optionally inserting debugging code in several ways. The ASSERT statement merely tests a predicate and raises a condition. When debugging, however, we generally like to optionally insert sequences of output statements to obtain intermediate results and provide for control flow tracing. The following technique may be used with some PL/I compilers. We enclose the debugging statements within DEBUG and ENDDEBUG statements, as in:

```
DEBUG;
      debugging statements;
ENDDEBUG;
```

where DEBUG and ENDDEBUG are preprocessor variables declared and initialized as

```
%DCL (DEBUG,ENDDEBUG) CHAR;
%ENDDEBUG = '/**/';
%DEBUG = described below;
```

Now if DEBUG = '' then the *debugging statements* are compiled. But if DEBUG = '/*' then the *debugging statements* become one large comment. (Note: The *debugging statements* must not contain any comments.) An alternate way to accomplish the same thing is

```
%INCLUDE DEBUG;
      debugging statements;
/**/;
```

where the included file DEBUG contains either a blank card (or no cards) or a /* card.

Unfortunately, neither of the above debugging tricks work with OS/360 PL/I F, since the F compiler does not allow preprocessor replacement strings or included files to contain unmatched comment delimiters. However, two debugging techniques can be used. In the first let DEBUGGING be a preprocessor variable declared as follows:

```
%DCL DEBUGGING FIXED;
%DEACTIVATE DEBUGGING;
%DEBUGGING = described below;
```

We set DEBUGGING to 1 to compile debugging code and set it to 0 to omit debugging code. One way to write the debugging code is

```
%IF DEBUGGING = 1 %THEN %DO;
      debugging statements;
      %END;
```

Another way is to include a preprocessor function DEBUG which takes the *debugging statements* as its argument and optionally generates or omits the statements, according to the value of DEBUGGING. Thus you would write

```
DEBUG((
        debugging statements;
));
```

Note that the double parentheses are necessary to force the *debugging statements* to be treated as one argument. The preprocessor code for DEBUG is

```
         %DCL DEBUG ENTRY(CHAR) RETURNS(CHAR);

%DEBUG: PROC(STMTS) RETURNS(CHAR);

         DCL STMTS CHAR;
         DCL I FIXED,
                (CODE,S) CHAR;

         IF DEBUGGING = 1
               THEN DO;
                       S = STMTS || '$@#*>+:&<$';
                       I = 0;

                       /* COMPUTE I = LENGTH(STMTS) + 1 */
                    L: I = I + 1;
                       IF SUBSTR(S,I,10) ¬= '$@#*>+:&<$' THEN
                               GO TO L;

                       /* REMOVE OUTER PARENTHESES */
                       CODE = SUBSTR(STMTS,2,I-3);
                       END;
               ELSE    CODE = '';

         RETURN(CODE);
         %END DEBUG;
```

We hope that you will adapt the ASSERT and DEBUG statements to your particular programming languages.

4.5 RECURSION

As a programming technique, recursion nicely meshes with top-down structured programming. Suppose our task is to solve a problem P, and suppose we find that we can solve P, provided we can solve a somewhat simpler form of the problem P. Then we should investigate the possible use of recursion. A common form for a recursive procedure is

```
SOLVE: PROC( P ) RECURSIVE;
           IF problem P is sufficiently simple
               THEN complete the solution of P
               ELSE DO;
                        reduce P somewhat;
                        CALL SOLVE( simpler-form-of-P );
                    END;
       END SOLVE;
```

To guarantee termination we need to answer the following question: If we call SOLVE for problem P and keep reducing the problem somewhat (and making further calls of SOLVE), then will the problem eventually be sufficiently simple to complete its solution?

This technique is especially applicable to working with data structures that are recursively defined, such as trees and linked lists. In Section 2.4 Example 5 is a recursive function procedure for searching a tree for the leftmost occurrence of a KEY. The function returns either the NULL pointer or a pointer to the appropriate tree node if it finds the KEY.

Using recursion can often enhance the clarity of code by eliminating redundant operations. In effect, recursion is a substitute for some standard uses of a push-down stack. Using a recursive procedure means the various invocations—activation records containing storage for parameters, local variables, return address, and so on—will be stacked until these calls have been completed. Recursion implicitly uses a stack. Accordingly, it is most appropriate for simplifying operations that require a stack, such as traversing a tree.

If a program uses recursion instead of code which explicitly performs the appropriate stacking operations, there should be some loss in execution and storage efficiency. This is simply because a specially tailored stack and its explicit management should execute faster than a more general stack (viz., the stack of invocations which have not yet returned) and its implicit management (by procedure calls and returns). In many cases, however, the gain in program clarity from the use of recursion, especially for computations on recursively defined data structures, more than offsets any loss in a program's efficiency of execution.

An elegant and natural use of recursive procedures with top-down programming is the recursive descent method for doing syntax recognition (in compilers). Here, for example, you might have a procedure

STATEMENT which can call the procedure DO_GROUP which, in turn, can call the procedure STATEMENT again. Recursive descent, then, uses a group of procedures, like STATEMENT, which can call themselves through a sequence of other procedure calls. Such a group of procedures is said to be mutually recursive.

We will now give an example of top-down structured programming using mutually recursive subroutines. Games and number theory are fertile sources of examples which embody general principles, can be stated concisely, and are easy to understand. Our example here is a classic puzzle game known as the "Chinese rings." Several versions of the game are available commercially. Martin Gardner in the "Mathematical Games" section of the August 1972 issue of *Scientific American*[4] shows how this puzzle (and also the Tower of Hanoi) can be solved using the binary Gray code. We will use a different tack—mutually recursive procedures—to solve the Chinese ring puzzle.

The puzzle consists of a number of rings, say six, mounted on a metal loop with a handle. If we imagine that we have grasped the handle in our right hand, then we can number the rings 1 to 6 from left to right. The object of the puzzle is to remove all six rings from the metal loop. There is a special rule for removing or mounting a ring: You can only remove or mount a ring provided the immediately preceding ring is on the loop and all other preceding rings are off. That is,

RULE: To remove or to mount ring N
(i) ring N − 1 must be *on*
and (ii) ring N − 2, ... ,ring 1 must all be *off*.

For example, to remove ring 5, we need ring 4 on and ring 3, ring 2, and ring 1 all off. Since ring 1 has no left neighbor, we can always remove or mount ring 1. Another consequence of the RULE is: when ring 1 is mounted, then we can remove or mount ring 2. (The RULE is physically embedded into the puzzle by linking ring N to a base *through* ring N + 1, as shown in Fig. 4.8.)

We proceed now to construct a PL/I program which solves the Chinese ring puzzle.

Start with the high-level PL/I-like program:

```
RINGS: PROC OPTIONS(MAIN);
        DCL puzzle-representation;
           %INCLUDE PROCS; /* INTERNAL PROCEDURES */
           Print("START GAME");
           CALL Remove-all-rings;
           Print("GAME OVER");
END RINGS;
```

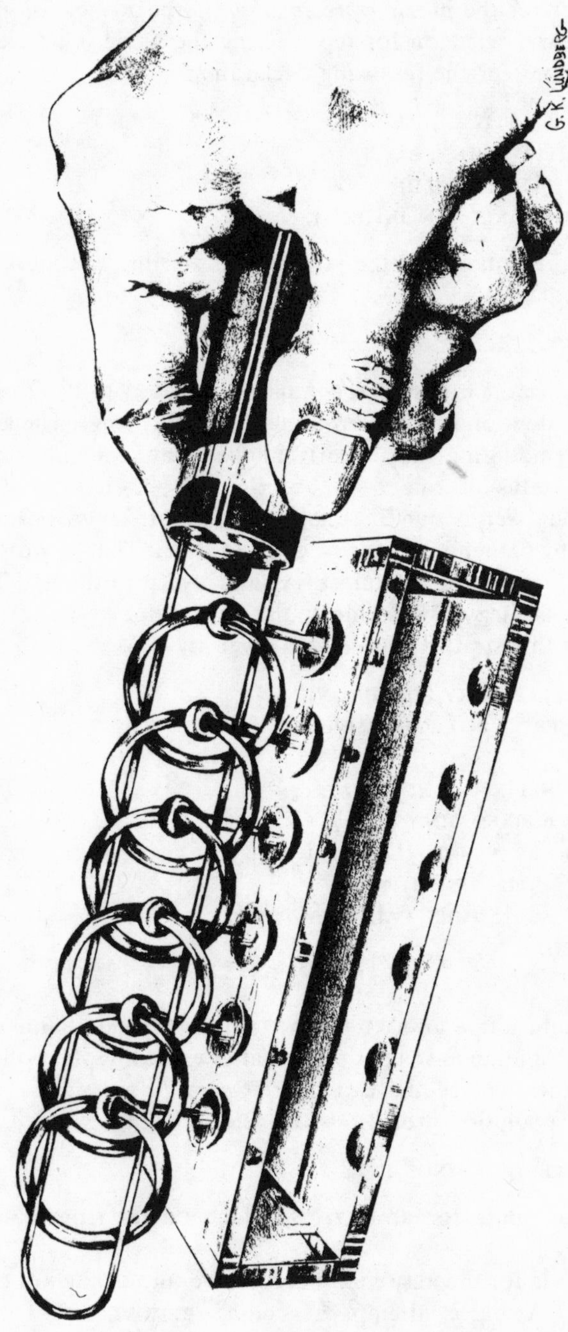

FIG. 4.8 The Chinese ring puzzle

Next, decide on either the *puzzle-representation* or the *Remove-all-rings* refinement. A natural selection for representing the game is to use an array of BITS. We opt for the following declarations:

```
DCL RING( 6 ) BIT( 1 ) ALIGNED;
DCL ON BIT(1) INIT('1'B),
    OFF BIT(1) INIT('0'B);
DCL #RINGS FIXED BIN INIT( 6 );
```

and we set our representation of the puzzle to its starting configuration with the assignment

```
RING = ON;
```

So the *puzzle-representation* has been completely reduced to PL/I code.

We turn our attention to the subroutine *Remove-all-rings*. The RULE for removing and mounting rings clearly implies that removing ring I might affect the status of ring I − 1, but ring I + 1 can be ignored. Therefore, we should set as our first major subgoal of *Remove-all-rings* the removing of ring 6, then removing ring 5, and so on. That is, we want to start removing rings at the rightmost ring and sweep to the left. This will be our general strategy. We decide upon a subroutine REM_LEFT(N) which implements this strategy; its code is given by

```
DCL REM_LEFT ENTRY (FIXED BIN);
REM_LEFT: PROC( N ) RECURSIVE;

        DCL N FIXED BIN;
        DCL I FIXED BIN;
           DO I = N TO 1 BY -1;
                 IF RING(I) = ON
                    THEN CALL REMOVE(I);
           END;
END REM_LEFT;
```

which calls on a subroutine REMOVE that we must write next. Note that when N is 0 the subroutine REM_LEFT returns after executing the DO loop zero times. We now replace the call on *Remove-all-rings* in our first approximation to a solution program with the statement

```
CALL REM_LEFT( #RINGS );
```

(The RECURSIVE attribute for REM_LEFT, in fact, comes from a later refinement step.)

To develop code for the REMOVE procedure, we turn to the RULE for removing a ring. A naïve attempt at coding REMOVE might look something like:

```
REMOVE: PROC( N );
        DCL N FIXED BIN;
            CALL MOUNT( N - 1 );
            CALL REM_LEFT( N - 2 );
            Print(" REMOVE " , N );
            RING(N) = OFF;
END REMOVE;
```

However, such code overlooks several points. First, if N is 1 (i.e., if we want to remove ring 1), then we don't want to mount ring 0. So, we should test N before calling MOUNT and REM_LEFT. Secondly, ring N might already be off. In that event we would want the call upon REMOVE to return immediately. Hence, the current status of RING(N) should also be checked.

Incorporating these considerations we obtain the code:

```
DCL REMOVE ENTRY (FIXED BIN);
REMOVE: PROC( N ) RECURSIVE;
        DCL N FIXED BIN;
            IF  RING(N) = ON  THEN
               DO;
                   IF N > 1 THEN
                      DO;
                          CALL MOUNT( N - 1 );
                          CALL REM_LEFT( N - 2 );
                      END;
                   PUT SKIP EDIT ('        REMOVE ', N ) (A,F(3) );
                   RING(N) = OFF;
               END;
END REMOVE;
```

which calls on an unspecified subroutine MOUNT. But the RULE for the puzzle applied to both removing *and* mounting a ring. So, there is a natural symmetry to the code for the two subroutines REMOVE and MOUNT. We have

```
DCL MOUNT ENTRY (FIXED BIN);
MOUNT: PROC( N ) RECURSIVE;
        DCL N FIXED BIN;
            IF RING(N) = OFF THEN
               DO;
                   IF N > 1 THEN
                      DO;
                          CALL MOUNT( N - 1 );
                          CALL REM_LEFT( N - 2 );
```

```
                    END;
                  PUT SKIP EDIT ('       MOUNT ', N ) (A,F(3) );
                  RING(N) = ON;
               END;
    END MOUNT;
```

This essentially completes the coding of the solution. If the three subroutines REM_LEFT, REMOVE, and MOUNT (and their ENTRY declarations) are included as internal subroutines by the "%INCLUDE PROCS;" statement, then the main procedure RINGS:

```
    RINGS: PROC OPTIONS(MAIN);
           DCL RING( 6 ) BIT( 1 ) ALIGNED;
           DCL ON BIT(1)  INIT('1'B),
               OFF BIT(1)  INIT('0'B);
           DCL # RINGS FIXED BIN INIT(6);
             %INCLUDE PROCS;
             RING = ON;
             PUT PAGE EDIT ( '      START GAME ' ) (A);
             PUT SKIP(2);
             CALL REM_LEFT( #RINGS );
             PUT SKIP(2);
             PUT EDIT ( '      GAME OVER ' ) (A);
    END RINGS;
```

when executed produces the following output which is a solution to the Chinese ring puzzle (in a minimum number of moves!).

```
    START GAME

       REMOVE  2
       REMOVE  1
       REMOVE  4
       MOUNT   1
       MOUNT   2
       REMOVE  1
       REMOVE  3
       MOUNT   1
       REMOVE  2
       REMOVE  1
       REMOVE  6
       MOUNT   1
       MOUNT   2
       REMOVE  1
       MOUNT   3
```

```
MOUNT   1
REMOVE  2
REMOVE  1
MOUNT   4
MOUNT   1
MOUNT   2
REMOVE  1
REMOVE  3
MOUNT   1
REMOVE  2
REMOVE  1
REMOVE  5
MOUNT   1
MOUNT   2
REMOVE  1
MOUNT   3
MOUNT   1
REMOVE  2
REMOVE  1
REMOVE  4
MOUNT   1
MOUNT   2
REMOVE  1
REMOVE  3
MOUNT   1
REMOVE  2
REMOVE  1

GAME OVER
```

The top-down development went from the main procedure RINGS to the subroutine REM_LEFT which calls REMOVE. And REMOVE, in turn, can call both MOUNT and REM_LEFT. The last subroutine MOUNT can also call itself and REM_LEFT. So we have three mutually recursive subroutines which solve the ring puzzle in a very "natural" way.

Starting with the call of REM_LEFT(#RINGS) in RINGS, there are 67 function calls in computing the solution. Of these 67 calls, 11 are calls on REM_LEFT with an argument value of zero. By adding a check for N = 1 to REMOVE and to MOUNT, such calls could be avoided. Further, REMOVE and MOUNT could be combined into a single subroutine, say PERFORM, which takes the appropriate action as determined by the call, say

```
CALL PERFORM( 'RMV', I );
```

But the gain in program clarity or quality by such "fine tuning" is debatable.

5. THE CHIEF PROGRAMMER TEAM CONCEPT

Data substantiating the practical payoff of structured programming's potential is still somewhat sketchy (as is most software engineering data). The best current documentation comes principally from IBM's highly successful Chief Programmer Team (CPT) projects which integrally used top-down segmented structured programming. But the CPT results pertain to a unified technical and operational methodology rather than just to structured programming per se. For instance, CPT's factor out the clerical overhead from programming in order to optimize an expert programmer's contributions.

In this chapter we first outline the origins of the CPT concept. Then we discuss the duties and functional relationships of team members. Next we indicate some advantages of a CPT over the traditional organization and management of a software project's personnel. We conclude with a fairly detailed description of the Programming Production Library, which forms the procedural foundation for the CPT method.

5.1 ORIGINS OF THE CPT CONCEPT

At a 1969 NATO conference on software engineering techniques J. D. Aron of IBM's Federal Systems Division (FSD) described an experimental "superprogrammer project."[1] The goal of this experiment was to have a single expert programmer, Dr. Harlan Mills, complete in 6 man-*months* a software system which was considered to be a 30 man-*year* undertaking for an "army of ants." About 50,000 instructions would be required.

The system, called Definitive Orbit Determination, was to be an interactive one using a large file. The programming task also required mastery of sufficient mathematics to develop (and code) the relevant orbit equations plus handling the interface problems associated with displays and analog input devices. Dr. Mills was to construct the program in its entirety from design down to the final coding and testing.

Mills implemented the project using top-down programming in PL/I. To avoid extensive referencing of manuals, he requested and was assigned both an expert PL/I programmer and an expert on the internal details of OS/360. He also had his secretary and a technician provide important clerical support by being his interface with the computer. This required him to rewrite the JCL and the linkage editor manuals and to build a small programming support system for clerical-level (rather than programmer-level) communication with the computer.

In the end the superprogrammer project took about six man-years. This (somewhat more modest) level of productivity still represented a substantial improvement over that of the parallel control group which was organized along traditional lines. Perhaps the most important results of the superprogrammer experiment were the practical insights into the assistance a senior programmer needs in order to perform optimally.

In his 1969 account J. D. Aron mentions that there was in progress a second experiment "dealing with an information bank for a New York City newspaper."[2] Of course he was referring to IBM's now famous *New York Times* project. As we mentioned in Chapter 1, this project affirmed the efficacy of structured programming in a practical production setting. The information bank system consisted of over 83,000 source code lines and was produced with only 11 man-years of effort. Moreover, the acceptance testing and the actual operation of the system have been almost error-free.

Top-down segmented structured programming was the design and implementation approach for the *New York Times* project. Much of the quality of both the programming effort and the final product is directly attributable to using this methodology. Also, the organization of the project's personnel and their operation as a team were essentially new. At that time the CPT represented a fundamentally different structure for the management of production programming.

Based upon his experiences in the superprogrammer project, Mills formulated the CPT concept. It involves the rigorous separation of programming activities from the attendant clerical tasks. This separation is reflected in the job specialization and in the operational details.

The basic personnel of a CPT consists of:

1. Chief programmer, the metamorphized superprogrammer.
2. Backup programmer, an expert assistant for technical design and programming strategy.

3. Librarian/secretary, a clerical assistant charged with input preparation and the filing of all output during program development.

Section 5.2 details their respective duties and relationships. Mills proposes an analogy between a CPT and a surgical team consisting of a head surgeon and specialists with supporting skills (both surgical and nonsurgical). The surgeon plans and performs the operation while directing team members to provide appropriate assistance.

There are two major technical procedures for CPT operations; naturally, one is for programming and the other is for clerical undertakings. As we have indicated, CPT's use a top-down segmented structured programming methodology. For a CPT a programming project *is* a set of internal and external libraries collectively called a Programming Production Library (PPL). Thus, a project is an evolving object that can be observed and measured. Section 5.4 discusses a PPL and associated human and computer procedures for using it.

IBM's *New York Times* project automated the newspaper's clipping file (morgue) by permitting users to browse through a large data base of article abstracts via a thesaurus. The original text of articles stored on microfiche could also be automatically retrieved and displayed at local terminals for the paper's editorial staff.

The system, consisting of over 83,000 source code lines, was developed in 22 calendar months (with 11 man-years of effort) and has been operational on a daily basis since November, 1971. Only the file maintenance subsystem (about 12,000 source lines) was complete after the first year. Most of the delivered code was written during the project's last 6 months.

Two articles were written by F. Terry Baker, the chief programmer on the *New York Times* project. His paper, "Chief Programmer Team Management of Production Programming,"[3] describes the project effort fully and documents the impressive productivity levels attained. And the article "System Quality Through Structured Programming"[4] provides an extensive error history covering acceptance testing and the first year of operation for the system.

Here we will cite just a few salient facts on this first CPT experiment.

Only 21 errors were found during five weeks of acceptance testing. Each error was fixed within a single day, and most of these errors were in (lower-level) code written during the project's last two months. Only 25 further errors surfaced during the information bank system's first year of operation.

The project's principal programmers averaged one detected error and 10,000 lines of source code per man-year.

The file maintenance subsystem (delivered only one week after coding was completed) operated 20 months before a single error was discovered in it.

About half of the subprograms (usually 200 to 400 source statements) were correct at the first compilation.

The CPT approach has subsequently been applied to many internal and contract projects by IBM's Federal Systems Center. The results thus far have strongly corroborated the conclusions drawn from the initial CPT experiment on the *New York Times* project. The principal conclusion is that a top-down segmented structured programming methodology employed within a CPT organization of project personnel leads to significantly improved programmer productivity and system reliability. In addition, top-down structured design and implementation makes for a more comprehensible software product which is, therefore, easier to maintain and to modify.

For example, the mission-simulation system for the Skylab operations was a large IBM project (about 400,000 source code lines) developed using top-down structured programming techniques. The system was produced within two years and delivered on schedule despite over 1,000 changes in the requirements.

Structured programming and the CPT approach are being widely adopted within IBM for production programming projects and are now regarded as technical and operational standards rather than as experimental concepts.

5.2 WHAT IS THE CPT CONCEPT?

The CPT concept is a combination of technical, organizational, and operational factors.[5,6] Although many of the factors have been known for some time, it is the total combination which gives such a striking increase in productivity, reliability, and manageability. The four major factors of the concept are:

1. Structured programming (coding).
2. Top-down design and integration.
3. The Programming Production Library and its associated machine and human procedures.
4. The organizational structure of the CPT.

The details of structured programming are discussed in Chapter 3, so we will merely summarize the key points here. In structured coding you restrict the flow of control of your programs to a few basic patterns. These patterns allow for sequential actions—"s1;s2;"—for conditional actions—"IF P THEN S1; ELSE S2;"—and for repetitive actions—"DO WHILE (P); S; END;". These basic forms of control flow are sufficient to express the flow of control needed for any program. Because these coding figures are based on sound mathematical principles, each figure has associated with it a correctness criterion or invariance relation which determines whether the figure correctly represents the desired function. You may use these correctness criteria not only for writing correct code, but for verifying the correctness of previously written code. Because each of the figures has a single-entry and a single-exit point, structured code, when properly indented to show the nesting of figures within other figures, is very easy to read and comprehend. As we shall see, code reading is an important part of the CPT concept.

We have discussed top-down design and integration in detail in Chapter 4. To review briefly, in the top-down approach you design, code, and integrate higher-level routines before doing the lower-level routines. Thus, if you are currently working on a functional module M at a certain level, then all of the higher-level modules which would lead to a call of M have already been coded, tested, and integrated together. You would design, code, test, and integrate M with the higher-level modules before you would begin coding any of the modules which might be called from M. The testing of M is done by substituting stubs (dummy programs) for each of the lower-level modules. These dummy programs may do as little as print a message indicating that they were called, or they may be primitive versions or simulations which may eventually be refined into final form. Because the higher-level routines are already coded and integrated, the interfaces with the higher-level routines are always clearly specified in the code. A corollary to the top-down approach is that routines at the same level are coded in the order in which they will be executed. This is because the earlier executed routines usually produce data required by the later routines.

The third factor in the CPT concept is the Programming Production Library (PPL) and its associated machine and human procedures. The PPL concept is designed to separate the clerical and intellectual tasks of programming. In addition the PPL makes the code produced more visible to the team members. It represents an organized and current status of the project the team is working on.

The PPL, as an information base, resides in two forms. The *internal library* is maintained in machine-legible form on disk, while the *external library* is maintained in human-legible form in listing binders. The clerical tasks of library maintenance are performed not by programmers but by a *librarian*. The internal library consists of job control statements, linkage editor statements, source language statements (PL/I, Assembly, etc.), object modules, load modules, test data, and utility control statements. The external library consists of listings of the internal library contents, along with output produced by compilations, assemblies, link edits, and test runs. The external library contains not only the current listings and output, but all output generated since the beginning of the project (in archives).

The programmer works only with the external library. By writing on the current listings or on coding forms, he indicates whatever changes or new information he wants added to the library. The librarian, by a combination of human and machine procedures, implements the desired changes to the internal and external libraries. When the programmer returns, he finds the resulting new listings in the current listing binders and the old listings at the top of the archive binders. This method of operation is illustrated in Fig. 5.1.

The librarian uses both human and machine procedures to accomplish library maintenance. The human procedures are clerical rules for accomplishing the following:

1. Preparation of machine input as directed by programmers writing in the external library or on coding forms.
2. Submission and pickup of computer runs.
3. Filing the output of runs in the current status binders and filing the superseded versions in the archives.

The human procedures are designed so that the input-preparation and output-filing rules are independent of the machine procedures and of the project content.

The PPL machine procedures consist almost entirely of job control statements and standard utility control statements. They provide for the following kinds of operations:

1. Updating of job control, link edit, and source program statements, and of test data.
2. Compilation or assembly of source programs into object modules, and link editing of object modules into load modules.
3. Housekeeping tasks like reclaiming internal library space and checkpointing the internal library onto backup tape.
4. Execution of test runs.

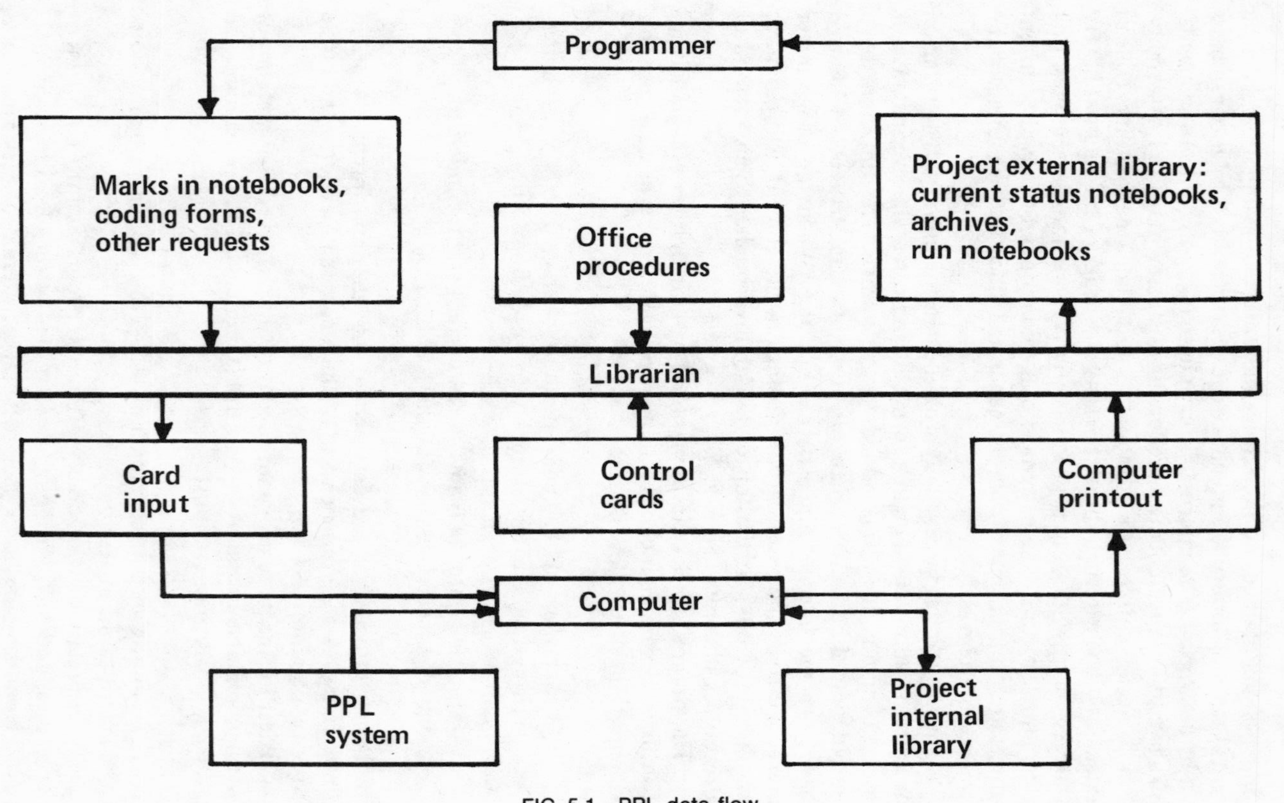

FIG. 5.1 PPL data flow

In addition to producing the source listings, compiler listings, load maps, test run output, and so on, the machine procedures also produce new library status listings.

The PPL approach has a number of advantages. All code and test results, both current and past, are completely visible to every team member. This enables and encourages the practice of code reading. By reading each other's code, programmers tend to resolve interface problems without the necessity of additional personal and written memos. The PPL method allows programmers to concentrate on programming, leaving the clerical duties to the librarian. Furthermore, the PPL enables the project manager to retain better control over costs, resources, and adherence to standards.

The fourth factor in the CPT concept is the functional organization of the team itself, which consists of a small number of skilled specialists who assist the chief programmer. The permanent members of the team are the chief programmer, the backup programmer, and the librarian/secretary. Additional programmers, systems analysts, and technicians are added to the team when needed, depending on the size and type of project. Fig. 5.2 illustrates the CPT organization. The lines represent lines of communication. The duties of the permanent members are described below.

The *chief programmer* is a senior-level programmer who is responsible for the development of the programming system project. He is the technical manager of the team. The chief programmer designs, codes, and integrates the critical parts of the programming system himself. If the system is large enough to require additional aid, he specifies and oversees the integration of all other programming as well.

The *backup programmer* is a senior-level programmer whose function is to provide full support for the chief programmer at a detailed level. He must be totally familiar with the development of the project, as he may be required to assume the chief programmer's responsibilities. Thus, he is active in all phases of the project, including design, coding, integration, and management. As directed by the chief programmer, the backup programmer will usually consider alternative designs and develop the testing plans.

As should be apparent from their functions, both the chief and backup programmers must be experienced professionals of proven ability, both in the technical aspects of programming and in project management. They must be technically competent and highly skilled in overall systems analysis, specification, design, and in the techniques of detailed programming, testing, and integration of the system. Since both the chief and backup programmers will be doing detailed coding of the

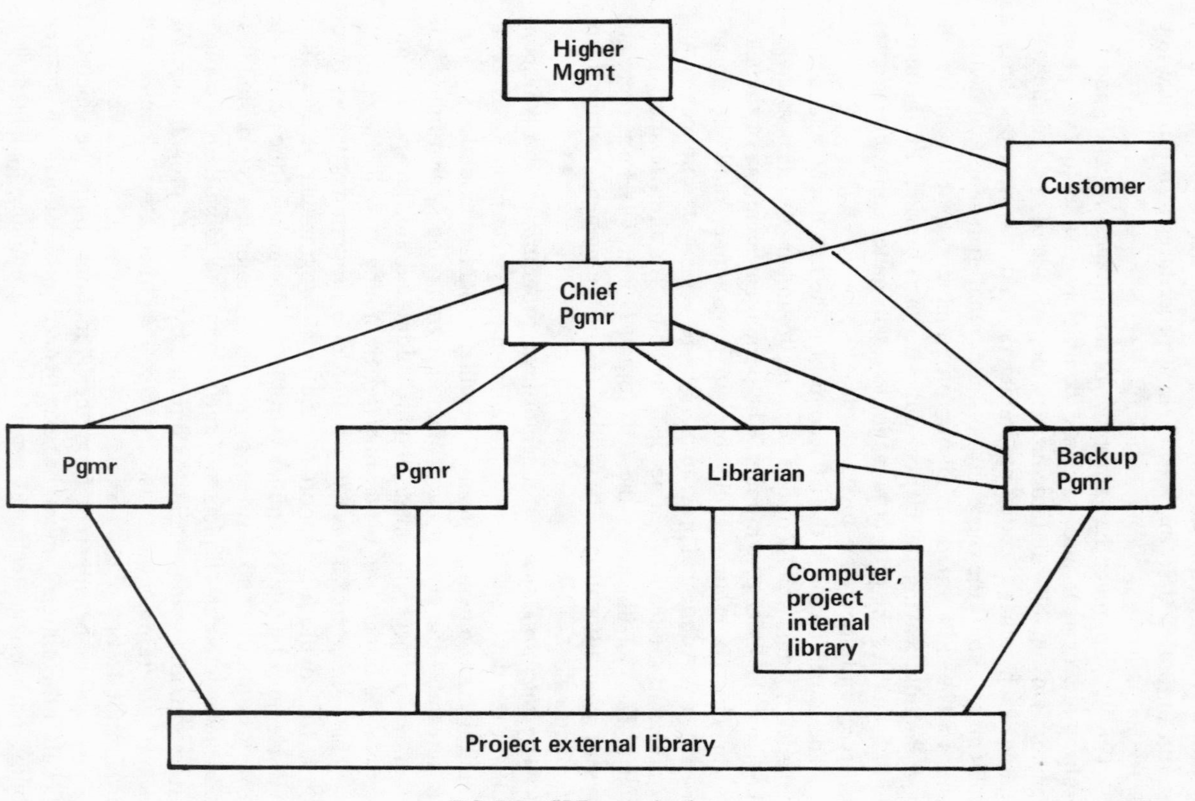

FIG. 5.2 CPT organization

critical parts of the system, they must be extremely proficient in using the operating system facilities and the programming language with which they are working. As managers, they must be capable not only of such internal team management tasks as developing programming production plans that meet cost, time, and resource requirements, but also of working with higher-level management and with the customer.

As discussed above, the *librarian* is responsible for maintenance of the PPL. This task is sufficiently straightforward so that it can be performed by a secretary who has had a small amount of PPL-oriented training. Note that the librarial and secretarial functions mesh nicely since the team members need librarial support when they are coding, testing, and integrating and need secretarial support when they are designing and documenting. In case of conflict, however, the PPL maintenance duties have priority. Although the job is independent of the project subject matter, because the PPL is such an important project asset, the librarian is a full team member instead of a pooled assistant.

For a small project the chief programmer, backup programmer, and librarian may produce the entire system. With a larger project the team may be augmented with additional programmers, analysts, or other specialists. These additional personnel provide specific functional capabilities of the system, as determined by the chief programmer. Specific assignments can range from coding a lower-order program stub to detailed design and coding of a high-level subsystem to complex mathematical analysis and development of algorithms. A project manager, who works in partnership with the chief programmer, is sometimes added to a CPT for projects involving large or complex legal and financial problems. This frees the chief programmer to concentrate on the technical management and development of the project.

It appears that 100,000 lines of source code is a practical upper bound for a single CPT augmented by about four programmers. For larger systems the concept can be extended into a hierarchy of teams. The top-level team is, of course, responsible for overall systems design and development of the critical system-control code. Some of its team members become chief programmers of teams at the next level down which develop specific functional subsystems. When the top-level team is finished with its critical coding, it monitors the developing subsystems and continuously integrates them with the overall system. Likewise, a team at the second level could spawn third-level teams to develop functional components for its subsystem. When a team in the hierarchy has completed its assignment, its members are free to go on to other projects, except for the chief programmer, who is probably a member of the higher-level team. Thus, the hierarchy of teams expands and contracts as the system is developed. Since chief programmers are also managers, the management structure is in direct correspondence with the functional structure of the system as currently developed. You should observe that the top-down design and integration approach is used throughout. Thus, when a team has completed its own critical code sections, it can immediately begin integrating the top-level code of its subordinate teams with its own critical code. By the same token, the top levels of its code are "simultaneously" being integrated with its superior team's code. A two-level team-of-teams approach is already being tried within IBM.

5.3 ADVANTAGES OF THE CPT APPROACH

In the preceding section we discussed what comprises the CPT. We now want to further illuminate the concept by discussing it in a number of contexts. First, we shall compare it with the more traditional approach to production programming. Since we have covered the advantages of structured coding and top-down design and integration in Chapters 3 and 4, we will be more concerned here with the advantages of the CPT organization and the PPL.

The traditional approach is illustrated in Fig. 5.3, where the lines represent lines of communication. If you compare this figure with Fig. 5.2, a few differences are immediately apparent. First of all, there are many more lines of communication in the traditional approach than in a CPT. The additional lines of interprogrammer communication appear in the form of extra memos and documents which specify such things as program interfaces. Additional problems arise because the program code does not agree with the memos and documents. A CPT reduces this communication overhead because of its disciplined functional structure and because the code listings in the external PPL are the primary method of communication.

Further examination of the two figures shows that in the traditional approach programmers communicate with both the external and internal project libraries. Each programmer usually maintains his own external and internal libraries, often in his own personal way. This leads to a number of problems. Because each programmer maintains his own card decks and listings, there is great variability in their quality and reliability. Card decks and listings are even sometimes misplaced or lost. Since each programmer has direct access to the computer and the internal project, there is a larger danger. Programmers must spend a great deal of time in the details of library maintenance, instead of concentrating on the

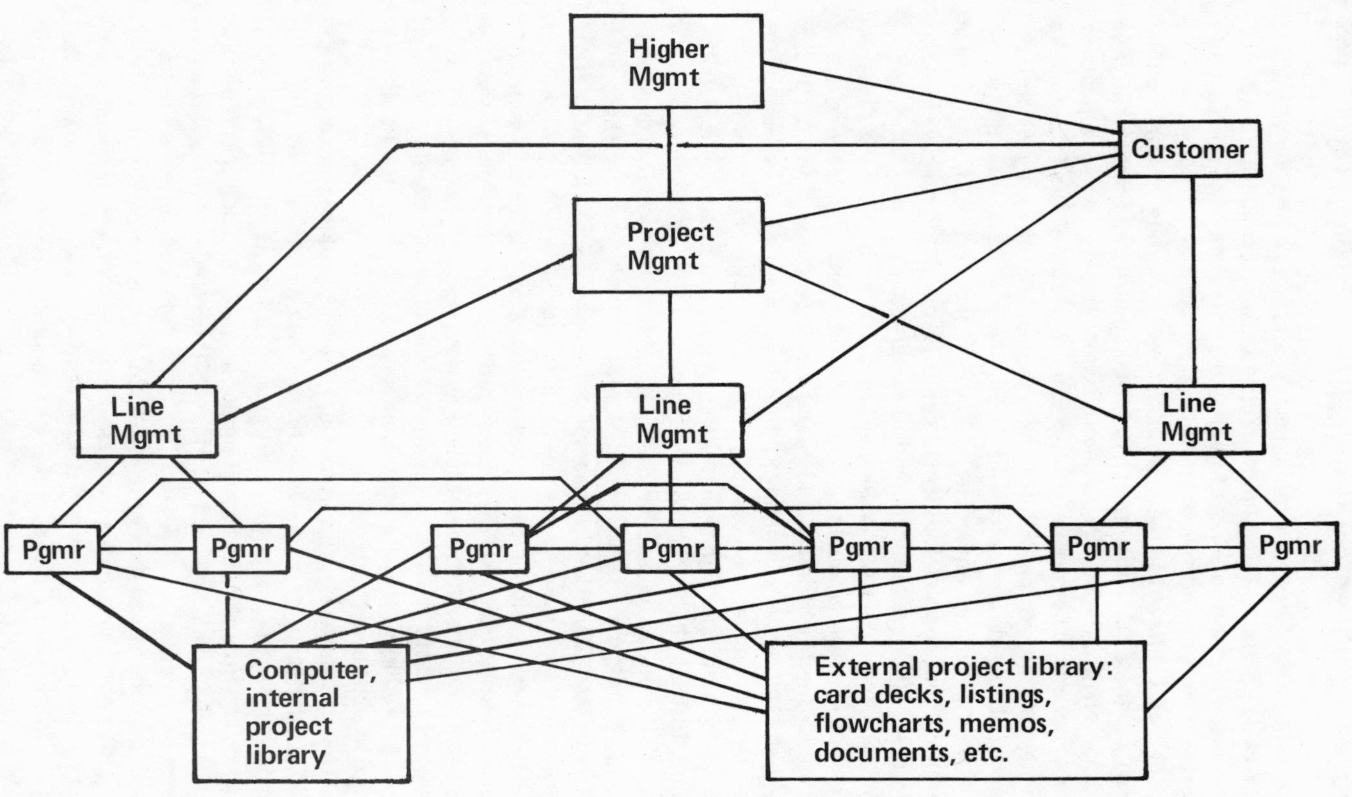

FIG. 5.3 Traditional organization

important tasks of design, coding, testing, and integration. Furthermore, since each programmer is maintaining his own personal libraries, it is very difficult for management to assess the true state of the project and to prevent budget and schedule overruns.

The PPL alleviates these problems by providing a single public library for the CPT. The librarian has total control and responsibility for the maintenance of the PPL, while the chief programmer is responsible for its contents. The internal and external libraries of the PPL and the machine and human procedures are highly standardized across all CPT projects. Thus, programmers may easily move from one project to another and yet get immediately down to the details of a particular project without concern for clerical details. Since the library is visible to the whole team, programmers tend to exercise more thought and care in their work, thereby further reducing errors. The visibility of the PPL also allows the chief programmer to maintain much better control over costs, resources, time schedules, and standards adherence. In a CPT the automated production facilities and disciplined functional organization allow the team members to concentrate on the customer's requirements.

In the traditional approach the managers do none of the detailed coding. Instead, the project is divided among the programmers, who do most of the design, coding, testing, and integration work on their own individual subparts of the system. Unfortunately, some of these programmers are junior-level personnel with insufficient skill and experience in handling the complexities of tools such as OS/360 and PL/I. In a CPT, however, it is the chief programmer who designs and codes the critical system sections. The chief programmer determines specific functions and assigns them to programmers who have the skills necessary to carry out the assignments. The chief programmer reviews the code produced by these programmers and integrates it with his own critical system code.

The traditional approach does not encourage the practice of code reading since each programmer maintains his own decks and listings. In contrast, in a CPT practically every line of code is examined by at least two people. When the chief programmer assigns a subfunction to a team member, that member must read over the chief's code in order to determine the interface. Likewise, the chief programmer reads the team member's code when reviewing it for integration with the higher-level code. Because the code is structured, the reading process is much easier and the reader is more likely to discover any errors in the program logic.

Dr. Mills points out that the PPL makes possible the practice of "development accounting."[7] In addition to "archiving" all computer-generated output, records would be kept of errors, testing patterns, and inspection activities. Thus, the PPL would be a complete information base describing the development of the project. Appropriate summaries would be generated for review by management. You might think that the number of listings and records generated would be overwhelming, even for a small project. But experience has shown that applying the CPT concept considerably reduces the number of errors and hence the number of computer runs required. Development accounting is similar to financial accounting. The librarian is in effect a management agent who maintains the PPL independently of the particular project and its programmers.

Another advantage of CPT's is in career development. The team provides a professional environment for senior people. It allows senior-level programmers to move up into management levels and yet to continue with detailed program development. It also provides a training ground for junior-level programmers who will eventually become chief programmers themselves. In addition, the librarian position is a step up from a secretarial position.

5.4 THE PPL

This section discusses in more detail the organization and procedures of a PPL. Although the discussion is based on an OS/360 version, we hope that you will see how to adapt a PPL to your own requirements. The OS/360 PPL is implemented almost entirely in terms of job control statements and standard utility control statements, and is designed for a batch processing environment.

The development of a system may require only one PPL or it may require several—one for each major subsystem or one for a standard checked-out system library and several for development libraries. Alternatively, one PPL could contain several small systems. In other words the organization and procedures of a PPL are independent of its content. In the remainder of this section we use "project" to mean a single pair of PPL internal and external libraries.

A PPL internal library consists of seven sections, each of which is a partitioned data set with a data set name of *projectname.sectionname*. The choice of sections reflects the fact that in OS/360 source modules are compiled into object modules, which are link edited into load modules, which are called into execution with test data by job control statements. The seven internal sections are:

1. SOURCE—This section contains all source coding (PL/I, Assembler, etc.). Each member is a code segment in the sense of

Chapter 4, Section 1. Individual members may be separately compiled or included by other members during compilation.

2. OBJECT—This section contains the object modules produced by compilation or assembly of SOURCE members.
3. LECL—This section contains linkage editor control language statements used to create load modules from OBJECT members.
4. LOAD—This section contains the load modules created by the linkage editor as directed by members of LECL.
5. JCL—This section contains the job control language statements used to execute the load modules of the developing system. Due to limitations of OS/360 the members of this section must be placed in a common procedure library PPL.PROCLIB before they can be executed. The PPL.PROCLIB is concatenated with the system cataloged procedure library SYS1.PROCLIB by a special reader procedure, so that in effect the procedures become cataloged under OS/360.
6. TEST—This section contains all programmer-coded system test data in card image format. Additional test data sets may be created and used by executing members of the JCL section.
7. UCL—This section contains the utility control language statements used by the PPL procedures. This section is established when the project PPL is first set up. It is normally not modified thereafter.

A PPL external library consists of current-status notebooks, archives, and run notebooks. Each PPL internal section has a corresponding current-status notebook. The SOURCE, LECL, JCL, TEST, and UCL sections contain listings of the section members. The OBJECT section contains the compiler and assembler listings of the corresponding OBJECT members. Likewise, the LOAD section contains the linkage editor listings of the corresponding LOAD members. The SOURCE, LECL, JCL, TEST, and UCL sections are usually kept in looseleaf notebooks. The listings are burst since each member is usually only one page. The OBJECT and LOAD listings are kept unburst in post binders. The listings within each current-status notebook are filed in alphabetical order by member name. Usually a current directory listing is kept at the front of each section.

For each current-status section of the library there is a corresponding archive section. When a member listing in a current-status section is replaced by a new listing, the old listing is placed at the top of the corresponding archive section. In addition to the SOURCE, OBJECT, LECL, LOAD, JCL, TEST, and UCL archives, there are also housekeeping and general archives. The housekeeping archive contains the output of PPL housekeeping functions such as library initiation, checkpoint, and space reallocation. The general archive contains any output which doesn't fit into one of the above categories. All archives are kept in reverse chronological order.

Run notebooks hold the execution output of system test runs. The listings are unburst and are kept in reverse chronological order. Often there is a run notebook for each subsystem in a project.

In addition to the project external library there is also a current-status notebook for each computing system used by PPL projects. The notebook contains, in alphabetical order by member name, listings of the current members of the common cataloged procedure library PPL.PROCLIB. Although this library is shared by several projects, a superseded member is placed in its particular project general archive.

There are two types of PPL computer procedures—normal operations and special operations. The librarian can perform normal operations with only a small amount of training; the special operations usually require some programming training or programmer assistance. The normal operations are updating, processing, housekeeping, and executing; the special operations are initiating, advanced housekeeping, and terminating. The normal and special operations available in each of these categories are summarized in the following paragraphs:

1. *Initiating.* Once a master PPL system is installed on a computing system, the initiating procedures allow you to establish a new PPL project. The procedures provide for cataloging the project name, generating the UCL data set, allocating space for internal sections, and cataloging the section names.
2. *Updating.* These procedures allow you to add or change members of a card image section (in particular SOURCE, LECL, JCL, and TEST), delete members from a section, print a section directory, copy JCL members to and delete them from the common procedure library PPL.PROCLIB, copy a member to another project or to the same project, and print all the members of a section. The editing of a member is done primarily by the standard utility program IEBUPDTE. However, since the utility only provides for replacement of an entire card image, a special editing program is used to allow for shifting the text of a group of cards left or right so many columns, and for changing a sequence of characters on a card to a different sequence of characters without repunching the whole card. These edit facilities make it much easier for the librarian to maintain the proper indentation of structured code.
3. *Processing.* For each programming language (PL/I, FORTRAN, COBOL, Assembly) there are three processing procedures: one to

syntax check a SOURCE member, one to compile a SOURCE member into an OBJECT member, and one to link edit OBJECT members into LOAD members, using the appropriate language subroutine library.

4. *Housekeeping.* The normal housekeeping procedures provide for checkpointing a PPL project onto a backup tape and for compacting the unused space in a section into one free space area. The special housekeeping functions provide for increasing the maximum space allocated to a section and for selectively restoring sections from a backup tape.
5. *Executing.* The execution procedures are those procedures which have been transferred from a JCL section to the common procedure library PPL.PROCLIB. They permit execution of load modules in the LOAD section.
6. *Terminating.* These procedures terminate a project by deleting the internal sections and uncataloging the section and project names.

```
//job-name JOB (acct-info),'user-name',MSGLEVEL=1
// EXEC EDIT,PROJECT=project-name,SECTION=section-name
//EDIT.SYSIN DD DATA
./ ADD LIST=ALL,NAME=member1-name
./ NUMBER NEW1=100,INCR=100
card deck for member1
./ CHANGE LIST=ALL,NAME=member2-name
./ NUMBER NEW1=100,INCR=100
a replacement or inserted card                          card-no
./ DELETE SEQ1=card-no,SEQ2=card-no
./ SHIFT LEFT=columns,FROM=card-no,TO=card-no
./ C card-no,RIGHT=columns,'old-text1', 'new-text1', ...
rest of modification cards for member2
/*
// EXEC PL1,PROJECT=project-name,MEMBER=member3-name
// EXEC PL1LE,PROJECT=project-name,MEMBER=member4-name
// EXEC member5-name,TEST=member6-name
```

FIG. 5.4 A typical PPL job

Fig. 5.4 illustrates a typical PPL job. The job consists of four job steps: EDIT, PL1, PL1LE, and *member5*. In the EDIT step, two members of section *section-name* are updated. First a new member *member1* is added, for which the NUMBER card specifies sequencing by 100 in columns 73-80.

Secondly, the CHANGE card specifies that *member2* is to be updated as directed by the following control cards. Replacement cards and newly inserted cards must have the appropriate card numbers in columns 73-80. The DELETE card specifies deletion of a sequence of cards from the member. The SHIFT card causes the text on a sequence of cards to be shifted left or right a certain number of columns. Lastly, the C card causes the text of a specific card to be optionally shifted and selectively replaced. Thus, *new-text1* replaces *old-text1*, etc. In the PL1 job step SOURCE *member3* is compiled into OBJECT *member3*. The PL1LE step link edits OBJECT members into LOAD members as directed by LECL *member4*, using the PL/I subroutine library SYS1.PL1LIB as the automatic call library. In the last job step *member5*—a JCL procedure copied to PPL.PROCLIB—is executed using TEST *member6* as input data.

The PPL office procedures instruct the librarian how to prepare input for jobs such as the example above and how to file the output of jobs in the appropriate notebooks and binders. Note that the office rules are independent of project content. Programmers indicate their changes to source code by writing on the current-status listings in a natural way, such as drawing a line through text to be deleted. New source or other members are submitted on coding forms. The librarian prepares the necessary control cards, submits the job for execution, and files the output. Note that the librarian is actually doing a simple, restricted type of programming. To make the filing process easier for the librarian, each PPL procedure begins with several identifiable JCL comment cards. Even so, the librarian must be able to recognize the different types of output produced by the procedures independently of the JCL since some systems, such as HASP, print the JCL separately from other output. The filing procedures are very detailed since practically all output is filed. For example, in an updating step the new member listings are filed in the section's current-status notebook, while the remainder of the job step output, such as the JCL header, is filed in the section archive, along with the superseded member listings. In addition, the job card deck is saved, at least until the next checkpoint onto a backup tape.

Besides the common user cataloged procedure library PPL.PROCLIB and the PPL cataloged procedures in SYS1.PROCLIB, a PPL system requires two other data sets, since they are referred to by some of the PPL procedures. PPL.LINKLIB contains load modules for those PPL functions which are not implemented directly in job control and utility control statements—for example, the special editor—and PPL.MACLIB contains the macro definitions used for structured Assembly coding (see Appendix B). Additional macro libraries for other programming languages could be added (see Appendix A for PL/I macros).

An improved PPL system called PPL2 is currently under development. Although some of its features are due to specially written programs, the following improvements can be accomplished primarily in JCL. The data set names have been expanded to include a library name component in the form *projectname.libraryname.sectionname,* thereby providing for a hierarchy of libraries within each project. For example, you could have a checked out system library and several development libraries. Furthermore, PPL2 allows user-named sections in addition to the standard project sections described above. The SOURCE section has been replaced by a separate section for each programming language. The OBJECT section contains load modules instead of object modules, thereby allowing it to be concatenated with the linkage editor automatic call library and reducing the amount of LECL required. Lastly, the UCL section has been eliminated. Some of the specially programmed features include automatic collection of program modification statistics and top-down/cross-reference listing of which segments CALL, INCLUDE, or COPY other segments.

6. RESOURCE MANAGEMENT AND PARALLEL PROCESSES

This chapter undertakes two large examples involving the use of parallel processes and management of resources. The concepts used in these examples (and their implementation) could form the basis for an operating system. In addition to illustrating the concepts of top-down design and modularity, we will introduce the concept of a *resource semaphore*, whose *request* and *release* primitives provide a mechanism for management of resources among cooperative parallel processes, i.e. for process synchronization. The resource semaphore concept was developed by Nelson Weiderman in his thesis, *Synchronization and Simulation in Operating System Construction*,[1] which in itself advocates a top-down structured approach to operating system design.

Just as the GO TO statement is an unstructured flow-of-control primitive, so too are the PL/I EVENT data type and WAIT statement unstructured synchronization primitives. Likewise, just as the SELECT-CASE, LOOP-EXITIF-ENDLOOP, etc. figures provide a more structured control flow, so too does the resource semaphore concept provide a better tool for structuring the interactions of cooperative parallel processes. In particular, critical sections, wherein several processes may be "simultaneously" accessing the same data fields, are not distributed throughout a program, but are confined to resource semaphore allocating and queuing routines.

In Section 6.1 we show the need for a process synchronization mechanism and introduce the resource semaphore concept. Sections 6.2, 6.3, and 6.4 develop a PL/I implementation (using tasks) of resource semaphores and the *request* and *release* primitives. Our implementation is adapted from Weiderman's BCPL/360 implementation (using coroutines). Sections 6.5 and 6.6 specify the first large example, a simple producer-consumer problem, and refine it into PL/I code. Lastly, in Section 6.7, we specify our second example, a simple multiprogrammed operating system, and refine it into PL/I pseudo-code. The example is derived from a similar system developed by Weiderman in his thesis from a term project specified by Shaw.[2]

By giving the implementation of *request* and *release* prior to either of the examples, we are departing slightly from a strict top-down approach. We do this because we view the resource semaphore concept as an end in itself, as a simple extension of our programming language (PL/I) to handle parallel programming applications. The producer-consumer problem illustrates one common, simple application. It also develops some basic allocating and queuing routines for use with resource semaphores. The operating system example provides a nontrivial illustration of structured design in a parallel processing situation.

In previous chapters we proceeded slowly through successive levels of minor refinement within a single procedure. In this chapter, however, we are primarily concerned with major refinements of a problem into a number of small procedures, each of which performs a single, simple function. In the producer-consumer example we develop the design directly in PL/I code. In fact, the initial design code is nearly identical to the final code, in part due to the simplicity and small size of the procedures. Consequently, only the final code is shown. Similar remarks apply to the operating system example, except that pseudo-code is used to accommodate abstract data types and operations.

6.1 LOGICAL RESOURCES

Parallel processes, called *tasks* in PL/I, represent a means whereby several computations may proceed either simultaneously on separate processors or by interleaved execution (multiprogramming) on a single processor. While parallelism can lead to considerable efficiency if the processes are essentially independent, it can also lead to some difficulties when the processes have to share resources. As an example of what can happen, consider the following example in which two parallel processes are attempting to update the same global variable:

```
UNSYNCH: PROC OPTIONS(TASK);

         DCL X FIXED BIN INIT(0);

      A: PROC;
         .....
         X = X + 1;
         .....
         END A;
```

```
B: PROC;
   .....
   X = X + 1;
   .....
   END B;

   CALL A EVENT(EA);
   CALL B EVENT(EB);
   WAIT (EA,EB);

   PUT LIST(X);
   END UNSYNCH;
```

In this example A and B are each separate tasks, both of which are trying to increment the global variable X. Since the processes make no attempt to synchronize their access to X, it is possible that either A or B will manage to store a new value for X before the other process fetches a value from X, in which case the final value printed for X will be 2. However, if both processes fetch a value from X before either of them stores a new value, then the final value of X will probably be 1, since each will have fetched a 0 and will try to store a 1. What is needed is a way to make sure that no more than one process is incrementing the cell for X at any time. This is done by the use of resource semaphores.

(Note: Technically, A and B are the names of procedures that are invoked as tasks. Since no TASK variables are specified in the CALL statements, the tasks have anonymous names. However, in discussing a task, we prefer to use the invoked procedure name to refer to it. We shall use A[*i*] to refer to a particular task invocation *i* of a procedure A when there is more than one task invocation of A.)

The variable X in the above example conceptually represents any resource which may be shared or accessed by more than one process. While it is obvious that physical things such as storage, tape drives, and time are resources, we want a more general definition. Thus, we introduce the concept of a *logical resource*. A *logical resource* is anything which can cause a process to become blocked. Each logical resource is assumed to consist of a finite number of resource units. Processes may request resource units and release them. If a process requests a resource and there is an insufficient amount of that resource available to satisfy the request, then that process becomes blocked—in PL/I it executes a WAIT statement. The process remains blocked until the request becomes satisfiable by some other process having released enough of the resource. A logical resource, then, is anything which a process may request, and whose absence may cause the process to become blocked.

For purposes of implementation some form of data structure is needed to contain the information about the status of a resource and the requests which are pending. Such a data structure will be called a *resource semaphore*. A *resource semaphore* consists of three items:

1. A *resource queue*, which contains the resource elements not currently allocated to a process.
2. A *wait queue*, which contains the processes that have made requests for resources from the resource semaphore, but whose requests have not yet been satisfied (such processes are logically blocked).
3. An *allocator routine*, which is a procedure that examines the resource and wait queues of the resource semaphore and attempts to allocate resources on the resource queue to processes on the wait queue. (Note that having the allocator routine as part of the resource semaphore allows each resource semaphore to have its own allocation strategy.)

As alluded to above, there are two primitive operations which a process may execute on a resource semaphore—*request* and *release*. A *request* primitive requires two parameters: the resource semaphore for which the request is made and an optional data parameter, which may be used by the allocator to qualify the request. (The request primitive must also be able to identify the process making the request, in case the process must be blocked.) The *release* primitive also requires two parameters: the name of the resource semaphore and the resource element which is being returned to the resource semaphore's resource queue.

Applying these concepts of resource semaphores and request/release synchronization primitives to the unsynchronized example given above, we obtain the following synchronized version (coded in pseudo-PL/I):

```
SYNCH: PROC OPTIONS(TASK);

       DCL X FIXED BIN INIT(0),
           RS resource_semaphore INIT(1 element);

    A: PROC;
       DCL E resource_element;
       .....
       E = request(RS,1);
```

```
        X = X + 1;
        release(RS,E);
        .....
        END A;

    B:  PROC;
        DCL E resource_element;
        .....
        E = request(RS,1);
        X = X + 1;
        release(RS,E);
        .....
        END B;

        CALL A EVENT(EA);
        CALL B EVENT(EB);
        WAIT (EA,EB);

        PUT LIST(X);
        END SYNCH;
```

Resource semaphore RS initially contains only one element. Thus, whichever process, A or B, is allocated the element first, will cause the other process to be blocked at the time it makes its request. It will remain blocked until the successful process releases the element, at which time the other process will then receive it. Thus, both processes manage to obtain exclusive access to X for the purpose of updating its value.

6.2 IMPLEMENTATION OF LOGICAL RESOURCES

Having illustrated the usefulness of the resource semaphore concept, we now proceed to an implementation of it in PL/I. We will be using the following extensions to PL/I throughout the rest of this chapter. These extensions, shown in Fig. 6.1, are implemented via the PL/I compile time preprocessor. The segment STRUCMAC contains the REPEAT, UNTIL, LOOP, EXITIF, ENDLOOP, SELECT, CASE, DEFAULT, and ENDSELECT macros discussed in Chapter 3 and Appendix A. The rest of the extensions are simply convenient abbreviations. The data type ROUTINE will be used for procedure entry point variables, as discussed in Section 6.4.

```
/* EXTENSIONS TO PL/I */

%INCLUDE STRUCMAC; /* STRUCTURED PROGRAMMING MACROS */

%DCL (INTG, BOOL, TRUE, FALSE, ROUTINE) CHAR;

%INTG = 'FIXED BIN (31,0)';
%BOOL = 'BIT(1)';
%TRUE = '''1''B';
%FALSE = '''0''B';
%ROUTINE = 'LABEL';
```

FIG. 6.1 EXTNSION

We will also be using a second form of extension to obtain the equivalent of new data types in PL/I. In this extension we assume the master declarations segment shown in Fig. 6.2 is global to all internal procedures. This master declarations segment gives the structure for each of the different kinds of control blocks that we will use. Then if we wish to declare, for example, PCB to be a process control block, we need merely write the following declaration:

```
DCL PCB BASED (PCB@) LIKE PROCESS_CONTROL_BLOCK;
```

We also adopt the convention that identifiers ending with '@' are pointer variables and are usually used as the base pointers of based structures declared like one of the master declarations.

```
/* MASTER DECLARATIONS */

%DCL (RES_SEMA, Q_HEAD, PROC_CB) FIXED;
%RES_SEMA = 1;
%Q_HEAD = 2;
%PROC_CB = 3;

DCL DP PTR;      /* DUMMY BASING POINTER */

DCL 1 RESOURCE_SEMAPHORE BASED(DP),
      2 TYPE INTG,   /* RES_SEMA */
      2 RES_Q PTR,
      2 WAIT_Q PTR,
```

```
        2 ALLOCATOR ROUTINE;

DCL 1 QUEUE_HEAD BASED(DP),
        2 TYPE INTG,   /* Q_HEAD */
        2 FIRST PTR,
        2 LAST PTR,
        2 IN ROUTINE,
        2 OUT ROUTINE;

DCL 1 QUEUE_ELEMENT BASED(DP),
        2 TYPE INTG,   /* ELEMENT TYPE */
        2 SUCC PTR,
        2 PRED PTR;
        /* ELEMENT DATA FIELDS */

DCL 1 PROCESS_CONTROL_BLOCK BASED(DP),
        2 TYPE INTG,   /* PROC_CB */
        2 SUCC PTR,
        2 PRED PTR,
        2 RQST INTG,
        2 GRANT PTR,
        2 AWAKEN EVENT;
```

FIG. 6.2 MASTDECL

As can be seen in the master declarations, a RESOURCE_SEMAPHORE contains four fields. The TYPE field is common to all of the structures used in our examples. It contains a code which indicates the type of structure involved. The codes are given at the beginning of the master declarations segment. The RES_Q and WAIT_Q fields will contain pointers to QUEUE_HEAD structures. These queue heads represent the resource queue and the wait queue of the resource semaphore. Lastly, the ALLOCATOR field contains the entry point of the allocator procedure.

Knowing that a resource semaphore contains pointers to two queues, we see that we will need some way of representing the queues. In our examples all queues will be represented as a bidirectional chain of elements. Thus, a *queue head* will contain a pointer to the first element on the queue and a pointer to the last element on the queue. Furthermore, each element of a queue will contain a pointer to its successor element and another pointer to its predecessor element. So, all structures which may appear on queues will contain TYPE, SUCC, and PRED fields as their first three fields, as shown in the declaration for QUEUE_ELEMENT in the master declarations. A QUEUE_HEAD structure will also contain two procedure entry points. The IN field specifies the routine to be called to add an element to the queue. The OUT field specifies the procedure to be called to delete an element from the queue.

When a process is blocked by a request, it is placed on the wait queue of the resource semaphore. This means that we need to have a PROCESS_CONTROL_BLOCK associated with each process. The first three fields are the standard fields for a queue element. The last three fields are used by the REQUEST and RELEASE procedures, as discussed below. Fig. 6.3 shows a resource semaphore and its resource and wait queues. Note that resource elements contain TYPE, SUCC, and PRED queuing fields as well as their own particular data fields.

6.3 IMPLEMENTATION OF REQUEST AND RELEASE

We are now ready to consider the implementation of the *request* and *release* primitives in more detail. First we need the functional specifications. REQUEST is to be a function which takes a process, namely the one calling REQUEST, a resource semaphore, and an optional data parameter, and which returns a resource element. The process is to remain in a blocked state until the resource allocator is able to fulfill the process's request, based on the elements on the resource queue. RELEASE is a procedure which takes a resource semaphore and a resource element, and which does not return a value. RELEASE is to place the resource element on the resource queue and then use the resource allocator to perform any possible allocations.

The PL/I code for REQUEST and RELEASE is given in Fig. 6.4. Examining the code for REQUEST, we see that the process making the request is represented by a pointer to its process control block, that the resource semaphore is represented by a pointer to its data structure, and that the optional data parameter is simply an integer. First, the DATA parameter is saved in the RQST field of the process control block. Secondly, the *pcb* will be placed on the wait queue of the resource semaphore. Since this involves a modification of the resource semaphore data structure, and since some other process may simultaneously be making a request on this resource semaphore, we must first gain exclusive access to the resource semaphore. This is accomplished by the procedure ENQUEUE, applied to the resource semaphore.

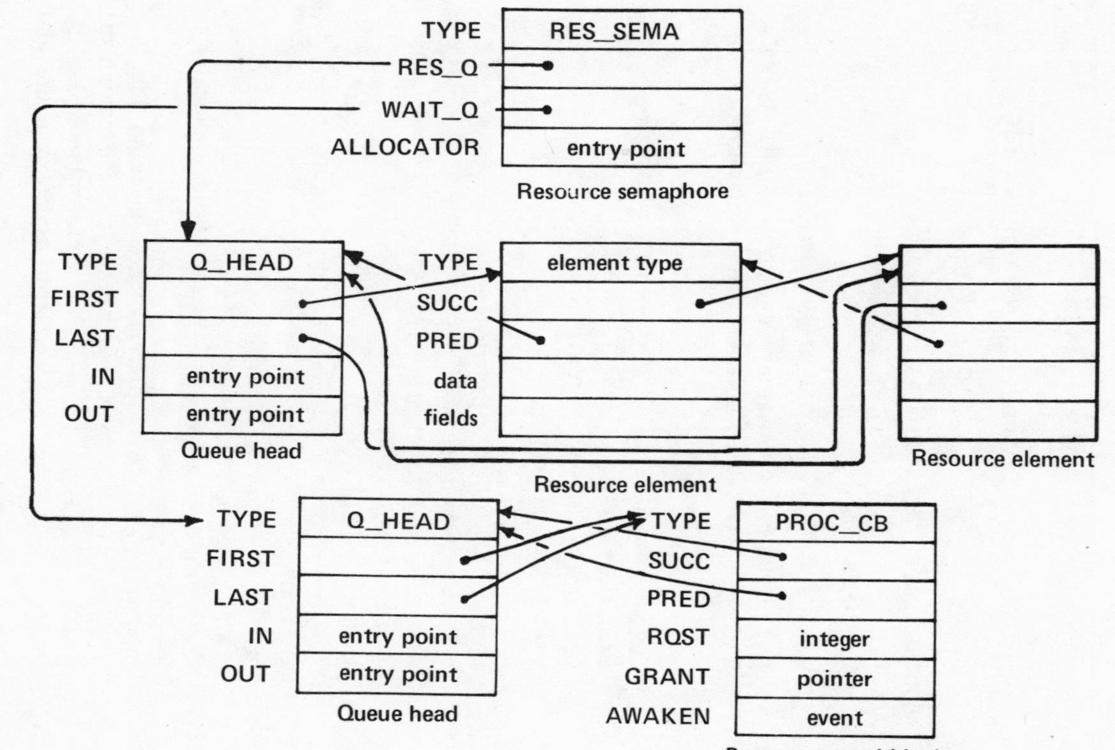

FIG. 6.3 A resource semaphore and its queues

```
        /* REQUEST, RELEASE PROCEDURES */

        DCL REQUEST ENTRY(PTR,PTR,INTG) RETURNS(PTR),
             RELEASE ENTRY (PTR,PTR);

REQUEST: PROC(PCB@,RS@,DATA) RETURNS(PTR);

        DCL (PCB@,RS@) PTR,
             DATA INTG;

        DCL 1 PCB BASED(PCB@) LIKE PROCESS_CONTROL_BLOCK,
             1 RS BASED(RS@) LIKE RESOURCE_SEMAPHORE,
             P PTR;

        PCB.RQST = DATA;
        CALL ENQUEUE(RS@);
        CALL INSERT(PCB@,RS.WAIT_Q);
        CALL DEQUEUE(RS@);

        LOOP;      /* ALLOCATION LOOP */
             CALL ENQUEUE(RS@);
             P = CALL_FN(RS.ALLOCATOR,RS@);
             CALL DEQUEUE(RS@);
        EXITIF(P=NULL);
             COMPLETION(P->PCB.AWAKEN = TRUE;
        ENDLOOP;

        WAIT (PCB.AWAKEN);
        COMPLETION(PCB.AWAKEN) = FALSE;
        RETURN(PCB.GRANT);
        END REQUEST;

RELEASE: PROC(RS@,RCB@);

        DCL (RS@,RCB@) PTR;

        DCL 1 RS BASED(RS@) LIKE RESOURCE_SEMAPHORE,
             P PTR,
             1 PCB BASED(P) LIKE PROCESS_CONTROL_BLOCK;

        CALL ENQUEUE(RS@);
        CALL INSERT(RCB@,RS.RES_Q);
        CALL DEQUEUE(RS@);
```

```
        LOOP;       /* ALLOCATION LOOP */
            CALL ENQUEUE(RS@);
            P = CALL_FN(RS.ALLOCATOR,RS@);
            CALL DEQUEUE(RS@);
        EXITIF(P=NULL);
            COMPLETION(PCB.AWAKEN) = TRUE;
        ENDLOOP;
        END RELEASE;
```

FIG. 6.4 RQSTRLSE

Functionally, ENQUEUE is a procedure which does not return control until it has guaranteed that the process calling it has exclusive access to the object pointed to by its parameter. There is no easy way to implement ENQUEUE in PL/I since a PL/I event cannot be simultaneously waited on by more than one process. However, the ENQ macro-instruction of OS/360 MVT provides exclusive access to objects for processes on a first-come-first-served basis. The S/360 Assembly code version of ENQUEUE given in Fig. 6.5 is our interface between PL/I and the ENQ macro-instruction.

```
ENQ      TITLE 'ENQUEUE PROCEDURE'
*   PROVIDE OS/360 ENQ SERVICE FOR PL/I F.
*   DCL ENQUEUE EXT ENTRY(PTR);
*   CALL ENQUEUE(P);
*        WHERE P POINTS TO THE ITEM TO BE ENQUEUED.
         PRINT  DATA
ENQUEUE  CSECT
R0       EQU    0
R1       EQU    1
R2       EQU    2
R11      EQU    11
R12      EQU    12
R13      EQU    13
R14      EQU    14
R15      EQU    15
*   STANDARD TASKING PL/I F PROCEDURE PROLOGUE.
         USING  *,R15
         SAVE   (14,12),,*
         LA     R0,DSALEN
```

```
         L        R15,=V(IHETSAD)
         BALR     R14,R15             GET DSA, ADD TO CHAIN
         MVI      0(R13),X'80'        PROCEDURE DSA
         MVI      96(R13),0           NO SUBTASKS
         USING    DSA,R13
         BALR     R11,0
         USING    *,R11
         DROP     R15
*   PROCEDURE BODY.  R1 -> PARAMETER LIST.
         MVC      QNAME(4),=CL4'ITEM'
         L        R2,0(R1)            R2 -> PARAMETER P
         L        R2,0(R2)            R2 = P
         LA       R2,0(R2)            CLEAR HIGH ORDER BYTE
         ST       R2,QNAME+4
         MVC      ENQLIST(LISTLEN),LIST
         ENQ      (QNAME,RNAME,,,),MF=(E,ENQLIST)
*   STANDARD TASKING PL/I F PROCEDURE EPILOGUE.
         L        R15,=V(IHETSAE)
         BR       R15                 FREE DSA AND RETURN
LIST     ENQ      (,,E,RNAMELEN,STEP),MF=L
LISTLEN  EQU      *-LIST
*   DYNAMIC STORAGE AREA.
DSA      DSECT
         DS       CL108               MIN TASKING PL/I F DSA
QNAME    DS       CL8                 QUEUE NAME
RNAME    EQU      QNAME+5             RESOURCE NAME
RNAMELEN EQU      3
ENQLIST  ENQ      (,,,,),MF=L
         DS       0D
DSALEN   EQU      *-DSA
         END
```

FIG. 6.5 ENQUEUE

Returning our attention to the REQUEST procedure, we see, following the insertion of the *pcb* on the wait queue, that exclusive control of the semaphore is released by the procedure DEQUEUE. Functionally, DEQUEUE is a procedure that releases its calling process's exclusive control of the object pointed to by its parameter. The Assembly code for DEQUEUE shown in Fig. 6.6 provides the interface between PL/I and the DEQ macro-instruction of OS/360 MVT.

```
DEQ      TITLE  'DEQUEUE PROCEDURE'
*   PROVIDE OS/360 DEQ SERVICE FOR PL/I F.
*   DCL DEQUEUE EXT ENTRY(PTR);
*   CALL DEQUEUE(P);
*        WHERE P POINTS TO THE ITEM TO BE DEQUEUED.
         PRINT  DATA
DEQUEUE  CSECT
R0       EQU    0
R1       EQU    1
R2       EQU    2
R11      EQU    11
R12      EQU    12
R13      EQU    13
R14      EQU    14
R15      EQU    15
*   STANDARD TASKING PL/I F PROCEDURE PROLOGUE.
         USING  *,R15
         SAVE   (14,12),,*
         LA     R0,DSALEN
         L      R15,=V(IHETSAD)
         BALR   R14,R15              GET DSA, ADD TO CHAIN
         MVI    0(R13),X'80'         PROCEDURE DSA
         MVI    96(R13),0            NO SUBTASKS
         USING  DSA,R13
         BALR   R11,0
         USING  *,R11
         DROP   R15
*   PROCEDURE BODY.  R1 -> PARAMETER LIST.
         MVC    QNAME(4),=CL4'ITEM'
         L      R2,0(R1)             R2 -> PARAMETER P
         L      R2,0(R2)             R2 = P
         LA     R2,0(R2)             CLEAR HIGH ORDER BYTE
         ST     R2,QNAME+4
         MVC    DEQLIST(LISTLEN),LIST
         DEQ    (QNAME,RNAME,,),MF=(E,DEQLIST)
*   STANDARD TASKING PL/I F PROCEDURE EPILOGUE.
         L      R15,=V(IHETSAE)
         BR     R15                  FREE DSA AND RETURN
LIST     DEQ    (,,RNAMELEN,STEP),MF=L
LISTLEN  EQU    *-LIST
*   DYNAMIC STORAGE AREA.
```

```
DSA       DSECT
          DS    CL108         MIN TASKING PL/I F DSA
QNAME     DS    CL8           QUEUE NAME
RNAME     EQU   QNAME+5       RESOURCE NAME
RNAMELEN  EQU   3
DEQLIST   DEQ   (,,,),MF=L
          DS    0D
DSALEN    EQU   *-DSA
          END
```

FIG. 6.6 DEQUEUE

INSERT is a general queue-handling routine whose functional specifications are as follows: it is to add its first parameter, a queue element, to its second parameter, a queue. As usual, we represent queue elements, queue heads, and resource semaphores by pointers to the respective data structures. Note that the actual insertion algorithm is part of the queue head structure.

Having placed the process on the wait queue, we now repeatedly call the resource allocator until no further allocations are possible. A resource allocator is a function whose parameter is the resource semaphore. The allocator examines the resource and wait queues of the semaphore and attempts to perform an allocation. If the available resources satisfy the request of one of the processes on the wait queue, then that process is removed from the wait queue and the selected resource is removed from the resource queue. The resource (i.e. a pointer to it) is to be placed in the GRANT field of the process control block. The value yielded by the allocator is the process control block (again a pointer to it). If no allocation is possible, the allocator is to return a NULL pointer. The function CALL_FN is a procedure which applies the allocator to its argument, the resource semaphore, and returns the result of the allocator. For each process control block returned by the allocator, we awaken the corresponding blocked process by posting the AWAKEN event field of the *pcb*.

Strictly speaking, this allocation loop should be executed by the operating system supervisor, and the process should actually be asleep. However, we don't have access to the operating system task scheduler, so we must simulate its effects. Thus, even though the process which has called REQUEST should be physically blocked at the time it placed itself on the resource semaphore wait queue, it is actually still executing the allocation loop; after all, someone has to call the allocator. However, now that the allocator has performed all of its allocations, we no longer need to keep the process active. Hence we now execute the WAIT statement on the AWAKEN field of the process's *pcb*. If in the previous allocation loop the allocator succeeded in fulfilling the request of the process, then the AWAKEN event for the process has already been posted, in which case the WAIT becomes a no-op and the process proceeds. Otherwise, the process remains in a physical wait state until another process, via a call on REQUEST or RELEASE, executes the allocator and successfully grants the waiting process's request, at which time the AWAKEN event is posted and the process is released from its wait state. Once the process is awakened, it must reset the AWAKEN event to FALSE so that the event variable can be reused for the process's next request. Lastly, the REQUEST procedure yields the resource pointed to by the GRANT field of the *pcb*.

The RELEASE procedure is less complicated. First, the resource element is placed on the resource queue via the call to INSERT. Then the same allocation loop as in REQUEST is used to perform as many allocations as possible.

6.4 PROCEDURE ENTRY POINT VARIABLES

Our discussion of REQUEST and RELEASE is complete except for one major point. By now you are probably wondering why we used ROUTINE as an abbreviation for LABEL and why we used CALL_FN to call the allocator. What we want is the ability to place procedure entry points in resource semaphores and queue heads, so that each resource semaphore can have its own allocator procedure and each queue head can have its own insertion and deletion procedures. However, the PL/I F implementation doesn't allow for entry variables. Fortunately, PL/I F does have label variables, the implementation of which is the same as for entry parameters.

What we would like to be able to do is the following: Suppose we have the declarations

```
DCL RS@ PTR,
    1 RS BASED(RS@) LIKE RESOURCE_SEMAPHORE,
    ALLOC ENTRY(PTR) RETURNS(PTR),
    P PTR;
```

We would like to be able to write the assignment statement shown below:

```
ALLOCATE RS;
RS.ALLOCATOR = ALLOC;
```

This assignment statement assigns the entry point of the allocator procedure called ALLOC to the ALLOCATOR field of the resource semaphore RS. Furthermore, we would like to be able to call the resource semaphore allocator by writing the statement:

```
P = RS.ALLOCATOR(RS@);
```

However, the two assignment statements are illegal since PL/I F does not have entry point variables.

Because of the implementation similarity between entry points and labels in PL/I F, we can get around this restriction by using label variables and assigning entry points to them. The three procedures shown in Fig. 6.7 implement our requirements, First, STORE_PROC is a procedure which stores its first parameter, an entry point, at the location given by its second parameter, a label variable. Thus, we can store the allocator in the ALLOCATOR field of a resource semaphore by writing

```
CALL STORE_PROC(ALLOC,RS.ALLOCATOR);
```

Second, CALL_FN is a procedure which takes a procedure value contained in a label variable, and a pointer, and which yields the result of applying the procedure to the pointer. Thus, the resource semaphore allocator is called by the statement

```
P = CALL_FN(RS.ALLOCATOR,RS@);
```

Third, CALL_PROC is a procedure which takes a procedure and two pointers and applies the procedure to the pointers. It is used to call the procedures stored in the IN and OUT fields of queue heads.

```
        /* STORE_PROC, CALL_PROC, CALL_FN PROCEDURES */

        DCL STORE_PROC ENTRY(ENTRY,ROUTINE),
            CALL_PROC ENTRY(ROUTINE,PTR,PTR),
            CALL_FN ENTRY(ROUTINE,PTR) RETURNS(PTR);


STORE_PROC: PROC(PROC_VAL,PROC_LOC);

        DCL (PROC_VAL,PROC_LOC) ROUTINE;
```

```
          PROC_LOC = PROC_VAL;
          END STORE_PROC;


     CALL_PROC: PROC(P,A,B);

          DCL P ENTRY(PTR,PTR),
               (A,B) PTR;

          CALL P(A,B);
          END CALL_PROC;


     CALL_FN: PROC(P,A) RETURNS(PTR);

          DCL P ENTRY(PTR) RETURNS(PTR),
               A PTR;

          RETURN(P(A));
          END CALL_FN;
```

FIG. 6.7 ENTRYVAR

Our implementation of procedure entry point variables is subject to the following usage restriction: When a procedure name is passed as an argument to another procedure, the value passed also points to the current top of the PL/I F run time stack (i.e., to the caller's environment). Hence, if you exit from the calling procedure, the passed procedure value (which you presumably have stored via STORE_PROC) becomes invalid and may not be used to call the (stored) procedure (via CALL_PROC or CALL_FN). The following example illustrates this restriction in more detail but is rather complex. Hence, you may skip to the last paragraph in this section.

Consider the program in Fig. 6.8. Execution begins with the creation of an activation record for EPVTEST on the PL/I run time stack. (Note: An activation record is created each time a procedure or begin block is entered and deleted when the procedure or begin block is exited. The record contains a register save area, automatic storage for the procedure or begin block, and other information particular to that activation.) Based variable N is allocated, set to 0, and printed. An activation record for Q is created and Q is entered. An entry point value for P is formed and assigned to R by the call of STORE_PROC.

```
        /* ENTRY POINT VARIABLE TEST */

EPVTEST: PROC OPTIONS(MAIN,REENTRANT,TASK);

        %INCLUDE EXTNSION;
        %INCLUDE ENTRYVAR;

        DCL R ROUTINE,
            N INTG BASED(N@),
            N@ PTR;

        DCL P ENTRY(PTR,PTR);

P: PROC(N@,DP);
        DCL (N@,DP) PTR;
        DCL N INTG BASED(N@);
        N = N + 1;
        END P;

        DCL Q ENTRY(PTR);

Q: PROC(N@);
        DCL N@ PTR;
        CALL STORE_PROC(P,R);
        CALL CALL_PROC(R,N@,NULL);
        PUT LIST(N);
        END Q;

        ALLOCATE N;
        N = 0;
        PUT LIST(N);
        CALL Q(N@);
L:      CALL CALL_PROC(R,N@,NULL);
        PUT LIST(N);
        END EPVTEST;
```

FIG. 6.8 EPVTEST

This entry point value actually consists of two parts, an instruction pointer (*ip*) and an environment pointer (*ep*). The *ip* points to the procedure body code to be executed; the *ep* indicates the environment (the set of activation records used for references to nonlocal AUTOMATIC variables) to be used when the procedure is executed. For PL/I F the *ep* formed for P (at the call to STORE_PROC) points to Q's activation record, since Q is the most recently entered procedure or begin block.

Having assigned P to R, we next execute the procedure stored in R (namely P) via the call to CALL_PROC. This causes N to be incremented to 1. After return to Q, Q prints the value of N (1). Q is exited and its activation record *deleted*. We are now about to execute statement L in EPVTEST. Now CALL_PROC is called, but when it attempts to call the procedure stored in R (P), we have an error. The error occurs because the *ep* of the procedure value in R points to Q's activation record, which no longer exists.

The code compiled for the CALL P(A,B) statement in CALL_PROC actually calls the library routine IHETSAN with arguments P, A, and B. IHETSAN is supposed to establish the proper environment from P's *ep* and transfer to P's entry point (*ip*). However, when the *ep* points to garbage, anything can happen. In particular, execution of EPVTEST yields a time limit exceeded error message (system completion code 322).

One solution to this problem is to move the call to STORE_PROC from Q to EPVTEST (prior to the call to Q). Then the *ep* will point to EPVTEST's activation record instead of Q's. An alternative is to pass P as an entry parameter in the call to Q—i.e., CALL Q(N@,P). Q would then pass its entry parameter on to STORE_PROC—i.e., if Q: PROC(N@,E), then CALL STORE_PROC(E,R). The *ep* is created at the call to Q and hence points to EPVTEST's activation record. The *ep* is passed on by Q to STORE_PROC and stored in R.

We point out that PL/I F is more restrictive than the PL/I language definition.[3] According to the definition, the *ep* formed by the "flawed" version of EPVTEST would point to EPVTEST's activation record, since P is statically (lexicographically) internal to EPVTEST. Note, however, that since P contains no references to nonlocal variables, its (necessary) environment could just as well be null. Thus, even the PL/I language definition is overly restrictive.

Before proceeding to an example of resource management, let us review what we have accomplished so far. Beginning with a PL/I machine, namely the PL/I F implementation, we have designed and implemented an abstract machine of slightly higher level, namely PL/I with *request* and *release* primitives for resource semaphores. In order to implement this higher level, we have used an intermediate-level machine, which is PL/I with procedure entry point variables. Our request-release machine, rather than PL/I, now becomes the bottom level or target machine in all our parallel processing examples.

6.5 A PRODUCER-CONSUMER EXAMPLE

We are now ready to consider our first major example of resource management and parallel processes. Here is the problem: We want to read a sequence of integers and to print a table whose first column contains the integers and whose second column contains the squares of the integers. At the end of the table we want to print the number of integers processed. As an additional requirement, we would like the rows of the output table to be in the same order as the input. The procedure PROBLEM shown in Fig. 6.9 is one possible solution to the problem. However, we now change the problem specifications to require the use of two parallel processes, one to be a producer of a resource and one a consumer of that resource. The producer process is to read the sequence of integers. For each integer in the sequence it is to release to a resource semaphore a resource containing the integer and the square of the integer. The consumer process is to request resources from the resource semaphore. For each resource it is to print the integer and the square of the integer contained in that resource element.

```
          /* PRODUCER-CONSUMER PROBLEM */

PROBLEM: PROC OPTIONS(MAIN);

          %INCLUDE EXTNSION;   /* EXTENSIONS */

          DCL N INTG,
               EOF BOOL INIT(FALSE),
               #SQUARES INTG INIT(0);

          ON ENDFILE(SYSIN) EOF = TRUE;

          PUT EDIT ('N', 'N*N') (X(3),A,X(7),A);
          PUT SKIP;

          LOOP;
               GET LIST(N);
          EXITIF(EOF);
```

```
            PUT SKIP EDIT (N,N*N) (F(5),F(10));
            #SQUARES = #SQUARES + 1;
        ENDLOOP;

        PUT SKIP(2) EDIT (#SQUARES,' SQUARES PROCESSED') (F(3),A);

        END PROBLEM;
```

FIG. 6.9 PROBLEM

We shall represent the resource elements by the structure SQUARES_QUEUE_ELEMENT shown below.

```
%DCL SQUARES_QE FIXED;
%SQUARES_QE = 4;

DCL 1 SQUARES_QUEUE_ELEMENT BASED(DP),
      2 TYPE INTG,   /* SQUARES_QE */
      2 SUCC PTR,
      2 PRED PTR,
      2 N INTG,
      2 N_SQR INTG;
```

The above code is to be appended to the master declarations segment in Fig. 6.2. Thus, we will have a resource semaphore SQUARES_RS whose elements are produced by the producer and consumed by the consumer.

Another resource which we must consider is storage space. The resource elements produced by the producer occupy a certain amount of storage space. The producer process should request the necessary space, form the resource element, and release it to the squares resource semaphore, whereupon the consumer process can request an element, utilize it (print it), and then release the space back to the space resource semaphore.

However, there is a slight problem here: It is possible for the producer process to consume all the space for squares resource elements and not leave any space for other processes. This can happen if the producer executes much more rapidly than any other process. To solve this problem, we will use a third resource semaphore which will contain empty squares elements. We will preallocate some number of squares queue elements and place them on the empty squares resource queue. Thus, the producer process will request an empty squares element, read an integer, fill in the integer and square fields of the resource element, and release it to the (full) squares resource semaphore. Meanwhile, the consumer process is requesting a full squares resource element, printing its contents, and releasing the element to the empty squares resource semaphore.

We envision that our program will have the overall multilevel structure given in Fig. 6.10. Level 1 is primarily concerned with initializing the processes and resource semaphores. Level 2 is actually the important level of our program, as it specifies the interactions between the processes and resource semaphores. Level 3 provides any supporting routines required by the processes and resource semaphores. In a larger problem, such as an operating system, this level would certainly be broken up into several levels of support. In fact, each process would have its own levels of refinement, as would each resource semaphore, although many of the resource semaphores might share the same basic queue-handling and allocation routines. Finally, at level 4 we have PL/I extended with *request* and *release* primitives.

Returning to level 2, we may specify the interactions between the processes and resource semaphores of our particular problem by the diagram in Fig. 6.11. In this diagram the boxes represent processes, the circles are resource semaphores, and the arrows indicate request and release actions. For instance, the producer releases full squares elements to the full squares resource semaphore, which are then requested by the consumer. The space resource semaphore has been omitted from this diagram because it will only be used by the main process to initialize the other resource semaphores.

We are now ready to begin developing our program. We see that we will be using three resource semaphores, one for storage space, one for empty squares, and one for full squares. Most of the work is to be done by two processes, producer and consumer. Thus, our main process must first allocate and set up the resource semaphores and second initiate the subprocesses. The main process then simply waits for the subprocesses to terminate, after which it may also terminate.

The PL/I code for the main process is shown in Fig. 6.12. The procedure RESMAN begins by first including the extensions and the master declarations. The compile time preprocessor provides a convenient way of setting various parameter values and limits. Thus MAX_EMPTY_SQUARES determines the number of preallocated squares resource elements that will be placed on the empty squares resource queue at the start of the job. The first DECLARE statement declares all of the identifiers which may be used in other internal procedures. In particular, it declares the pointers to the space, full, and empty squares resource semaphores,

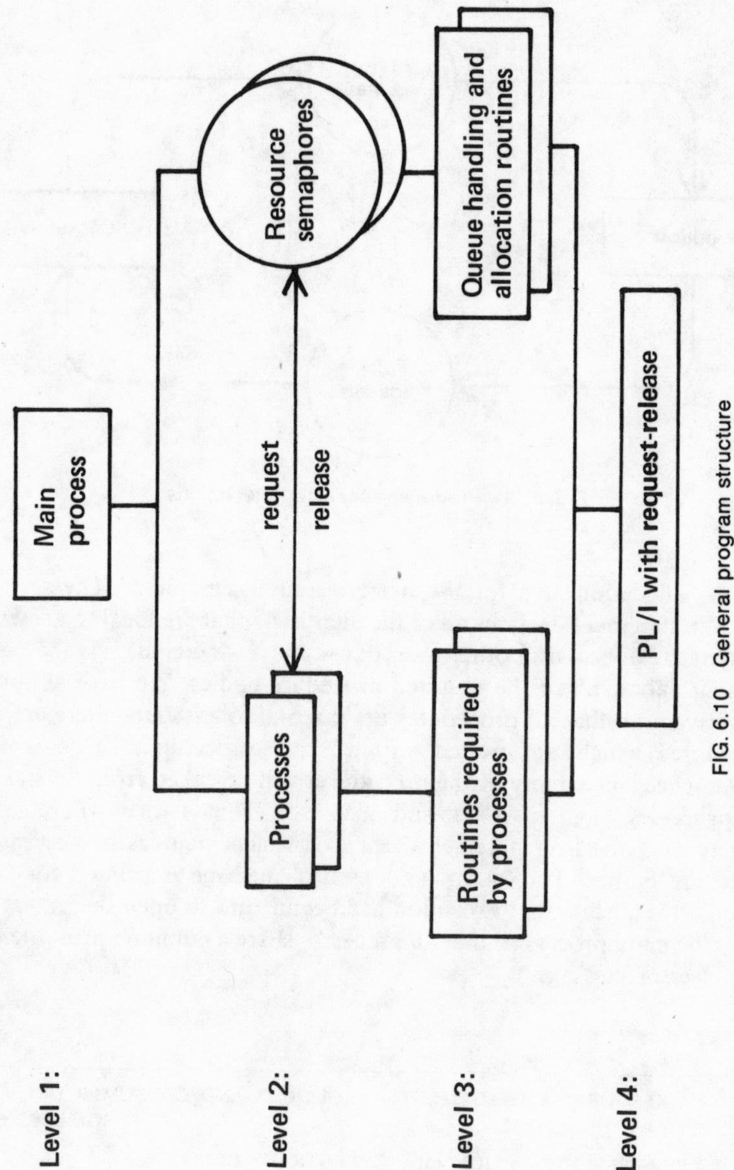

FIG. 6.10 General program structure

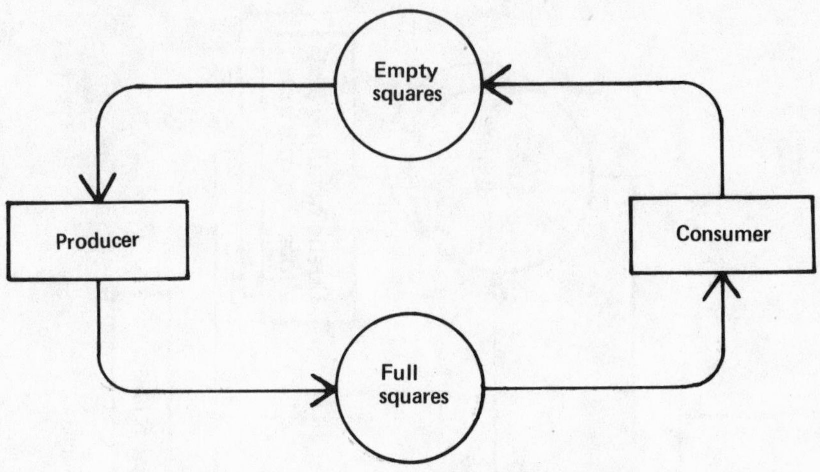

FIG. 6.11 Producer-consumer interactions

and the allocation area for the space resource semaphore. The second DECLARE statement declares all of the identifiers that are local to RESMAN, i.e., that are not used in other procedures. Next we include, via the code segment PROCS, all of the required procedure bodies. We have adopted the convention that all procedures are internal to RESMAN—there are no procedures which are nested within other procedures. This is for convenience since many of the procedures will be called from several of the processes (e.g., REQUEST and RELEASE). Thus PROCS will consist entirely of %INCLUDE statements, each of which includes one or more procedure bodies. The 'BEGIN PROCESSING' message is printed for two reasons: to indicate that execution has begun, and to open the SYSPRINT file in the main process so that all processes share a common print file (in case of error messages).

```
/* RESOURCE MANAGEMENT -- PRODUCER AND CONSUMER OF
                                          SQUARES */

RESMAN: PROC OPTIONS(MAIN,REENTRANT,TASK);

   %INCLUDE EXTNSION;   /* EXTENSIONS */
   %INCLUDE MASTDECL;   /* MASTER DECLARATIONS */

   %DCL MAX_EMPTY_SQRS FIXED;
   %MAX_EMPTY_SQRS = 5;
```

```
DCL  (ENQUEUE, DEQUEUE) EXT ENTRY(PTR),
     (SPACE_RS@, SQUARES_RS@, EMPTY_SQRS_RS@) PTR,
     SPACE_AREA AREA(10000);

DCL  I INTG,
     1 PCB BASED(PCB@) LIKE PROCESS_CONTROL_BLOCK,
     (PCB@, RQ@, WQ@, RCB@) PTR,
     (PROD_PCB@, CONS_PCB@) PTR,
     (PROD_EVT, CONS_EVT) EVENT;

%INCLUDE PROCS;     /* PROCEDURES */

PUT LIST ('BEGIN PROCESSING');

/* SET UP PCB FOR MAIN PROCESS */

PCB@ = ALLOC_SPACE(PROC_CB);
COMPLETION(PCB.AWAKEN) = FALSE;

%INCLUDE SETUPRS;  /* SET UP RESOURCE SEMAPHORES */

/* SPAWN PROCESSES */

PROD_PCB@ = CREATE_PCB(PCB@);
CONS_PCB@ = CREATE_PCB(PCB@);

CALL PRODUCER(PROD_PCB@) EVENT(PROD_EVT);
CALL CONSUMER(CONS_PCB@) EVENT(CONS_EVT);

WAIT (PROD_EVT,CONS_EVT);

/* CLEAN UP */

PUT SKIP(3) LIST ('END PROCESSING');
END RESMAN;
```

FIG. 6.12 RESMAN

We would now like to set up the resource semaphores. Since resource semaphores and queues require storage space, we would like to set up the storage space resource semaphore first. Then we will be able to request space from it in order to set up the other resource semaphores. Since each process should have a process control block associated with it, so that it can call REQUEST, we thus must first set up a *pcb* for the main process. The call of the function ALLOC_SPACE returns a pointer to the space for the *pcb*. The next statement initializes the *pcb* so that it is ready to be used in a call to REQUEST. Next, the included file SETUPRS causes the resource semaphores to be created and initialized.

We are now ready to initiate the individual subprocesses. First, we must create a *pcb* for each process. The function CREATE_PCB is a routine which requests space from the space resource semaphore for a *pcb*, initializes the *pcb*, and returns a pointer to it. Since REQUEST requires the *pcb* of the process making the request, we must pass the main process *pcb* as an argument to CREATE_PCB, so that it can pass it on to REQUEST. At last we are able to initiate the subprocesses PRODUCER and CONSUMER, by means of the task CALL statements. We then immediately wait for each of the subprocesses to terminate, after which we print out a termination message and cease execution.

As our next point of refinement, we consider the code which sets up the resource semaphores. The PL/I code is given in Fig. 6.13. As stated before, we first want to set up the space resource semaphore so that we may then use it to set up the other resource semaphores. All of our storage elements are represented by based variables, and PL/I provides two choices for allocating based variable storage. The storage may either be allocated local to the task in which the allocate statement is executed or it may be allocated within a specific area variable. This area variable is local to the procedure in which it is declared. Since storage for resource elements may be requested in one process and passed to another process, and since we don't always know the order of termination of processes, we want all storage to be allocated in an area variable declared in the main process. This way, the storage will exist at least as long as any of the subprocessses. Thus, we will be using the area variable SPACE_AREA, declared in the main procedure RESMAN, for all of our storage requests.

```
/* SET UP RESOURCE SEMAPHORES */

/* SET UP SPACE RESOURCE SEMAPHORE */

RQ@ = ALLOC_SPACE(Q_HEAD);
CALL INIT_Q(RQ@,FREE_SPACE,ALLOC_SPACE);
WQ@ = ALLOC_SPACE(Q_HEAD);
CALL INIT_Q(WQ@,LAST_IN,UNQUEUE);
SPACE_RS@ = ALLOC_SPACE(RES_SEMA);
CALL INIT_RS(SPACE_RS@,RQ@,WQ@,SPACE_ALLOCATOR);

/* SET UP OTHER RESOURCE SEMAPHORES */
```

```
EMPTY_SQRS_RS@ = CREATE_RS (PCB@,LAST_IN,UNQUEUE,LAST_IN,
                            UNQUEUE,BASIC_ALLOCATOR);
DO I = 1 TO MAX_EMPTY_SQRS;
      RCB@ = REQUEST(PCB@,SPACE_RS@,SQUARES_QE);
      CALL RELEASE(EMPTY_SQRS_RS@,RCB@);
      END;
SQUARES_RS@ = CREATE_RS(PCB@,LAST_IN,UNQUEUE,LAST_IN,
                         UNQUEUE,BASIC_ALLOCATOR);
```

FIG. 6.13 SETUPRS

You should note, however, that although SPACE_AREA is global to all our procedures, we restrict access to it to the queuing routines and allocator of the space resource semaphore. A resource semaphore is conceptually an independent module or level of abstraction, and as such it is entitled to its own internal data and routines. Thus, SPACE_AREA must be considered to be an internal or local variable of the space resource semaphore, even though its declaration makes it accessible (according to PL/I identifier scope rules) to all of our program. Once the space resource semaphore is established, the proper way to obtain and give up storage space is by way of the *request* and *release* primitives. *Request* and *release* represent the interface between a resource semaphore and a process.

In order to set up the space resource semaphore, we must allocate space for and initialize the resource queue head, the wait queue head, and the resource semaphore itself. The function ALLOC_SPACE is assumed to take an integer parameter indicating the type of based variable we wish to allocate, to allocate the requested amount of space in SPACE_AREA, and to return a pointer to it. The INIT_Q procedure takes a queue head, a queue insertion routine, and a queue deletion routine, and initializes the IN and OUT fields of the queue head to the insertion and deletion routines. Thus, FREE_SPACE is the routine that will return space to the resource queue of the space resource semaphore, and ALLOC_SPACE is the routine that will obtain space from the resource queue. Likewise, LAST_IN is the routine that will place a *pcb* on the wait queue of the resource semaphore, and UNQUEUE is the routine that will remove a *pcb* from the wait queue. The INIT_RS procedure initializes its first parameter, a resource semaphore, to the values of its remaining parameters—namely, to the resource queue head, the wait queue head, and the resource allocator routine. For the space resource semaphore, the queue heads are the ones previously created and described above.

The space allocator routine is SPACE_ALLOCATOR. Now that the space resource semaphore is set up, all further requests for space will be made via REQUEST. In such a request, the data parameter will be one of the TYPE codes defined in the master declarations (Fig. 6.2).

The other resource semaphores are now easy to set up. We use a function CREATE_RS to allocate the space for a resource semaphore and its queue heads and to initialize all of the appropriate fields. CREATE_RS is a function which takes the *pcb* of the calling process, a resource queue insertion routine, a resource queue deletion routine, a wait queue insertion routine, a wait queue deletion routine, and an allocator routine. For most of our queues we will use LAST_IN as the insertion routine and UNQUEUE as the deletion routine. All of our insertion and deletion routines take two parameters, the first of which is the queue element to be inserted or deleted and the second of which is the queue head. LAST_IN is to be a routine which places its queue element at the end of the queue; UNQUEUE is a routine which is to delete its element from the queue. Both the full and empty squares resource semaphores use BASIC_ALLOCATOR as their allocation routine. The basic allocation strategy is to allocate the first resource on the resource queue to the first process on the wait queue. Thus, by using LAST_IN as the queue insertion routine for both queues and BASIC_ALLOCATOR as the allocation routine, both the resource and wait queues of a resource semaphore are first-in-first-out (FIFO) queues. In particular the empty and full squares resource semaphores are created with FIFO queues. The empty squares resource semaphore must be initialized to contain MAX_EMPTY_SQUARES number of resource elements. This is accomplished by requesting the space for a squares queue element and releasing it to the resource semaphore MAX_EMPTY_SQUARES number of times. The full squares resource semaphore is to start out with an empty resource queue.

We may now quickly dispense with the PRODUCER and CONSUMER processes, the coding for which is given in Fig. 6.14. Each process takes as a parameter the *pcb* that was created for it. Functionally, the PRODUCER process is to read each integer of the input sequence, request an empty squares resource, fill in the integer and the square of the integer fields of the resource, and release the resource to the full squares resource semaphore. The process will terminate when it reaches an end-of-file condition on the input data set. It passes this end signal on to the CONSUMER process by releasing a resource whose integer field is set to −1. Since the resource queue of the full squares resource semaphore is a FIFO queue, we have guaranteed that the CONSUMER process must process the items in the same order that the PRODUCER has processed the input sequence. The CONSUMER process is to initialize the table heading, then request full square elements from the full squares resource semaphore, print the integer and its square, and release the resource element to the empty squares resource semaphore. It will continue to do this until it has obtained the end signal element, at which time it is to print out the number of squares processed and terminate.

```
            /* PRODUCER, CONSUMER PROCESSES */

            DCL  PRODUCER ENTRY(PTR),
                 CONSUMER ENTRY(PTR);

    PRODUCER: PROC(PCB@);

            DCL PCB@ PTR;

            DCL SQE@ PTR,
                1 SQE BASED(SQE@) LIKE SQUARES_QUEUE_ELEMENT,
                EOF BOOL INIT(FALSE);

            ON ENDFILE(SYSIN) EOF = TRUE;

            REPEAT;
                SQE@ = REQUEST(PCB@,EMPTY_SQRS_RS@,0);
                GET LIST(SQE.N);
                IF EOF THEN SQE.N = -1;
                       ELSE SQE.N_SQR = SQE.N * SQE.N;
                CALL RELEASE(SQUARES_RS@,SQE@);
            UNTIL(EOF);
            END PRODUCER;

    CONSUMER: PROC(PCB@);

            DCL PCB@ PTR;

            DCL SQE@ PTR,
                1 SQE BASED(SQE@) LIKE SQUARES_QUEUE_ELEMENT,
                #SQUARES INTG INIT(0),
                DONE BOOL INIT(FALSE);

            PUT PAGE EDIT ('N','N*N') (X(3),A,X(7),A);
            PUT SKIP;

            REPEAT;
                SQE@ = REQUEST(PCB@,SQUARES_RS@,0);
                IF SQE.N >= 0
```

```
                    THEN DO;
                         PUT SKIP EDIT (SQE.N,SQE.N_SQR)
                                        (F(5),F(10));
                         #SQUARES = #SQUARES + 1;
                         END;
                    ELSE DONE = TRUE;
                 CALL RELEASE(EMPTY_SQRS_RS@,SQE@);
             UNTIL(DONE);

             PUT SKIP(2) EDIT (#SQUARES,' SQUARES PROCESSED') (F(3),A);
             PUT PAGE;
             END CONSUMER;
```

FIG. 6.14 PRODCONS

6.6 QUEUING AND ALLOCATION ROUTINES

We now have several possible points of refinement open to us—the *pcb*, resource semaphore, and queue creation routines, the queue insertion and deletion routines, and the resource allocators. First, let us dispense with the *pcb* creation routine. As stated previously, the CREATE_PCB procedure allocates space for a *pcb*, initializes it, and returns the *pcb* as its value. The code for CREATE_PCB is shown in Fig. 6.15.

```
        /* CREATE_PCB PROCEDURE */

        DCL CREATE_PCB ENTRY(PTR) RETURNS(PTR);

    CREATE_PCB: PROC(PCB@) RETURNS(PTR);

        DCL PCB@ PTR;

        DCL NEW_PCB@ PTR,
            1 PCB BASED(NEW_PCB@) LIKE PROCESS_CONTROL_BLOCK;

        NEW_PCB@ = REQUEST(PCB@,SPACE_RS@,PROC_CB);
        COMPLETION(PCB.AWAKEN) = FALSE;
        RETURN(NEW_PCB@);
        END CREATE_PCB;
```

FIG. 6.15 CREATPCB

The procedures CREATE_RS, INIT_RS, CREATE_Q, and INIT_Q given in Figs. 6.16 and 6.17 are used to create and initialize resource semaphores and queue heads. We will simply give the functional specifications for each of the procedures since the coding is quite straightforward. The CREATE_RS function takes the *pcb* of the calling process, a resource queue insertion routine, a resource queue deletion routine, a wait queue insertion routine, a wait queue deletion routine, and a resource allocator routine, and returns a pointer to the created and initialized resource semaphore. The INIT_RS procedure initializes its first parameter, a resource semaphore, to the values of its remaining parameters, a resource queue, a wait queue, and an allocator routine. The CREATE_Q function takes the process control block of the calling process, a queue insertion routine, and a queue deletion routine, and returns a pointer to the created and initialized queue head. Lastly, INIT_Q is a procedure which initializes the IN and OUT fields of its first parameter, a queue head, to the queue insertion routine and queue deletion routine which constitute its second and third parameters. It also sets the queue head to indicate an empty queue.

```
/* CREATE_RS, INIT_RS PROCEDURES */

DCL  CREATE_RS ENTRY(PTR,ENTRY,ENTRY,ENTRY,ENTRY,ENTRY)
                    RETURNS(PTR),
     INIT_RS ENTRY(PTR,PTR,PTR,ENTRY);

CREATE_RS: PROC(PCB@,RQI,RQO,WQI,WQO,ALLOC) RETURNS(PTR);

          DCL  PCB@ PTR,
               (RQI,RQO,WQI,WQO,ALLOC) ENTRY;

          DCL  (RS@,RQ@,WQ@) PTR;

          RS@  = REQUEST(PCB@,SPACE_RS@,RES_SEMA);
          RQ@  = CREATE_Q(PCB@,RQI,RQO);
          WQ@ = CREATE_Q(PCB@,WQI,WQO);
          CALL INIT_RS(RS@,RQ@,WQ@,ALLOC);
          RETURN(RS@);
          END CREATE_RS;


INIT_RS: PROC(RS@,RQ@,WQ@,ALLOC);

          DCL  (RS@,RQ@,WQ@) PTR,
               ALLOC ENTRY;
```

```
        DCL 1 RS BASED(RS@) LIKE RESOURCE_SEMAPHORE;

        RS.RES_Q = RQ@;
        RS.WAIT_Q = WQ@;
        CALL STORE_PROC(ALLOC,RS.ALLOCATOR);
        END INIT_RS;
```

FIG. 6.16 CREATERS

```
        /* CREATE_Q, INIT_Q PROCEDURES */

        DCL CREATE_Q ENTRY(PTR,ENTRY,ENTRY) RETURNS(PTR),
            INIT_Q ENTRY(PTR,ENTRY,ENTRY);

CREATE_Q: PROC(PCB@,QI,QO) RETURNS(PTR);

        DCL PCB@ PTR,
            (QI,QO) ENTRY;

        DCL QH@ PTR;

        QH@ = REQUEST(PCB@,SPACE_RS@,Q_HEAD);
        CALL INIT_Q(QH@,QI,QO);
        RETURN(QH@);
        END CREATE_Q;

INIT_Q: PROC(QH@,QI,QO);

        DCL QH@ PTR,
            (QI,QO) ENTRY;

        DCL 1 QH BASED(QH@) LIKE QUEUE_HEAD;

        QH.FIRST = QH@;
        QH.LAST = QH@;
        CALL STORE_PROC(QI,QH.IN);
        CALL STORE_PROC(QO,QH.OUT);
        END INIT_Q;
```

FIG. 6.17 CREATEQ

The remaining procedures to be refined are the queue insertion and deletion routines and the resource allocators. We first refine the basic queue insertion and deletion routines, LAST_IN and UNQUEUE. As stated previously, all queue handling routines take two parameters, the first of which is the queue element to be inserted or deleted and the second of which is the queue head. The LAST_IN procedure places an element at the end of a queue. As can be seen from the code in Fig. 6.18, this is accomplished by setting both the SUCC field of the previous last element on the queue and the LAST field of the queue head to point to the element to be inserted. The SUCC and PRED fields of the inserted element are set to point to the queue head and the previous last element, respectively. The UNQUEUE procedure removes an element from a queue. This is accomplished by updating both the PRED field of the successor of the element to be deleted and the SUCC field of the predecessor of the element to be deleted, so that they no longer point to the element, but to each other instead.

```
          /* LAST_IN, UNQUEUE PROCEDURES */

          DCL LAST_IN ENTRY(PTR,PTR),
              UNQUEUE ENTRY(PTR,PTR);


LAST_IN: PROC(QE@,QH@);

          DCL (QE@,QH@) PTR;

          DCL 1 QE BASED(QE@) LIKE QUEUE_ELEMENT,
              1 QH BASED(QH@) LIKE QUEUE_HEAD,
              P PTR;

          QE.SUCC = QH@;
          QE.PRED = QH.LAST;
          P = QH.LAST;
          P->QE.SUCC = QE@;
          QH.LAST = QE@;
          END LAST_IN;

UNQUEUE: PROC(QE@,QH@);

          DCL (QE@,QH@) PTR;

          DCL 1 QE BASED(QE@) LIKE QUEUE_ELEMENT,
              P PTR;

          IF QE.TYPE ¬= Q_HEAD THEN DO;
              P = QE.SUCC;
```

```
        P->QE.PRED = QE.PRED;
        P = QE.PRED;
        P->QE.SUCC = QE.SUCC;
        END;
    END UNQUEUE;
```

FIG. 6.18 BASICQ

Next we choose to refine the BASIC_ALLOCATOR routine. An allocator is a procedure which takes a pointer to a resource semaphore and returns either NULL or a pointer to the *pcb* that it has allocated. If it performs a successful allocation, then it must remove the *pcb* and resource element allocated from the wait and resource queues of the resource semaphore, and put a pointer to the resource element in the GRANT field of the *pcb*. The basic allocator strategy is to allocate the first resource on the resource queue to the first process on the wait queue. The PL/I code for BASIC_ALLOCATOR is given in Fig. 6.19. We begin by setting RCB to the first element on the resource queue and PCB to the first element on the wait queue. Now if either RCB or PCB is a queue head rather than a queue element, then the corresponding queue is empty. Hence, the allocator is to yield NULL to indicate that no allocation is possible. However, if both RCB and PCB are queue elements, then we set the GRANT field of PCB to point to the resource element. Lastly, we delete the resource element from the resource queue and the *pcb* from the wait queue. The allocated *pcb* is then yielded as the result of BASIC_ALLOCATOR.

```
    /* BASIC_ALLOCATOR PROCEDURE */

    DCL BASIC_ALLOCATOR ENTRY(PTR) RETURNS(PTR);

BASIC_ALLOCATOR: PROC(RS@) RETURNS(PTR);

    DCL RS@ PTR;

    DCL 1 RS BASED(RS@) LIKE RESOURCE_SEMAPHORE,
          (RQ@,WQ@,RCB@,PCB@) PTR,
          1 RQ BASED(RQ@) LIKE QUEUE_HEAD,
          1 WQ BASED(WQ@) LIKE QUEUE_HEAD,
          1 RCB BASED(RCB@) LIKE QUEUE_ELEMENT,
          1 PCB BASED(PCB@) LIKE PROCESS_CONTROL_BLOCK;
    RQ@ = RS.RES_Q;
```

```
        RCB@ = RQ.FIRST;
        WQ@ = RS.WAIT_Q;
        PCB@ = WQ.FIRST;

        IF RCB.TYPE=Q_HEAD | PCB.TYPE=Q_HEAD
             THEN PCB@ = NULL;
             ELSE DO;
                  PCB.GRANT = RCB@;
                  CALL DELETE(RCB@,RQ@);
                  CALL DELETE(PCB@,WQ@);
                  END;

        RETURN(PCB@);
        END BASIC_ALLOCATOR;
```

FIG. 6.19 BASICALL

We have made use of two generalized queue insertion and deletion routines, namely INSERT and DELETE. INSERT was used in the REQUEST and RELEASE procedures, while DELETE was used in BASIC_ALLOCATOR. As usual, the first parameter of these routines is the element to be inserted or deleted. The second parameter is the queue head. INSERT performs the insertion by calling the queue insertion routine stored in the IN field of the queue head. Likewise, DELETE performs the deletion by calling the queue deletion routine stored in the OUT field of the queue head. The code for INSERT and DELETE is given in Fig. 6.20. The call of the stored queue handling routines is accomplished by the procedure CALL_PROC described previously.

```
        /* INSERT, DELETE PROCEDURES */

        DCL INSERT ENTRY(PTR,PTR),
            DELETE ENTRY(PTR,PTR);


   INSERT: PROC(QE@,QH@);

        DCL (QE@,QH@) PTR;

        DCL 1 QH BASED(QH@) LIKE QUEUE_HEAD;

        CALL CALL_PROC(QH.IN,QE@,QH@);
        END INSERT;


   DELETE: PROC(QE@,QH@);
```

```
DCL (QE@,QH@) PTR;

DCL 1 QH BASED(QH@) LIKE QUEUE_HEAD;

CALL CALL_PROC(QH.OUT,QE@,QH@);
END DELETE;
```

FIG. 6.20 INSDEL

The only procedures remaining to be refined are the queue handling and allocator routines for the space resource semaphore. The code for the insertion and deletion routines, FREE_SPACE and ALLOC_SPACE, is shown in Fig. 6.21. Since all of our allocations take place in the area variable SPACE_AREA, PL/I automatically maintains its own queue of free elements in the area variable. Thus, our resource queue never actually contains any elements, only the queue head. However, the queue head is necessary because RELEASE will call INSERT to attempt to insert an element on the queue, and INSERT will call FREE_SPACE. Since we will be allocating and freeing based variables which have different storage size requirements, and since PL/I provides no convenient implementation-independent way of determining the size of a based variable, the easiest way of allocating and freeing the various based variables is to have separate ALLOCATE and FREE statements for each based variable. Thus, in both FREE_SPACE and ALLOC_SPACE we use the SELECT statement with a separate case for each type of based variable. In FREE_SPACE the type code is taken from the TYPE field of the element to be freed. Thus, the FREE_SPACE routine has merely to select the appropriate FREE statement and free the corresponding based variable. PL/I automatically maintains the queue of free elements in SPACE_AREA. Likewise, ALLOC_SPACE has only to allocate space for the appropriate based variable, according to the space type code which is passed as its parameter. If the type code is invalid or the area has insufficient free space for the allocation, ALLOC_SPACE returns a NULL pointer. Otherwise, it returns a pointer to the successfully allocated element, after having filled in the TYPE field of the element to indicate the kind of element allocated.

```
/* FREE_SPACE, ALLOC_SPACE PROCEDURES */

DCL FREE_SPACE ENTRY(PTR,PTR),
    ALLOC_SPACE ENTRY(INTG) RETURNS(PTR);


FREE_SPACE: PROC(QE@,QH@);
```

```
        DCL (QE@,QH@) PTR;

        DCL 1 QE BASED(QE@) LIKE QUEUE_ELEMENT;

        SELECT(QE.TYPE);
              CASE(RES_SEMA):      FREE QE@->RESOURCE_SEMAPHORE
                                         IN(SPACE_AREA);
              CASE(Q_HEAD):        FREE QE@->QUEUE_HEAD
                                         IN(SPACE_AREA);
              CASE(PROC_CB):       FREE QE@->PROCESS_CONTROL_BLOCK
                                         IN(SPACE_AREA);
              CASE(SQUARES_QE):    FREE QE@->SQUARES_QUEUE_ELEMENT
                                         IN(SPACE_AREA);
        ENDSELECT;
        END FREE_SPACE;

ALLOC_SPACE: PROC(SPACE_TYPE) RETURNS(PTR);

        DCL SPACE_TYPE INTG;

        DCL QE@ PTR,
            1 QE BASED(QE@) LIKE QUEUE_ELEMENT;

        ON AREA GO TO NOSPACE;

        SELECT(SPACE_TYPE);
              CASE(RES_SEMA):      ALLOCATE RESOURCE_SEMAPHORE
                                         SET(QE@) IN(SPACE_AREA);
              CASE(Q_HEAD):        ALLOCATE QUEUE_HEAD
                                         SET(QE@) IN(SPACE_AREA);
              CASE(PROC_CB):       ALLOCATE PROCESS_CONTROL_BLOCK
                                         SET(QE@) IN(SPACE_AREA);
              CASE(SQUARES_QE):    ALLOCATE SQUARES_QUEUE_ELEMENT
                                         SET(QE@) IN(SPACE_AREA);
              DEFAULT:
              NOSPACE:             QE@ = NULL;
        ENDSELECT;

        IF QE@ ¬= NULL THEN QE.TYPE = SPACE_TYPE;
        RETURN(QE@);
        END ALLOC_SPACE;
```

FIG. 6.21 SPACEQ

If you observe closely, you will notice that there is a GO TO statement in the ON AREA on-unit in ALLOC_SPACE. In PL/I the AREA condition is raised and the current AREA on-unit executed whenever an ALLOCATE statement fails because of insufficient free space in the area variable. A normal return from the on-unit causes the ALLOCATE statement to be retried. This would be useful if our area variable (SPACE_AREA) were a based variable and the on-unit changed the basing pointer to point to another area with sufficient space. In our situation, however, there is no additional space available to allocate. Hence, we must make an exceptional exit from the AREA on-unit to prevent an infinite sequence of allocation attempts and failures.

The point of this digression is that structured programming does not necessarily mean GO TO-less programming. Rather, it is a highly disciplined use of control flow. You should therefore restrict yourself to certain standard forms of control flow as much as possible. However, on those occasions when limitations in the programming language require exceptional control flow, you should still try to retain as much clarity and structure as possible.

Lastly, we select our only unrefined procedure, SPACE_ALLOCATOR. Since PL/I automatically maintains the queue of free elements in the area variable, there is nothing on the resource queue for us to examine. Thus, SPACE_ALLOCATOR will simply pick the first *pcb* on the wait queue and attempt to allocate its request for space. The code for SPACE_ALLOCATOR is given in Fig. 6.22. We begin by setting PCB to be the first *pcb* on the wait queue. If PCB is a queue head, the wait queue is empty. So the allocator must return NULL to indicate no allocation is possible. Otherwise, we call ALLOC_SPACE and give it the RQST field of PCB, which contains the type of request being made. You should recall that the RQST field was previously set to the DATA parameter of the REQUEST procedure. If ALLOC_SPACE is unable to allocate any space, then SPACE_ALLOCATOR returns NULL. Otherwise, it deletes the *pcb* from the wait queue and sets the GRANT field to point to the allocated space. You should note that whereas we used DELETE for the wait queue, and since there is no resource queue, we have called the resource queue deletion routine ALLOC_SPACE directly rather than via DELETE. We make this direct call because the parameters of ALLOC_SPACE are not the usual queue element and queue head parameters.

```
/* SPACE_ALLOCATOR PROCEDURE */

DCL SPACE_ALLOCATOR ENTRY(PTR) RETURNS(PTR);
```

```
SPACE_ALLOCATOR: PROC(RS@) RETURNS(PTR);

        DCL RS@ PTR;

        DCL 1 RS BASED(RS@) LIKE RESOURCE_SEMAPHORE,
              (WQ@,PCB@) PTR,
              1 WQ BASED(WQ@) LIKE QUEUE_HEAD,
              1 PCB BASED(PCB@) LIKE PROCESS_CONTROL_BLOCK;

        WQ@ = RS.WAIT_Q;
        PCB@ = WQ.FIRST;

        IF PCB.TYPE = Q_HEAD
              THEN PCB@ = NULL;
              ELSE DO;
                    PCB.GRANT = ALLOC_SPACE(PCB.RQST);
                    IF PCB.GRANT = NULL
                          THEN PCB@ = NULL;
                          ELSE CALL DELETE(PCB@,WQ@);
                    END;

        RETURN(PCB@);
        END SPACE_ALLOCATOR;
```

FIG. 6.22 SPACEALL

Although all of our procedures are now refined, we still have the code segment PROCS left to do. PROCS is to INCLUDE all of the internal procedure bodies within the main procedure. The code for PROCS is shown in Fig. 6.23.

```
/* INCLUDE INTERNAL PROCEDURES */

%INCLUDE PRODCONS;  /* PRODUCER, CONSUMER */
%INCLUDE CREATPCB;  /* CREATE_PCB */
%INCLUDE CREATERS;  /* CREATE_RS, INIT_RS */
%INCLUDE CREATEQ;   /* CREATE_Q, INIT_Q */
%INCLUDE INSDEL;    /* INSERT, DELETE */
%INCLUDE BASICQ;    /* LAST_IN, UNQUEUE */
%INCLUDE BASICALL;  /* BASIC_ALLOCATOR */
%INCLUDE SPACEQ;    /* FREE_SPACE, ALLOC_SPACE */
```

```
%INCLUDE SPACEALL;  /* SPACE_ALLOCATOR */
%INCLUDE RQSTRLSE;  /* REQUEST, RELEASE */
%INCLUDE ENTRYVAR;  /* STORE_PROC, CALL_PROC, CALL_FN */
```

FIG. 6.23 PROCS

Given the input data

```
1  2  3  4  5
6  7  8
9  10  11  12  13  14  15  16
17  18
19  20  21
22  23  24  25
```

the program produces the output shown in Fig. 6.24, where the solid lines denote page boundaries.

```
BEGIN PROCESSING
```

```
 N    N*N

 1      1
 2      4
 3      9
 4     16
 5     25
 6     36
 7     49
 8     64
 9     81
10    100
11    121
12    144
13    169
14    196
15    225
16    256
17    289
```

```
18   324
19   361
20   400
21   441
22   484
23   529
24   576
25   625

25 SQUARES PROCESSED
```

```
END PROCESSING
```

FIG. 6.24 RESMAN output

Our first example of resource management and parallel processing is now complete. We have successfully refined and modularized the problem into a number of small functions, each of which performs one small part of the problem. We have presented the concept of resource semaphores, a very general method for resource management and process synchronization. In the next section, we will use this concept to develop the design of a multiprogrammed operating system.

6.7 A MULTIPROGRAMMED, MULTIPROCESSING OPERATING SYSTEM

In this section, we develop the design of a multiprogrammed, multiprocessing operating system using the resource semaphore concept. We undertake this large example not only to show a nontrivial instance of resource management and parallel processing, but also to illustrate the application of top-down segmented structured design to a complex problem. We first specify the problem down to an appropriate level of detail. We then present the high-level design in terms of charts which give the data flow between processes and resource semaphores. Lastly, we give structured PL/I pseudo-code for all of the processes. We make extensive use of abstractions in the form of abstract operations and data types for abstract machines.

We assume herein that you are familiar with the basic concepts of operating systems, in particular with multiprogramming, multiprocessing, spooling, and paging. In order to keep this example within reasonable bounds, we completely avoid such topics as on-line file systems, sharing of user information, interactive terminals, time sharing, and advanced algorithms for job scheduling, paging, and deadlock prevention. Many of these topics (including resource semaphores) are discussed in *The Logical Design of Operating Systems* by Alan Shaw.[4] Although our system is basically a multiprogrammed batch-processing system, it can be extended to incorporate any or all of the above topics.

We begin with a specification of the hardware the system is to run on. The hardware consists of central processing units (CPU's), peripheral processing units (PPU's), a peripheral processor controller (PPC), an input-output controller (IOC), pagable core memory, card readers, line printers, and drums. Fig. 6.25 shows a typical configuration using two PPU's and one of everything else. Descriptions of the individual components follow. Note that whereas all of these hardware components could actually be built, we intend to simulate them via PL/I F, OS/360 MVT, and S/360 hardware.

Since we want to write our system in tasking PL/I using request-release on resource semaphores, we shall consider the machine language of our CPU's to be tasking PL/I. Thus, a CPU is directly simulated by PL/I F (with request-release), OS/360 MVT, and a S/360. We use the CPU's to execute our system programs. As in the producer-consumer example, our system will consist of several independent processes which are executing "continuously" and "simultaneously." Since tasking PL/I already provides a process scheduler—the MVT task scheduler—we do not have to write that part of our system. In fact, our system design is such that we don't care (and can't tell) whether our system processes are multiprogrammed on one CPU or multiprocessed on several CPU's. Hence, we shall hereafter refer to *the* CPU.

The PPU's execute the user programs, and so they are restricted versions of the CPU. In effect, the CPU corresponds to system or master mode of an S/360 CPU, where all instructions are nonprivileged and executable, whereas a PPU corresponds to user or slave mode, where some instructions (like I/O and halt instructions) are privileged and cause some form of interruption. Since we intend to simulate the PPU's with PL/I processes, we restrict the PPU instruction set to a read, a write, a halt, and a few computational instructions such as load accumulator, add, store, branch if positive. A PPU has an appropriate set of internal registers, such as an accumulator and an instruction pointer (which contains the address of the next instruction to be

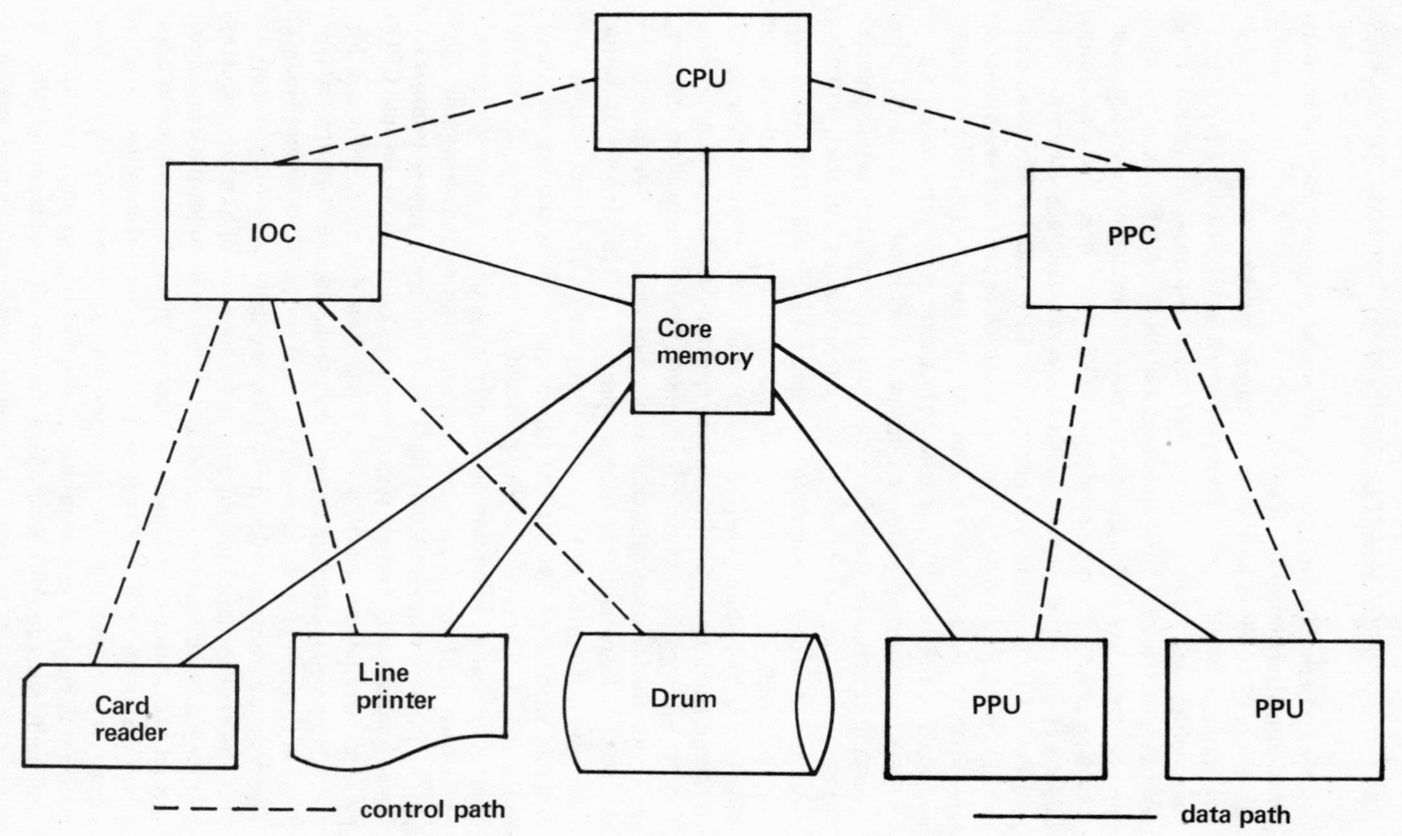

FIG. 6.25 A typical hardware configuration

executed). Each PPU also has an instruction timer which it decrements for each instruction it executes.

Each PPU has a core memory paging mechanism, consisting of a page table location register (containing the absolute core address of a page table) and the hardware necessary to translate virtual core addresses into actual core addresses via the page table. A page table contains the actual core address of a page of virtual core memory when that page is actually in core memory. Otherwise, it contains the drum address of the virtual page or an indication that the page does not exist.

The PPC is the interface between the CPU and the PPU's. In fact, the PPC is a hardware version of two resource semaphores (and hence is simulated by two resource semaphores), one for CPU-to-PPU messages and one for PPU-to-CPU messages. Thus, when a system process wants to execute a user program, it releases a command to the PPC. The command contains all the information (accumulator, instruction pointer, page table pointer, and timer contents) necessary to initialize a PPU for execution of a user program. An available PPU requests a command, initializes itself, and begins executing the user program. Execution by the PPU continues until a privileged instruction is encountered or an error condition (such as illegal instruction, page fault, or time expired) arises. The PPU then releases status information—final contents of its registers, the reason for terminating execution, and possibly other information—to the PPC. Meanwhile, the system process is requesting this status information from the PPC. Having obtained it, the system process, for example, carries out the user I/O request and releases another command to the PPC to continue the user program; in case of error, the system process terminates execution of the user program.

Our system design partitions the core memory into two parts. One part, the system core, is used by the CPU for executing system programs. It also contains I/O buffers, system control blocks, and so on. The other part, the user core, is used by PPU's, via their paging mechanisms, for executing user programs. We may simulate the user core either as a large array of core pages or as a set of individual core page resource elements. The system core is provided directly by the underlying PL/I machine.

The card readers, line printers, and drums are all basically standard I/O devices. Each device requests a command, executes the command, and releases status information. A card reader reads a card into a core page (usually an input buffer in system core) and then responds with a successful completion status signal (or with an end-of-file signal if the reader was empty). A line printer prints a core page as a line of text (optionally preceded by a forms page ejection) and signals completion. A drum transfers a page of data between an actual core memory page and an actual drum memory track (page) and signals completion. We simulate the I/O devices by PL/I processes, using PL/I input/output statements for the actual card reading and line printing. The drum memory can be treated like the user core memory.

The IOC is the interface between the CPU and the I/O devices and is similar to the PPC in form and function. Thus, we also represent the IOC as two resource semaphores, one for each direction of communication. The basic difference is that the I/O devices connected to the IOC have different characteristics, so that the commands and status information are device dependent. Each I/O command and status response must contain the address of a particular I/O device (for instance, one particular card reader, not just any reader). Each command also needs an absolute core page address. Line printer commands also need a page eject flag. Drum commands additionally need an absolute drum track address and the direction of data transfer. The normal status response for all devices is a completion signal. The card reader may also signal end of file.

Specification of the hardware is now complete. We now continue with a specification of the system as viewed by a user. The user sees only a very simple batch-processing system running on the following hardware: a central processing unit, core memory, a card reader, and a line printer. A user job consists of a $JOB card, a program, a $DATA card, the program's input data, and an $ENDJOB card. The $JOB card contains the user's name and the execution time and output line limits for the job. The $DATA card is not required when there is no program input data.

The batch system processes each user job in the input job stream as follows: It reads the job card and establishes the time and line limits. It loads the user's program intc memory and prints a copy of the program. (For simplicity, we may require the program to be written in an easily loaded absolute machine code format.) If loading is successful, the system initiates execution of the program. The user program terminates execution either normally or as the result of an error condition such as too much time. The system purges the job with appropriate termination messages and prepares for the next job.

The operating system design is largely independent of the particular instruction set and internal registers of the user's central processing unit. From the user's point of view, his CPU has a read, a write, a halt, and a number of computational instructions, all of which are nonprivileged. Actually, the user CPU is a virtual machine. His program is really executed by a PPU.

Our operating system has several goals. Using the above described hardware, we want the system to appear to a user to be the simple batch system specified above. In reality, however, we want the system to make more optimum use of its resources in order to maximize job throughput and minimize job turnaround time. Our system is now sufficiently specified so that we may begin with its design.

At the very top level we may view the system as a single "black box" with a number of job input streams, one per card reader, and a number of job output streams, one per line printer. Looking inside the box, we see several PPU's and drums. Experience with other operating systems has shown us that a good way to achieve our system performance objectives is to multiprogram/multiprocess the user jobs on the PPU's. Thus, when one job is delayed by an I/O operation, another job may be executing. Since such a design requires a supply of readily available jobs, we also want to spool jobs from the card readers to the drums, which are considerably faster I/O devices. Thus, user jobs are taken from drum memory for execution by PPU's in user core. The user I/O is actually between user core and drum, so that all output accumulates on drum memory. After a user program terminates execution, the job output is spooled from drum to one of the line printers, which, like card readers, are relatively slow I/O devices.

We thus have partitioned our system into three parts, as shown in Fig. 6.26. *SpoolIn Service* is to transfer user jobs from a card reader to drum memory. When a job is transferred, *SpoolIn* is to release a job control block (*jcb*) to the *Load* resource semaphore. The *jcb* contains all of the pertinent information about the job that will be needed by the later parts of the job processing path. In particular, it contains the location of the job on the drum. The *jcb* represents the job's current status and is passed along from *SpoolIn* to *Execute* to *SpoolOut* and updated by each as the job progresses through the system.

Execute Service is to perform the loading and execution of user jobs. It obtains a job from the *Load* resource semaphore, loads the user program into user core, prints the user program, establishes job time and line limits, causes a PPU to execute the user program, performs user I/O operations (using drum for the user card reader and line printer), and cleans up when the user program terminates execution. Lastly, it releases the job (*jcb*) to the *Output* resource semaphore. Note that all job output is to be saved on drum, both user program execution output and system message output.

SpoolOut Service is to transfer user job output from drum to line printer. It obtains a job from the *Output* resource semaphore, prints the job output, and purges the job from the system by releasing the job's remaining resources, such as drum space.

So far we have considered only a single job stream. We intend to

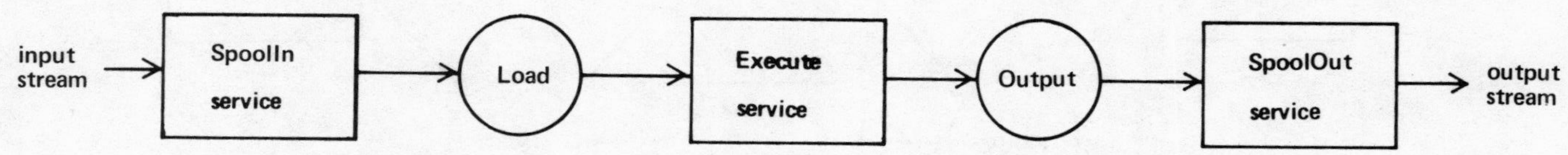

FIG. 6.26 The basic system services (as before, rectangles represent processes and circles represent resource semaphores).

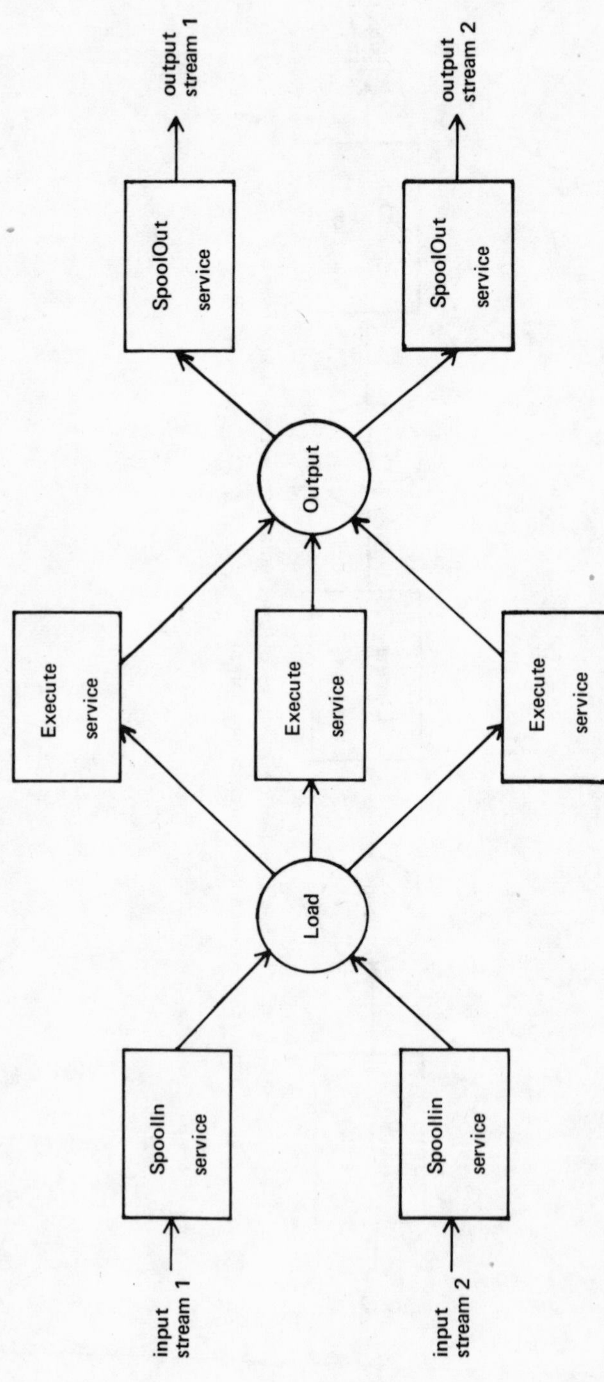

FIG. 6.27 The basic system services for multiple I/O streams

have exactly one *Load* resource semaphore, which contains all jobs that are spooled in and ready for loading/executing. We also want exactly one *Output* resource semaphore, which holds all jobs that have completed execution and are ready for printing. However, we want multiple copies of each of the service processes. In particular, we want a separate *SpoolIn Service* associated with each card reader and a separate *SpoolOut Service* associated with each line printer. Thus, each spooling service takes as a parameter the address of the I/O device with which it is associated. However, an *Execute Service* needs no long-term association with any particular PPU since all of the PPU's are identical and hence interchangeable. (Card readers and line printers are interchangeable only between jobs, not during the spooling of a job.) Since each *Execute Service* is to completely process one job before undertaking another, the number of *Execute Services* determines the maximum number of user jobs that may be multiprogrammed/multiprocessed on the PPU's, assuming sufficient resources exist. Fig. 6.27 illustrates the basic system services for a system with two card readers and two line printers and which allows a maximum of three jobs to be "simultaneously" in execution.

Our discussion of the system so far has been concerned only with how it appears after it has been fired up. We still need an initialization process. We adopt the approach used in the producer-consumer example, in which the main PL/I task (RESMAN, see Fig. 6.12) is the initialization process. As such, it is to first set up and initialize all of the resource semaphores. Then it is to start all of the processes as subtasks. Next it must wait for all of the processes to terminate so that it can terminate last. Fig. 6.28 gives the PL/I pseudo-code for our operating system initialization process. Note that as we refine the system into more processes and resource semaphores, we must include them in the initialization process.

```
OpSys: PROC OPTIONS(MAIN,REENTRANT,TASK);

        %INCLUDE Extensions;
        %INCLUDE MasterDeclarations;

        DCL  (Enqueue, Dequeue) EXT ENTRY(PTR),
             SpaceArea AREA(large size);

        DCL  all resource semaphores;
```

```
DCL  all process PCBs,
     all process events;

DCL  all local variables;

%INCLUDE all procedures;

PUT LIST('BEGIN PROCESSING');

Set up PCB for OpSys process;

Set up Space resource semaphore;
Set up and initialize all other resource semaphores;

Creat PCBs for processes;

Initiate each process by
     CALL process(processPCB,other args)
          EVENT(processEvent);

WAIT (all system process events);

Send EndSignals to all drum, line printer, and PPU
     processes; /* terminate simulation */
WAIT (all hardware process events);

PUT SKIP LIST('END PROCESSING');
END OpSys;
```

FIG. 6.28 Initialization process

We may now proceed to refine each of the three service processes. We begin with *SpoolIn*, which is charged with transferring jobs from a particular card reader to drum memory. Since there is no direct data path between the two I/O devices, the transfer must use core memory as an intermediate buffer. Furthermore, although drums are much faster than card readers, the other system processes are also heavily using the drums. Hence, we want to use several core buffers to try to smooth out the spooling process. We thus split (each) *SpoolIn Service* into two processes: *Reader*—a card-reading process—and *Input*—a drum writing process.

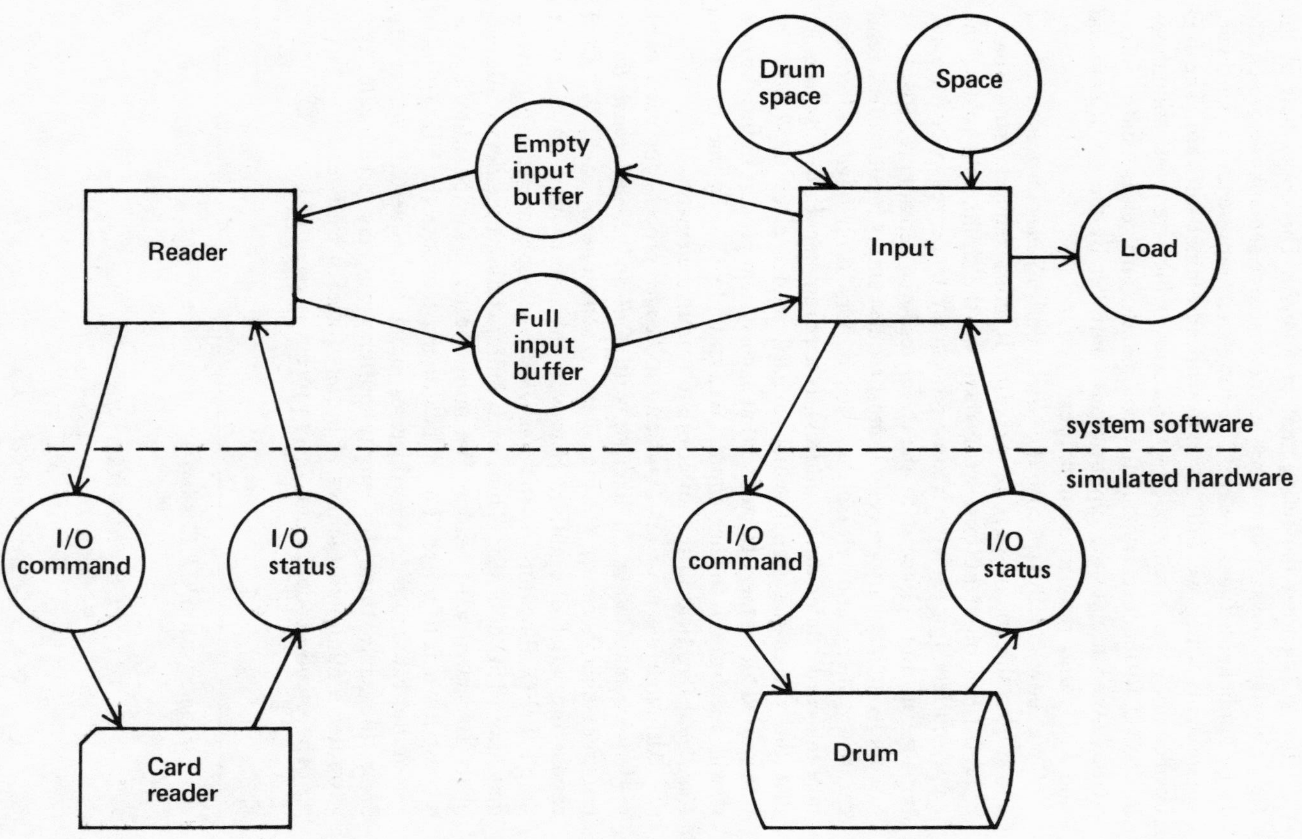

FIG. 6.29 *SpoolIn Service* refined

Fig. 6.29 shows the refinement of *SpoolIn*. The upper half of the figure contains the system processes and resource semaphores which are to be implemented as software. The lower half represents the hardware components which we will simulate with additional software. The I/O devices may be simulated by processes which request commands addressed to them, carry out the commands, and release status information. We simulate the input-output controller by the *I/O Command* and *I/O Status* resource semaphores.

We now briefly specify the *Input* and *Reader* processes. *Input* constitutes the major part of *SpoolIn*. It must request drum space, request filled input buffers, write them on the drum, and release the empty buffers. For each job it must request (system core) space for a *jcb*, initialize it, and release it to the *Load* resource semaphore. *Reader* is essentially an auxiliary process. It must request empty input buffers, read cards into them, and release the filled buffers. Both *Input* and *Reader* take the card reader device address as a parameter. Lastly, we require that the end-of-file signal which a card reader gives to *Reader* be transmitted along the job path so that each system process in turn knows it will receive no further input. We may do this by means of an *EndSignal* flag field in the appropriate resource elements.

Although we have an *Input* and a *Reader* process for each card reader, we may either do likewise with *Full* and *Empty Input Buffer* resource semaphores or we may have exactly one of each. We shall choose the latter alternative. However, this means that instead of a simple FIFO allocator for the *Full Buffer* semaphore, we must use a matching FIFO allocator. Thus, each buffer contains the device address of its associated card reader. We must specify a device address in a request for a full buffer. The allocator must choose (in FIFO order) among buffers whose device addresses match the requested address. By doing the same thing for empty buffers, we may preallocate and guarantee a minimum number of buffers for each card reader.

The pseudo-code for the *Input* process is given in Fig. 6.30.

```
Input: PROC(PCB,RdrAddr);

        DCL PCB ProcessControlBlock,
            RdrAddr DeviceAddress;

        DCL JCB JobControlBlock,
            Buf InputBuffer;
```

```
LOOP;
    Request JCB from SpaceRS;

    LOOP; /* skip to next $JOB card */
        Request Buf[RdrAddr] from FullInBufRS;
    EXITIF(Buf = $JOB card | EndSignal);
        Release Buf to EmptyInBufRS;
    ENDLOOP;

EXITIF(EndSignal);

    Fill in JCB with name, time, line limits;
    Release Buf to EmptyInBufRS;

    Set up empty files for JCB.ProgramFile, JCB.InputFile,
        and JCB.OutputFile;
    Buf = WriteInputFile(PCB,RdrAddr,JCB.ProgramFile);

    IF Buf = $DATA card THEN DO;
        Release Buf to EmptyInBufRS;
        Buf = WriteInputFile(PCB,RdrAddr,JCB.InputFile);
        END;

    IF Buf = $ENDJOB card
        THEN Release Buf to EmptyInBufRS;
        ELSE Request Buf be placed at front of FullInBufRS
                resource queue; /* may be $JOB card */

    Release JCB to LoadRS;
ENDLOOP;

Release Buf to EmptyInBufRS;
Release EndSignal JCB to LoadRS;
END Input;
```

FIG. 6.30 *Input* process

It uses the additional master declarations (data type templates) shown in Fig. 6.31 (see also Fig. 6.2).

```
%DCL QueueElemFields CHAR;
%QueueElemFields =
        'QEFields,3 Type INTG,3 Succ PTR,3 Pred PTR';

DCL  1  JobControlBlock BASED(DP),
        2 QueueElemFields,
        2 JobCard,
          3 Name CHAR(length),
          3 TimeLimit INTG,
          3 LineLimit INTG,
        2 Files,
          3 ProgramFile DrumTrackList,
          3 InputFile DrumTrackList,
          3 OutputFile DrumTrackList,
        2 PageTable UserCoreAddress,
        2 EndSignal BOOL;

DCL  1  InputBuffer BASED(DP),
        2 QueueElemFields,
        2 Device DeviceAddress,
        2 Buffer(PageSize) Word,
        2 EndSignal BOOL;
```

FIG. 6.31 Additional master declarations

Most of the code should be self-explanatory, except for the following: Firstly, we expect that variables such as *PCB, JCB,* and *Buf* will be implemented in PL/I as pointers to based structures declared LIKE the appropriate master template. Secondly, items in square brackets in request statements are data parameters used to qualify the requests. Thus

Request *Buf* [*RdrAddr*] from *FullInBufRS*;

becomes

```
BUF = REQUEST(PCB@,FULL_IN_BUF_RS@,RDR_ADDR);
```

in PL/I. Lastly, *Input* spools user programs and user input data as separate files on drum. We represent a file by a list of its drum tracks (pages). *Input* uses the routine *WriteInputFile* to transfer a file's cards from core to drum.

WriteInputFile is a procedure which takes a process control block, a card reader device address, and a file drum track list as parameters. It is to transfer program or data cards from full input buffers to empty drum tracks and append the tracks to the file track list. When it encounters a $ card or *EndSignal*, it is to yield the input buffer as its result.

The pseudo-code for *WriteInputFile* is shown in Fig. 6.32.

```
WriteInputFile: PROC(PCB,RdrAddr,File) RETURNS(InputBuffer);

        DCL  PCB ProcessControlBlock,
             RdrAddr DeviceAddress,
             File DrumTrackList;

        DCL  Buf InputBuffer,
             IOCmnd IOCommandStatus,
             Track DrumTrack;

        Request IOCmnd from SpaceRS;

        LOOP;
             Request Buf[RdrAddr] from FullInBufRS;
        EXITIF(Buf = $ card EndSignal);
             Request Track from DrumSpaceRS;
             Set up IOCmnd to write Buf onto Track;
             Release IOCmnd to IOCommandRS;
             Request IOCmnd[IOCmnd] from IOStatusRS;
             Release Buf to EmptyInBufRS;
             Append Track to File;
        ENDLOOP;

        Release IOCmnd to SpaceRS;
        RETURN(Buf);
        END WriteInputFile;
```

FIG. 6.32 *WriteInputFile* procedure

It uses the additional master template given in Fig. 6.33.

```
DCL  1  IOCommandStatus BASED(DP),
        2 QueueElemFields,
        2 Command,
```

```
        3 Common,
          4 Device DeviceAddress,
          4 Core CoreAddress,
        3 LinePrinter,
          4 PageEject BOOL,
        3 Drum,
          4 ReadOrWrite BOOL,
          4 Track DrumTrackAddress,
      2 Status,
        3 CompletedOrEOF BOOL,
      2 EndSignal BOOL;
```

FIG. 6.33 Additional master declaration

Note that an I/O command contains fields for both the command and the status response. Hence, system processes release I/O commands to the IOC (*I/O Command* resource semaphore) and request the same commands back from the IOC (*I/O Status* resource semaphore) to obtain the corresponding status response. The allocators for the *I/O Command* and *I/O Status* semaphores must both be matching allocators. *I/O Command* matches device addresses and *I/O Status* matches command addresses.

Figs. 6.34, 6.35, and 6.36 give the pseudo-code for the *Reader, CardReader,* and *Drum* processes. *Reader* is a straightforward system process for reading cards into empty buffers. The two hardware simulation processes, *CardReader* and *Drum,* illustrate how an I/O device requests an I/O command from the IOC (*I/O Command* resource semaphore), executes the command, and returns status information by releasing the command to the IOC (*I/O Status* resource semaphore).

```
Reader: PROC(PCB,RdrAddr);

      DCL PCB ProcessControlBlock,
          RdrAddr DeviceAddress;

      DCL Buf InputBuffer,
          IOCmnd IOCommandStatus;

      Request IOCmnd from SpaceRS;
```

```
LOOP;
      Request Buf [RdrAddr] from EmptyInBufRS;
      Set up IOCmnd to read RdrAddr into Buf;
      Release IOCmnd to IOCommandRS;
      Request IOCmnd [IOCmnd] from IOStatusRS;
EXITIF(EndOfFile status signal);
      Release Buf to FullInBufRS;
ENDLOOP;

Release IOCmnd to SpaceRS;
Release EndSignal Buf to FullInBufRS;
END Reader;
```

FIG. 6.34 ***Reader* process**

```
CardReader: PROC(PCB,RdrAddr);

      DCL  PCB ProcessControlBlock,
           RdrAddr DeviceAddress;

      DCL  IOCmnd IOCommandStatus,
           EOF BOOL INIT(FALSE),
           Rdr STREAM INPUT INTERNAL,
           Card CHAR(80);

      OPEN FILE(Rdr) TITLE('RDR' || RdrAddr);
      ON ENDFILE(Rdr) EOF = TRUE;

      LOOP;
            Request IOCmnd [RdrAddr] from IOCommandRS;
            GET FILE(Rdr) EDIT(Card)   (A);
      EXITIF(EOF);
            Copy relevant portion of Card into buffer specified by
                  IOCmnd;
            Mark IOCmnd with Completed status;
            Release IOCmnd to IOStatusRS;
      ENDLOOP;
```

```
        Mark IOCmnd with EndOfFile status;
        Release IOCmnd to IOStatusRS;
        CLOSE FILE(Rdr);
        END CardReader;
```

FIG. 6.35 *CardReader* process

```
Drum: PROC(PCB,DrumAddr);

        DCL  PCB ProcessControlBlock,
             DrumAddr DeviceAddress;

        DCL  IOCmnd IOCommandStatus;

        LOOP;
             Request IOCmnd [DrumAddr] from IOCommandRS;
        EXITIF(EndSignal);
             Transfer data between core and drum as specified by
                 IOCmnd;
             Mark IOCmnd with Completed status;
             Release IOCmnd to IOStatusRS;
        ENDLOOP;

        Release IOCmnd to SpaceRS;
        END Drum;
```

FIG. 6.36 *Drum* process

We turn now to the refinement of *Execute Service,* whose specification was given previously. While our design permits us to use advanced scheduling and paging policies, these topics go beyond the scope of this book. Therefore, we adopt the following simple approach, which illustrates basic multiprogramming/multiprocessing of user jobs. Having loaded a user program into user core, we leave it there until it completes execution. However, execution is temporarily suspended (and the PPU relinquished) whenever a user program needs system service, such as for input/output.

We thus split *Execute Service* into three processes: *Load, Execute,* and *Unload,* as shown in Fig. 6.37. A *Load* process is to obtain jobs from

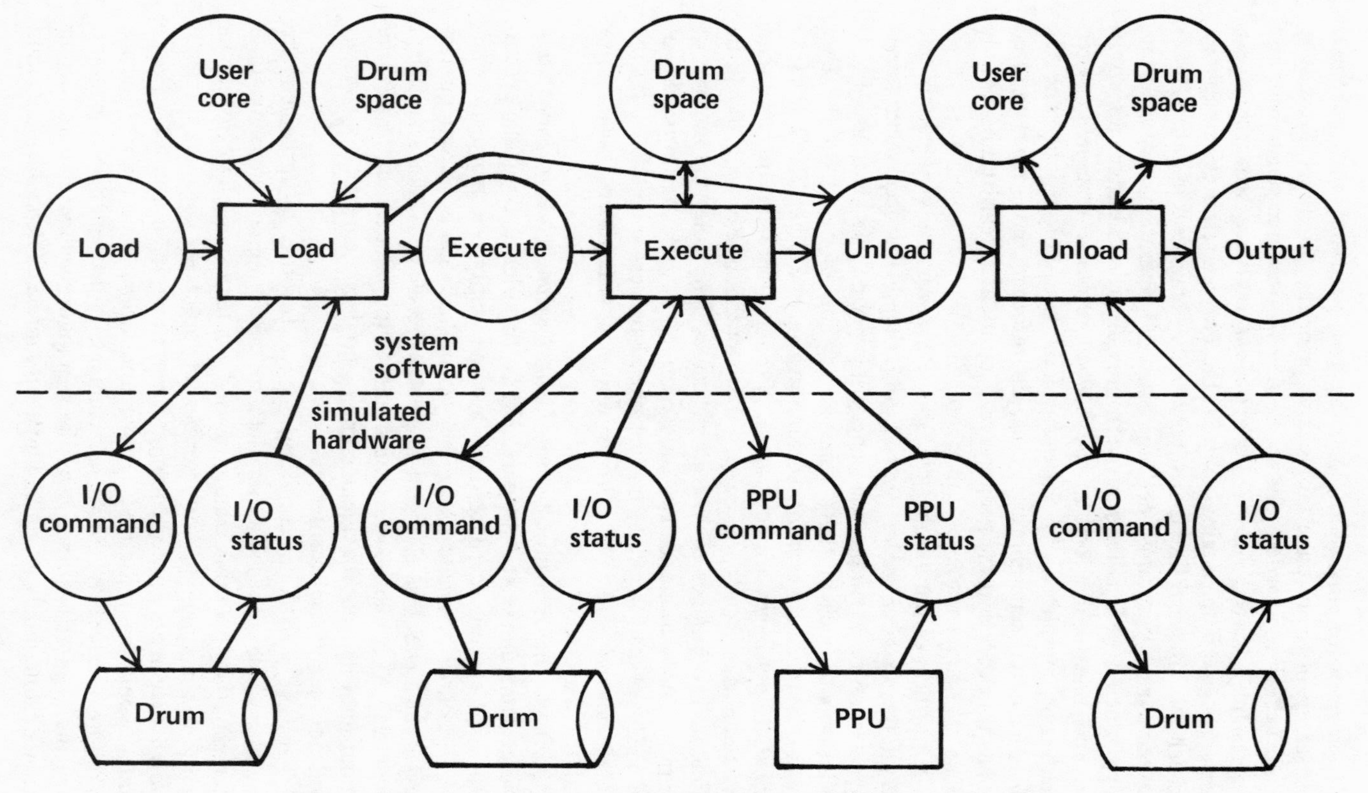

FIG. 6.37 *Execute Service* refined

the *Load* resource semaphore, load the user programs into empty user core, set up program page tables, and print the programs. *Load* is to release successfully loaded jobs to the *Execute* resource semaphore and unsuccessfully loaded jobs to the *Unload* resource semaphore. An *Execute* process is to obtain jobs from the *Execute* resource semaphore, establish job time and line limits, repeatedly obtain and initialize PPU's to execute user programs, perform user I/O operations (using drum, during which a PPU is relinquished), provide error messages for errant jobs, and release the jobs to the *Unload* resource semaphore when execution is completed. An *Unload* process is to obtain jobs from the *Unload* resource semaphore, release job resources no longer required (such as user core and the program and input data files), and release the jobs to the *Output* resource semaphore.

Regardless of the number of *Execute Services,* we want exactly one each of the *Load, Execute, Unload,* and *Output* resource semaphores. Since we desire a simple job scheduling policy, we shall use FIFO allocators with each of these semaphores. The allocators for the *User Core* and *Drum Space* resource semaphores may be either FIFO or LIFO since all empty pages are equivalent. Although there can be more than one *Load* and one *Unload* process, we expect that one of each should be sufficient. The number of *Execute* processes determines the number of user programs "simultaneously" in execution. As to the hardware side of Fig. 6.37, we shall simulate the peripheral processor controller by the *PPU Command* and *PPU Status* resource semaphores, just as we simulated the IOC.

Actually the allocators for the *Load, Execute, Unload,* and *Output* resource semaphores are not quite FIFO. In order to drain the system when input streams (card readers) become empty, we propagate *End-Signal* resource elements along the job path. When a system process receives an *EndSignal* element, it passes the element along and then terminates. A resource semaphore must not allocate an *EndSignal* element until its resource queue contains no data elements *and* it knows it will not receive any further data elements.

The first part of the condition is easy. In order to implement the second part, we add a counter field to the resource semaphore data structure. When the initialization process creates a semaphore, it sets the semaphore's counter to the number of processes that may release *EndSignal* elements to the semaphore. For example, in Fig. 6.27, *Load*'s counter would be initialized to two and *Output*'s to three. When a semaphore receives an *EndSignal* element, it decrements its counter. When the counter becomes zero, the semaphore will receive no further elements. Semaphores which can give out more *EndSignal* elements than they will receive, such as *Load* in Fig. 6.27, must be preallocated by the initialization process with sufficient additional *EndSignal* elements.

```
Load: PROC(PCB);

      DCL PCB ProcessControlBlock;

      DCL JCB JobControlBlock,
          IOCmnd IOCommandStatus,
          Core UserCorePage,
          Track DrumTrack,
          I INTG;

      Request IOCmnd from SpaceRS;

      LOOP;
          Request JCB from LoadRS;
      EXITIF(EndSignal);
          OutputLine('$JOB ' || JCB.Name);

          Request JCB.PageTable from UserCoreRS;
          Set PageTable entries to Null;

          Track = first track in JCB.ProgramFile;
          DO I = 1 TO PageTableSize WHILE(Track ≠ Null);
             Request Core from UserCoreRS;
             Set up IOCmnd to read Track into Core;
             Release IOCmnd to IOCommandRS;
             Request IOCmnd[IOCmnd] from IOStatusRS;
             PageTable(I) = Core;
             Track = next track in ProgramFile;
             END;

          OutputLine('PROGRAM:');
          Append ProgramFile to OutputFile; /* print program */
          JCB.ProgramFile = Null;

          IF PageTable(1) = Null | Track≠Null
             THEN DO;
                    OutputLine('NO PROGRAM OR PROGRAM TOO BIG');
                    Release JCB to UnloadRS;
```

```
                END;
            ELSE Release JCB to ExecuteRS;
    ENDLOOP;

    Release IOCmnd to SpaceRS;
    Release EndSignal JCB to ExecuteRS;
    END Load;
```

FIG. 6.38 *Load* process

```
        %DCL OutputLine ENTRY(CHAR) RETURNS (CHAR);

%OutputLine: PROC(Line) RETURNS(CHAR);
        DCL Line CHAR;
        RETURN('CALL WriteOutputLine(PCB,JCB.OutputFile,' ||
                Line || ')');
        %END OutputLine;



WriteOutputLine: PROC(PCB,File,Line);

        DCL PCB ProcessControlBlock,
            File DrumTrackList,
            Line CHAR(*) VAR;

        DCL IOCmnd IOCommandStatus,
            Buf IOBuffer,
            Track DrumTrack;

        Request Buf from SpaceRS;
        Buf = Line;

        Request Track from DrumSpaceRS;

        Request IOCmnd from SpaceRS;
        Set up IOCmnd to write Buf onto Track;
        Release IOCmnd to IOCommandRS;
        Request IOCmnd [IOCmnd] from IOStatusRS;

        Append Track to File;
```

```
        Release IOCmnd to SpaceRS;
        Release Buf to SpaceRS;
        END WriteOutputLine;
```

FIG. 6.39 *OutputLine* and *WriteOutputLine* procedures

We now give our pseudo-code for the *Execute Service* processes. The code for the *Load* process is shown in Fig. 6.38 and should be self-explanatory. All of the *Execute Service* processes use the procedure *OutputLine,* defined in Fig. 6.39, to place system messages in users' output files (on drum). The *Execute* process, shown in Fig. 6.40, is quite straightforward. It uses the additional master template given in Fig. 6.41. Just as for an I/O command, a PPU command contains fields for both the command and the status response. The PPC and PPU's are treated in a manner analogous to that of the IOC and I/O devices. Fig. 6.42 gives the system actions performed by *Execute* when a PPU terminates execution of a user program.

```
Execute: PROC(PCB);

    DCL PCB ProcessControlBlock;

    DCL JCB JobControlBlock,
        IOCmnd IOCommandStatus,
        PPUCmnd PPUCommandStatus,
        #Lines INTG,
        Track DrumTrack,
        Stop BOOL;

    Request PPUCmnd from SpaceRS;
    Request IOCmnd from SpaceRS;

    LOOP;
        Request JCB from ExecuteRS;
    EXITIF(EndSignal);
        OutputLine('EXECUTION BEGUN:');

        PPUCmnd.PageTable = JCB.PageTable;
        PPUCmnd.InstructionPtr = 0;
        PPUCmnd.Timer = JCB.TimeLimit;
```

```
            PPUCmnd.EndSignal = FALSE;

            #Lines = 0;
            Stop = FALSE;

            REPEAT;
               Release PPUCmnd to PPUCommandRS;
               Request PPUCmnd[PPUCmnd] from PPUStatusRS;
               %INCLUDE PerformSystemAction;
            UNTIL(Stop);

            Release JCB to UnloadRS;
        ENDLOOP;

        Release IOCmnd to SpaceRS;
        Release PPUCmnd to SpaceRS;
        Release EndSignal JCB to UnloadRS;
        END Execute;
```

FIG. 6.40 *Execute* process

```
DCL 1 PPUCommandStatus BASED(DP),
      2 QueueElemFields,
      2 Command,
        3 PageTable UserCoreAddress,
        3 InstructionPtr UserCoreAddress,
        3 Accumulator Word,
        3 Timer INTG,
      2 Status,
        3 TerminationCode INTG,
        3 Core UserCoreAddress,
        3 PageTableIndex INTG,
      2 EndSignal BOOL;
```

FIG. 6.41 Additional master declaration

```
SELECT(PPUCmnd.TerminationCode);
    CASE(HaltInstruction):
        Stop = TRUE;
```

```
CASE(ReadInstruction):
        Track = first track in JCB.InputFile;
        IF Track ≠ Null
          THEN  DO;
                Set up IOCmnd to read Track into
                   PPUCmnd.Core;
                Release IOCmnd to IOCommandRS;
                Request IOCmnd[IOCmnd] from IOStatusRS;
                Remove Track from InputFile;
                Release Track to DrumSpaceRS;
                END;
          ELSE  DO;
                OutputLine('END OF INPUT');
                Stop = TRUE;
                END;

CASE(WriteInstruction):
        IF #Lines < JCB.LineLimit
          THEN  DO;
                Request Track from DrumSpaceRS;
                Set up IOCmnd to write PPUCmnd.Core onto
                   Track;
                Release IOCmnd to IOCommandRS;
                Request IOCmnd[IOCmnd] from IOStatusRS;
                Append Track to JCB.OutputFile;
                #Lines = #Lines + 1;
                END;
          ELSE  DO;
                OutputLine('LINE LIMIT EXCEEDED');
                Stop = TRUE;
                END;

CASE(PageFault):
        OutputLine('ADDRESS TOO BIG');
        Stop = TRUE;
CASE(BadOpCode):
        OutputLine('ILLEGAL INSTRUCTION');
        Stop = TRUE;
CASE(BadData):
        OutputLine('INVALID DATA');
        Stop = TRUE;
CASE(TimeExpired):
```

```
        OutputLine('TIME LIMIT EXCEEDED');
        Stop = TRUE;
ENDSELECT;
```

FIG. 6.42 *PerformSystemAction* segment

Although we did not completely specify the PPU hardware, Fig. 6.43 provides a reasonable PPU simulation process. The inner LOOP is the usual "fetch instruction," "increment instruction pointer," "decode instruction," and "execute operation" cycle. Note that we have omitted the *"PPUCmnd."* qualifier from such field names as *"TerminationCode"* (*"TC"*), *"Timer"*, *"InstructionPtr"*. The procedure *AbsoluteAddress,* shown in Fig. 6.44, translates virtual addresses into absolute addresses (or page faults) via the page table. It is a lexicographically internal procedure of the PPU simulation procedure and accesses the *PPUCmnd* fields and *AbsAddr* as global variables. Fig. 6.45 gives the "execute operation" portion of the cycle.

```
PPU: PROC(PCB);

        DCL PCB ProcessControlBlock;

        DCL PPUCmnd PPUCommandStatus,
            AbsAddr UserCoreAddress,
            Instruction Word,
            OpCode OperationCode,
            Addr UserCoreAddress;

        %DCL TC CHAR;
        %TC = 'TerminationCode';

        %INCLUDE AbsAddrProc;

        LOOP;
            Request PPUCmnd from PPUCommandRS;
        EXITIF(EndSignal);
                    TC = 0;

            LOOP; /* Interpret instructions */
                IF Timer ≤ 0 THEN TC = TimeExpired;
            EXITIF(TC≠0);
```

```
                CALL AbsoluteAddress(InstructionPtr);
        EXITIF(TC≠0);
                Instruction = UserCore(AbsAddr);
                (OpCode,Addr) = Instruction;
                CALL AbsoluteAddress(Addr);
        EXITIF(TC≠0);
                InstructionPtr = MOD(InstructionPtr+1,
                                          VirtualCoreSize);
                %INCLUDE PerformOperation;
                Timer = Timer - InstructionTime(OpCode);
        EXITIF(TC≠0);
        ENDLOOP;

        Release PPUCmnd to PPUStatusRS;
    ENDLOOP;

    Release PPUCmnd to SpaceRS;
    %DEACTIVATE TC;
    END PPU;
```

FIG. 6.43 *PPU* process

```
    DCL AbsoluteAddress ENTRY(UserCoreAddress);

AbsoluteAddress: PROC(Addr);

    DCL Addr UserCoreAddress;

    DCL I INTG;

    I = HigherOrderPart(Addr);

    IF PageTable(I) is a UserCoreAddress
        THEN AbsAddr = PageTable(I) + LowOrderPart(Addr);
        ELSE DO;
            TC = PageFault;
            PageTableIndex = I;
            END;

    END AbsoluteAddress;
```

FIG. 6.44 *AbsAddrProc* segment

```
SELECT(OpCode);
    CASE(Halt):
                TC = HaltInstruction;

    CASE(Read):
                TC = ReadInstruction;
                Core = AbsAddr;

    CASE(Write):
                TC = WriteInstruction;
                Core = AbsAddr;

    CASE(Load,Store,Add,etc.):
                /* may use Accumulator, UserCore(AbsAddr)
                   may set Accumulator, UserCore(AbsAddr)
                   may set TC = BadData */

    CASE(branch instructions):
                /* may use Accumulator
                   may set InstructionPtr = Addr
                   may set TC = BadData */

    DEFAULT:
              TC = BadOpCode;
ENDSELECT;
```

FIG. 6.45 *PerformOperation* segment

The pseudo-code for the *Unload* process is shown in Fig. 6.46. *Unload* uses the procedure *FreeFile,* defined in Fig. 6.47, to release the tracks of a file to the *Drum Space* resource semaphore.

```
Unload: PROC(PCB);

    DCL PCB ProcessControlBlock;

    DCL JCB JobControlBlock,
        I INTG;
```

```
LOOP;
      Request JCB from UnloadRS;
EXITIF(EndSignal);

      DO I = 1 TO PageTableSize;
            IF JCB.PageTable(I) is UserCoreAddress THEN
                  Release PageTable(I) to UserCoreRS;
            ELSE IF PageTable(I) is DrumTrackAddress THEN
                  Release PageTable(I) to DrumSpaceRS;
            END;

      Release JCB.PageTable to UserCoreRS;
      CALL FreeFile(PCB,JCB.ProgramFile);
      CALL FreeFile(PCB,JCB.InputFile);
      OutputLine('$ENDJOB');
      Release JCB to OutputRS;
ENDLOOP;

Release EndSignal JCB to OutputRS;
END Unload;
```

FIG. 6.46 *Unload* process

```
FreeFile: PROC(PCB,File);

      DCL PCB ProcessControlBlock,
          File DrumTrackList;

      DCL Track DrumTrack;

      DO WHILE(File≠Null);
            Track = first track in File;
            Remove Track from File;
            Release Track to DrumSpaceRS;
            END;

      END FreeFile;
```

FIG. 6.47 *FreeFile* procedure

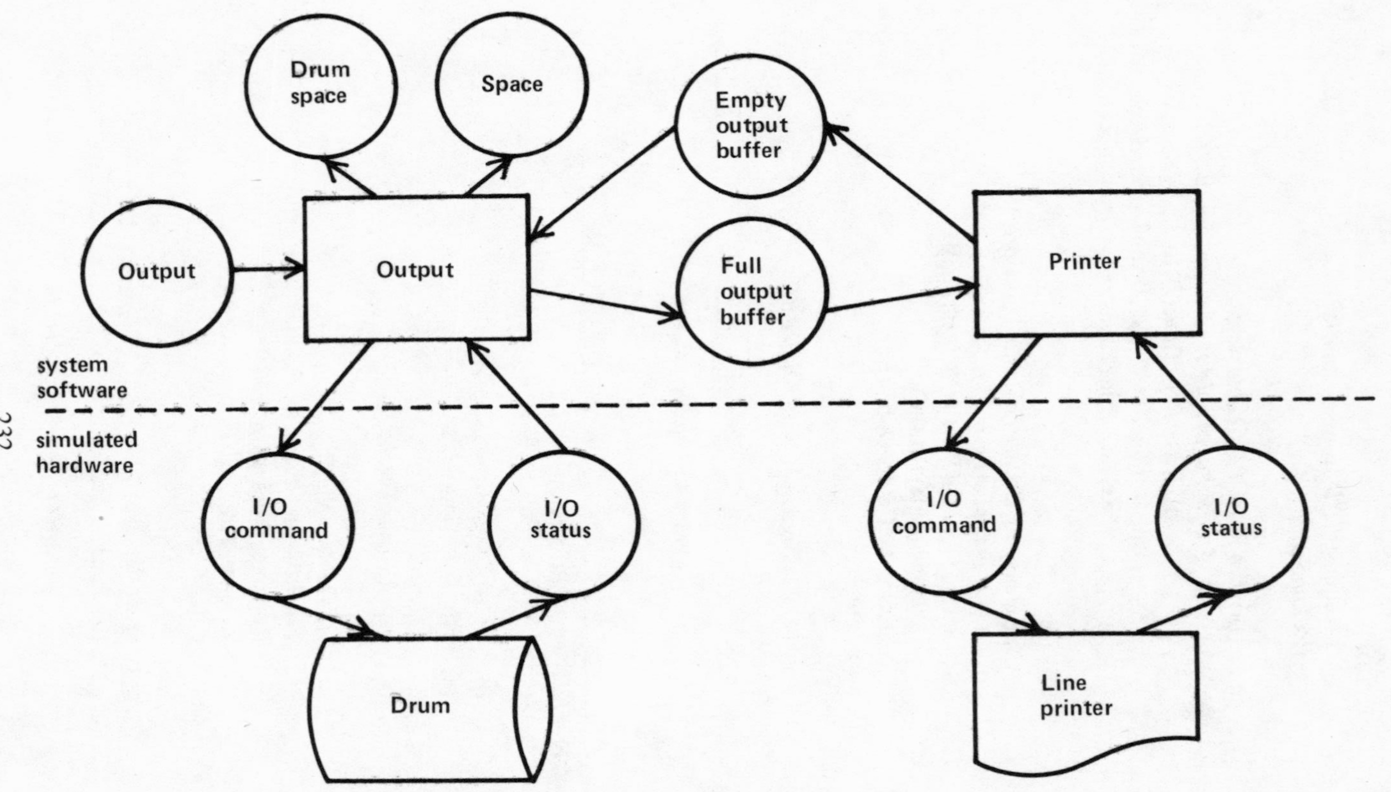

FIG. 6.48 *SpoolOut Service* refined

Turning now to the refinement of *SpoolOut Service,* we note that *SpoolOut* is similar to *SpoolIn,* except that the flow of data and resources is reversed. We quickly split *SpoolOut* into the processes and resource semaphores shown in Fig. 6.48. The *Output* process forms the main part of *SpoolOut*. *Output* is to obtain jobs from the *Output* resource semaphore and to transfer user output from drum to empty output buffers, yielding full output buffers. It must also release all of a user job's remaining resources—namely, the output file drum space and the *jcb.* The *Printer* process is an auxiliary process that is to print full output buffers and yield empty output buffers. As with *SpoolIn,* we have one *Output* and one *Printer* process for each line printer, but exactly one *Empty* and one *Full Output Buffer* resource semaphore, shared by all *SpoolOut Services*. The pseudo-code for the *Output, Printer,* and *Line-Printer* processes is given in Figs. 6.49, 6.50, and 6.51, respectively. They use the following additional master template.

```
DCL 1 OutputBuffer BASED(DP),
      2 QueueElemFields,
      2 Device DeviceAddress,
      2 PageEject BOOL,
      2 Buffer(PageSize) Word,
      2 EndSignal BOOL;
```

```
Output: PROC(PCB,PrtrAddr);

        DCL PCB ProcessControlBlock,
            PrtrAddr DeviceAddress;

        DCL JCB JobControlBlock,
            Buf OutputBuffer,
            IOCmnd IOCommandStatus,
            Track DrumTrack,
            Eject BOOL;

        Request IOCmnd from SpaceRS;

        LOOP;
            Request JCB from OutputRS;
        EXITIF(EndSignal);
            Eject = TRUE;
```

```
        DO WHILE(JCB.OutputFile≠Null);
            Track = first track in OutputFile;
            Request Buf[PrtrAddr] from EmptyOutBufRS;
            Set up IOCmnd to read Track into Buf;
            Release IOCmnd to IOCommandRS;
            Request IOCmnd[IOCmnd] from IOStatusRS;
            Buf.PageEject = Eject;
            Release Buf to FullOutBufRS;
            Remove Track from OutputFile;
            Release Track to DrumSpaceRS;
            Eject = FALSE;
            END;

        Release JCB to SpaceRS;
    ENDLOOP;

    Release JCB to SpaceRS;
    Release IOCmnd to SpaceRS;
    Request Buf[PrtrAddr] from EmptyOutBufRS;
    Release EndSignal Buf to FullOutBufRS;
    END Output;
```

FIG. 6.49 ***Output* process**

```
Printer: PROC(PCB,PrtrAddr);

    DCL PCB ProcessControlBlock,
        PrtrAddr DeviceAddress;

    DCL Buf OutputBuffer,
        IOCmnd IOCommandStatus;

    Request IOCmnd from SpaceRS;

    LOOP;
        Request Buf[PrtrAddr] from FullOutBufRS;
    EXITIF(EndSignal);
        Set up IOCmnd to print Buf on PrtrAddr;
        IOCmnd.PageEject = Buf.PageEject;
        Release IOCmnd to IOCommandRS;
```

```
        Request IOCmnd[IOCmnd] from IOStatusRS;
        Release Buf to EmptyOutBufRS;
    ENDLOOP;

    Release Buf to EmptyOutBufRS;
    Release IOCmnd to SpaceRS;
    END Printer;
```

FIG. 6.50 *Printer* process

```
LinePrinter: PROC(PCB,PrtrAddr);

    DCL PCB ProcessControlBlock,
        PrtrAddr DeviceAddress;

    DCL IOCmnd IOCommandStatus,
        Prtr STREAM OUTPUT PRINT INTERNAL,
        Line CHAR(120);

    OPEN FILE(Prtr) TITLE('PRTR' || PrtrAddr);

    LOOP;
        Request IOCmnd[PrtrAddr] from IOCommandRS;
    EXITIF(EndSignal);
        Copy relevant portion of buffer specified by IOCmnd
            into Line;
        IF IOCmnd.PageEject
            THEN PUT FILE(Prtr) PAGE;
            ELSE PUT FILE(Prtr) SKIP;
        PUT FILE(Prtr) EDIT(Line) (A);
        Mark IOCmnd with Completed status;
        Release IOCmnd to IOStatusRS;
    ENDLOOP;

    Release IOCmnd to SpaceRS;
    CLOSE FILE(Prtr);
    END LinePrinter;
```

FIG. 6.51 *LinePrinter* process

Our refinement of the operating system design has proceeded as far as it will go in this book. In order to transform our pseudo-code into PL/I code, we need a more detailed specification of the system and especially the hardware—$JOB card format, number of words per core page and bytes (or bits) per word, PPU instructions. We can then decide how to represent abstract data types such as *UserCorePage* with PL/I's data types. Once the PL/I data representations are known, we can easily translate the abstract operations encoded in pseudo-code into equivalent PL/I code, while retaining the structured control flow given by the pseudo-code.

The pseudo-code we have presented here represents only the basic framework of the system. Although one of our goals was to optimize job throughput and turnaround time, we have not included any code for measuring system performance. There are a number of places in our design where useful statistics may be obtained. You need only to augment the resource semaphore, queue head, and resource element data structures with additional fields, and appropriately modify the allocators, queuing routines, and processes (system and/or hardware) to collect and produce the desired information.

APPENDIX A. STRUCTURED PROGRAMMING EXTENSIONS TO PL/I

In this appendix we present the PL/I preprocessor code for the implementation of the REPEAT-UNTIL, LOOP-EXITIF-ENDLOOP, and SELECT-CASE figures. First, we give the functional specifications for the figures, then the general implementation strategy, and finally the code for the procedures involved.

The REPEAT-UNTIL figure is similar to the DO-WHILE figure in that it allows a block of code to be executed repeatedly, subject to a termination predicate. With DO-WHILE the predicate is tested before the first execution of the contained block. However, with REPEAT-UNTIL the contained block is always executed at least once. The termination test comes at the end of each execution of the block. Thus you may write something such as

```
REPEAT;
        group;
UNTIL(pred);
```

where *group* is one or more PL/I statements and *pred* is a boolean expression. This is to expand into the following PL/I code:

```
R#uniq: DO;
            group;
            IF ¬(pred) THEN GO TO R#uniq;
            END R#uniq;
```

In this expansion *uniq* stands for an integer which is unique to this particular expansion. Thus R#*uniq* is an identifier used here as a unique label.

The LOOP-EXITIF-ENDLOOP figure is a combination of the DO-WHILE and REPEAT-UNTIL figures. It allows a block of code to be repeatedly executed until one of possibly several termination predicates is satisfied.

The block of code consists of groups of PL/I statements separated by termination test statements. In the following example there are three code groups separated by two termination predicates:

```
LOOP;
        group1;
EXITIF(pred1);
        group2;
EXITIF(pred2);
        group3;
ENDLOOP;
```

The figure is usually used with only two groups and one predicate; *group1* reads an input file, the *predicate* tests for end of file, and *group2* processes the item read. The example above is to expand into the following PL/I code:

```
L#uniq: DO;
          group1;
          IF pred1 THEN GO TO E#uniq;
          group2;
          IF pred2 THEN GO TO E#uniq;
          group3;
          GO TO L#uniq;
E#uniq: END L#uniq;
```

As before, *uniq* is a decimal integer which is unique to the expanded figure.

The SELECT-CASE figure is an extension of the IF-THEN-ELSE statement of PL/I. Instead of having only true and false alternatives, we may have an arbitrary number of alternatives, each associated with a distinct integer. Suppose you write the following:

```
SELECT(intg_expr);
        CASE(2):          group2;
        CASE((3,1,5)):    group315;
        DEFAULT:          group0;
ENDSELECT;
```

The SELECT statement evaluates the integer expression and transfers control to the group of statements labeled by a CASE label with the appropriate integer value. If such a case label does not exist, control is given to the group labeled by DEFAULT. The selected group is executed, after which control passes to the ENDSELECT statement. As can be seen in the example, the cases may be listed in any order and do not have to be consecutive integers. Thus, case 4 above is missing, even though there are cases 3 and 5. The parameter to the CASE macro is either a positive fixed decimal integer or a list of such integers enclosed in an extra pair of parentheses. Since the preprocessor processes the argument of CASE before calling the macro procedure, you may also use compile time variables and preprocessor procedures to generate the CASE argument. Such usage is illustrated in the FREE_SPACE and ALLOC_SPACE routines in Chapter 6. Note that blanks in the argument of CASE will be ignored by CASE. The CASE groups are optional. The DEFAULT group is also optional, but if it occurs, it must be placed after all of the case groups. If the DEFAULT label is omitted, it is assumed to label the ENDSELECT statement. Each CASE or DEFAULT may label one or more PL/I statements, which comprise the associated group. The example above will expand into the following PL/I code:

```
S#uniq: DO;
        I#uniq = intg_expr;
        IF I#uniq<=0 | I#uniq>M#uniq
             THEN GO TO D#uniq;
             ELSE GO TO C#uniq(I#uniq);

       C#uniq(2): group2;
                  GO TO E#uniq;

       C#uniq(3):
       C#uniq(1):
       C#uniq(5): group315;
                  GO TO E#uniq;

       D#uniq:
       C#uniq(4): group0;

  E#uniq: END S#uniq;
          DCL (I#uniq,
               M#uniq STATIC INIT(5)) FIXED BIN,
               C#uniq(5) LABEL;
```

As before, *uniq* is a decimal integer which is unique to the expanded figure. Lastly, you should note that the REPEAT-UNTIL, LOOP-EXITIF-ENDLOOP, and SELECT-CASE figures may be nested within each other and within themselves.

The general implementation strategy is as follows. Each of the keywords REPEAT, UNTIL, LOOP, EXITIF, ENDLOOP, SELECT, CASE, DEFAULT, and ENDSELECT is the name of the preprocessor procedure to be invoked for that keyword. These identifiers are always activated. In addition, there are some global compile time variables and a unique number generator procedure, the identifiers for which are always deactivated. Since the figures may be nested, a stack is used for each of the figures, so that whenever the initial keyword—REPEAT, LOOP, or SELECT—of a figure is encountered, the current status of the global control variables for that figure is pushed onto the stack. The global control variables are then initialized for the new occurrence of the figure. The figure is completely processed, during which the current values of the global control variables are used to process the keywords EXITIF, CASE, and DEFAULT. When the termination keyword—UNTIL, ENDLOOP, or ENDSELECT—is encountered, then the termination code is produced and the stack for the figure is popped to restore the status of the enclosing figure, if any.

The OS/360 PL/I F preprocessor allows only a very restricted subset of PL/I to be used. The only data types are FIXED DECIMAL(5,0) integers and VARYING CHAR(*) strings. Thus, the stacks have to be represented as character strings. An element is pushed onto the stack by concatenating it onto the front of the string. The element is popped by using SUBSTR to extract the element and the rest of the stack. The size of each element placed on the stack should be known in advance, since SUBSTR requires the length of the substring to be extracted. Note the SUBSTR is the only built-in function available to preprocessor procedures. (The LENGTH function ought to be provided, as should arrays.) The only built-in structured looping figure is the ITERATIVE-DO, namely

```
%DO var = expr1 TO expr2 BY expr3;
        group;
        %END;
```

Lastly, since there is no error signaling facility (such as MNOTE in OS/360 Assembler Language), the following implementation does not check for user errors.

```
/* STRUCTURED PROGRAMMING EXTENSIONS */

/* REPEAT-UNTIL, LOOP-EXITIF-ENDLOOP, SELECT-CASE */

%DCL REPEAT ENTRY RETURNS(CHAR),
```

```
        UNTIL ENTRY(CHAR) RETURNS(CHAR),
        (R_LAB, RU_STAK) CHAR;

%DCL    LOOP ENTRY RETURNS(CHAR),
        EXITIF ENTRY(CHAR) RETURNS (CHAR),
        ENDLOOP ENTRY RETURNS(CHAR),
        (L_#UNIQ, L_STAK) CHAR;

%DCL    SELECT ENTRY(CHAR) RETURNS(CHAR),
        CASE ENTRY(CHAR) RETURNS(CHAR),
        DEFAULT ENTRY RETURNS(CHAR),
        ENDSELECT ENTRY RETURNS(CHAR),
        DEFAULT1 ENTRY RETURNS(CHAR),
        S_MAX FIXED,
        (S_#UNIQ, S_CASES, S_STAK) CHAR;

%DCL    #UNIQUE ENTRY RETURNS(CHAR),
        UNIQ# FIXED;

%DEACTIVATE R_LAB, RU_STAK, L_#UNIQ, L_STAK,
            DEFAULT1, S_MAX, S_#UNIQ, S_CASES, S_STAK,
            #UNIQUE, UNIQ#;

%R_LAB = '######';
%RU_STAK = '#';
%L_#UNIQ = '#####';
%L_STAK = '#';
%S_MAX = 0;
%S_#UNIQ = '#####';
%S_CASES = 'U';
%S_STAK = '#';
%UNIQ# = 1000;

%INCLUDE REPUNTIL;  /* REPEAT, UNTIL, #UNIQUE */
%INCLUDE LOOPENDL;  /* LOOP, EXITIF, ENDLOOP */
%INCLUDE SELENDSL;  /* SELECT, ENDSELECT */
%INCLUDE CASEMAC;   /* CASE */
%INCLUDE DEFLT;     /* DEFAULT, DEFAULT1 */
```

FIG. A.1 STRUCMAC

Fig. A.1. shows the declaration and initialization code for the REPEAT-UNTIL, LOOP-EXITIF-ENDLOOP, and SELECT-CASE extensions. The only global information required for REPEAT-UNTIL is the unique label used by each of the keywords in their expansions. This label is contained in the variable R_LAB. R_LAB is saved on RU_STAK when REPEAT-UNTIL figures are nested. Similarly, LOOP-EXITIF-ENDLOOP requires only the unique number of the current LOOP-EXITIF-ENDLOOP figure. This number is contained in L_#UNIQ, which is saved on L_STAK when LOOP-EXITIF-ENDLOOP figures are nested. The SELECT-CASE figure requires three items of global information: S_#UNIQ contains the unique number for the current SELECT-CASE figure; S_MAX contains the current maximum case encountered for the current SELECT-CASE figure; S_CASES is a string of 'U's and 'D's. It is treated as an array of single characters. The bounds of the array are 0 to the current value of S_MAX. Thus, the upper bound increases as new maximum cases are encountered. The *i*th entry of the array is either 'U' or 'D'. 'U' indicates that case *i* is undefined—i.e., it has not yet been encountered. 'D' indicates that case *i* is defined—i.e., a CASE label for integer *i* has been encountered. Whenever SELECT-CASE figures are nested, the current values of S_MAX, S_#UNIQ, and S_CASES are saved in the stack S_STAK. Lastly, the global variable UNIQ# contains the last generated unique number.

```
            /* REPEAT, UNTIL, #UNIQUE MACROS */

    %REPEAT: PROC RETURNS(CHAR);

            RU_STAK = R_LAB || RU_STAK;
            R_LAB = 'R' || #UNIQUE;
            RETURN(R_LAB || ': DO');
            %END REPEAT;

    %UNTIL: PROC(PRED) RETURNS(CHAR);

            DCL PRED CHAR;

            DCL CODE CHAR;

            CODE = 'IF ¬(' || PRED || ') THEN GO TO ' || R_LAB ||
                        '; END ' || R_LAB;

            R_LAB = SUBSTR(RU_STAK,1,6);
            RU_STAK = SUBSTR(RU_STAK,7);
            RETURN(CODE);
            %END UNTIL;
```

```
%#UNIQUE: PROC RETURNS(CHAR);

        UNIQ# = UNIQ# + 1;
        RETURN('#' || SUBSTR(UNIQ#,5));
        %END #UNIQUE;
```

FIG. A.2 REPUNTIL

The code for the REPEAT, UNTIL, and #UNIQUE macros is shown in Fig. A.2. The REPEAT macro pushes its global information R_LAB onto RU_STAK. It then generates a new label for R_LAB by calling #UNIQUE to obtain a new unique number. Lastly, it yields the required PL/I code using the new unique label. The UNTIL macro generates the appropriate termination test code, using the current label in R_LAB. It then pops RU_STAK to restore the saved value of R_LAB. The #UNIQUE macro increments UNIQ# to obtain a new unique number and returns a string beginning with '#' and followed by a unique four-digit number.

The code for the LOOP, EXITIF, and ENDLOOP macros is given in Fig. A.3. The LOOP macro saves its global information L_#UNIQ on the stack L_STAK. It then generates a new unique number. Lastly, it produces the required PL/I code. The EXITIF macro expands into the required termination test code, using the current LOOP-EXITIF-ENDLOOP figure number in L_#UNIQ. The ENDLOOP macro generates the necessary looping and end code for the current figure. It then pops L_STAK to restore the saved value of L_#UNIQ.

```
        /* LOOP, EXITIF, ENDLOOP MACROS */

%LOOP: PROC RETURNS(CHAR);

        L_STAK = L_#UNIQ || L_STAK;
        L_#UNIQ = #UNIQUE;
        RETURN('L' || L_#UNIQ || ': DO');
        %END LOOP;

%EXITIF: PROC(PRED) RETURNS(CHAR);

        DCL PRED CHAR;

        DCL CODE CHAR;

        CODE = 'IF ' || PRED || ' THEN GO TO E' || L_#UNIQ;
        RETURN(CODE);
        %END EXITIF;
```

```
%ENDLOOP: PROC RETURNS(CHAR);

        DCL CODE CHAR;

        CODE = 'GO TO L' || L_#UNIQ || '; E' || L_#UNIQ ||
                 ': END L' || L_#UNIQ;

        L_#UNIQ = SUBSTR(L_STAK,1,5);
        L_STAK = SUBSTR(L_STAK,6);
        RETURN(CODE);
        %END ENDLOOP;
```

FIG. A.3 LOOPENDL

Fig. A.4 contains the code for the SELECT and ENDSELECT macros. SELECT saves the current values of S_#UNIQ, S_MAX, and S_CASES on the stack S_STAK. It then reinitializes the global variables for the current SELECT-CASE figure. Lastly, it expands into the required PL/I code. ENDSELECT first sets the upper bound for the label array. Then it tests to see whether case 0 is defined or undefined. If case 0 is undefined, no DEFAULT label was encountered for this figure. Hence, ENDSELECT generates the required default labels via DEFAULT1. If case 0 is defined, the DEFAULT label was present and missing case labels have already been generated. Next, ENDSELECT generates the required PL/I termination code. Lastly, it pops the saved values of S_#UNIQ, S_MAX, and S_CASES from S_STAK.

```
        /* SELECT, ENDSELECT MACROS */

%SELECT: PROC(EXPR) RETURNS(CHAR);

        DCL EXPR CHAR;

        DCL CODE CHAR;

        S_STAK = S_#UNIQ || S_MAX || S_CASES || S_STAK;
        S_#UNIQ = #UNIQUE;
        S_MAX = 0;
        S_CASES = 'U';

        CODE = 'S' || S_#UNIQ || ': DO; I' || S_#UNIQ || ' = ' ||
                 EXPR || '; IF I' || S_#UNIQ || '<=0 | I' || S_#UNIQ ||
                 '>M' || S_#UNIQ || ' THEN GO TO D' || S_#UNIQ ||
                 '; ELSE GO TO C' || S_#UNIQ || '(I' || S_#UNIQ || ')';
```

```
        RETURN(CODE);
        %END SELECT;

    %ENDSELECT: PROC RETURNS(CHAR);

        DCL  BOUND FIXED,
             CODE CHAR;

        IF S_MAX > 0 THEN BOUND = S_MAX;
                      ELSE BOUND = 1;

        IF SUBSTR(S_CASES,1,1) = 'U' THEN CODE = DEFAULT1 || ': ';
                                      ELSE CODE = '';
        CODE = CODE || 'E' || S_#UNIQ || ': END S' || S_#UNIQ ||
               '; DCL (I' || S_#UNIQ || ', M' || S_#UNIQ ||
               ' STATIC INIT(' || S_MAX || ')) FIXED BIN, C' ||
               S_#UNIQ || '(' || BOUND || ') LABEL';

        S_#UNIQ = SUBSTR(S_STAK,1,5);
        S_MAX = SUBSTR(S_STAK,6,8);
        S_CASES = SUBSTR(S_STAK,14,S_MAX+1);
        S_STAK = SUBSTR(S_STAK,S_MAX+15);
        RETURN(CODE);
        %END ENDSELECT;
```

FIG. A.4 SELENDSL

The CASE macro is shown in Fig. A.5. If S_MAX > 0, a previous case group has already been encountered. Hence, the terminating GO TO E#*uniq* statement must be generated first before the code for this case group can be generated. The next chunk of code in CASE skips over any leading blanks and '(' in the argument of CASE and forces the argument to end with ')'. The label EACH_CASE indicates the start of a loop. Each pass through the loop processes the next case in the argument list. The first part of the loop locates the terminating ',' or ')' and extracts the case integer. Next, the code for the case label is generated. Then, the appropriate entry is S_CASES is changed from 'U' to 'D'. If the closing delimiter is ',' then the next case is processed. Otherwise, CASE is finished.

```
        /* CASE MACRO */

    %CASE: PROC(CASES) RETURNS(CHAR);
```

```
        DCL CASES CHAR;

        DCL (I,J,N) FIXED,
            (CODE,C,COLON,NC,U) CHAR;

        IF S_MAX > 0 THEN CODE = 'GO TO E' || S_#UNIQ || '; ';
                     ELSE  CODE = '';

        DO I = 1 TO 99999;
            C = SUBSTR(CASES,I,1);
            IF C ¬= ' ' THEN GO TO L1;
            END;
L1:     IF C = '(' THEN CASES = SUBSTR(CASES,I+1);
               ELSE  CASES = SUBSTR(CASES,I) || ')';
        COLON = '';

EACH_CASE:
        DO I = 1 TO 99999;
            C = SUBSTR(CASES,I,1);
            IF C=')' | C=',' THEN GO TO L2;
            END;
L2:     NC = SUBSTR(CASES,1,I-1);
        CODE = CODE || COLON || 'C' || S_#UNIQ || '(' || NC || ')';
        COLON = ': ';

        N = NC;
        IF N > S_MAX
            THEN DO;
                U = '';
                DO J = 1 TO N-S_MAX-1;
                    U = U || 'U';
                    END;
                S_CASES = S_CASES || U || 'D';
                S_MAX = N;
                END;
            ELSE S_CASES = SUBSTR(S_CASES,1,N) || 'D' ||
                           SUBSTR(S_CASES,N+2);

        IF C = ',' THEN DO;
            CASES = SUBSTR(CASES,I+1);
            GO TO EACH_CASE;
            END;
        RETURN(CODE);
        %END CASE;
```

FIG. A.5 CASEMAC

Fig. A.6 gives the code for the DEFAULT macro. DEFAULT first generates a GO TO E#*uniq* if any cases have previously been generated. It then generates the required default labels via the macro DEFAULT1. Lastly, it changes case 0 in S_CASES from 'U' to 'D'. The DEFAULT1 macro generates a case label for each case in S_CASES which is still undefined ('U').

```
        /* DEFAULT, DEFAULT1 MACROS */

   %DEFAULT: PROC RETURNS(CHAR);

        DCL CODE CHAR;

        IF S_MAX > 0 THEN CODE = 'GO TO E' || S_#UNIQ || '; ';
                    ELSE CODE = '';
        CODE = CODE || DEFAULT1;
        IF S_MAX > 0 THEN S_CASES = 'D' || SUBSTR(S_CASES,2);
                    ELSE S_CASES = 'D';
        RETURN(CODE);
        %END DEFAULT;

   %DEFAULT1: PROC RETURNS(CHAR);

        DCL I FIXED,
            CODE CHAR;

        CODE = 'D' || S_#UNIQ;
        DO I = 1 TO S_MAX;
            IF SUBSTR(S_CASES,I+1,1) = 'U' THEN
               CODE = CODE || ': C' || S_#UNIQ || '(' || I || ')';
            END;
        RETURN(CODE);
        %END DEFAULT1;
```

FIG. A.6 DEFLT

APPENDIX B. STRUCTURED PROGRAMMING IN ASSEMBLY LANGUAGE

In this appendix we present a set of macros which implement in Assembly Language the structured programming figures of Chapter 3—IF-THEN-ELSE, SELECT-CASE, DO-WHILE, REPEAT-UNTIL, LOOP-EXITIF-ENDLOOP, and ITERATIVE-DO. We assume that you are familiar with the purpose and use of the various figures (see Chapter 3). It would also be helpful if you are familiar with their implementation in PL/I (see Appendix A), since the general ideas and approach are similar. Although the macros as presented here are oriented to OS/360 Assembler Language (Assembler F), you should concentrate on the ideas and concepts involved so that you may adapt the approach to other assembly languages.

We will begin by specifying how the various macros are to realize the structured figures and by illustrating their usage. We then discuss in a general way the implementation of the macros, in particular the local and global information structures required and the macro and assembly time facilities needed in the assembler. The macros we present here are based on the *CONCEPT* 14 macros[1] developed by Marvin Kessler and used within IBM Federal Systems Division for over three years. Note that even if you don't use the macros, you can still simulate the structured figures by writing the code that the macros would have generated.

B.1 THE IF-THEN-ELSE FIGURE

The IF-THEN-ELSE figure is implemented by the macros IF, ELSE, and ENDIF. Thus, the PL/I version

IF *predicate* THEN DO;
　　group1;

```
        END;
ELSE DO;
        group2;
        END;
```

is expressed in Assembly Language (AL) code as

```
IF predicate THEN
   group1
ELSE
   group2
ENDIF
```

where *predicate* is defined below and each *group* is a sequence of AL statements. As in PL/I the ELSE and *group2* statements may be omitted.

The form of the *predicate* depends to some extent on the particular assembly language. For S/360, many instructions set a condition code which may then be tested by a branch on condition (BC) instruction. Thus, the predicate must indicate what condition to use. Furthermore, for efficiency the predicate may be compounded from several basic predicates by ANDing/ORing them together so that only as many basic predicates are tested as are necessary to determine the overall value of the predicate. Since there is only one condition code register (part of the program status word (PSW)) in the hardware, basic predicates will usually need to specify the instruction which sets the condition code as well as the condition to test for. Thus we have three forms of basic predicates:

1) *condition*
2) *compare-instruction,operand1,condition,operand2*
3) *instruction-mnemonic,operand1,operand2,condition*

where *condition* is either a numeric condition code from 1 through 14 or is one of the extended mnemonics in Table B.1. Each form may be optionally enclosed in parentheses, except that forms 2 and 3 must be enclosed in parentheses when used in compound predicates.

The first form of basic predicate is used when the condition code has been set by an instruction prior to the IF macro. Thus, for example, the sequence

```
IF cond THEN
   group1
ELSE
   group2
ENDIF
```

where *cond* is a condition such as GT or 2, should expand into

```
         BC     15-cond,L#1
            group1
         B      L#2
L#1      EQU    *
            group2
L#2      EQU    *
```

where each L#*n* denotes a unique label created by the macros. (Note: The order in which labels are numbered in the following examples is not necessarily the order in which they are numbered by a particular implementation of the macros; the only requirement is that each label be unique.)

Table B.1

After type instruction	*Mnemonic*	*Code*	*Meaning*	*Complement mnemonic*	*Code*
arithmetic	P	2	plus	NP	13
	M	4	minus	NM	11
	Z	8	zero	NZ	7
	O	1	overflow	NO	14
test under mask	O	1	ones	NO	14
	M	4	mixed	NM	11
	Z	8	zeros	NZ	7
compare	H, GT	2	high, greater than	NH, LE	13
	L, LT	4	low, less than	NL, GE	11
	E, EQ	8	equal	NE	7

The second and third forms of basic predicate specify the instruction which sets the condition code as well as the condition to be tested. The second form is used for compare instructions and the third form for all other instructions. The instructions and their operands are written in the normal manner. Thus

```
IF CLC,FIELD(19),EQ,25(R7) THEN
   group1
ELSE
   group2
ENDIF
```

expands into

```
        CLC   FIELD(19),25(R7)
        BC    15-8,L#1
          group1
        B     L#2
L#1     EQU   *
          group2
L#2     EQU   *
```

and

```
        IF TM,FLAGBYTE,X'80',O THEN
          group
        ENDIF
```

expands into

```
        TM    FLAGBYTE,X'80'
        BC    15-1,L#1
          group
L#1     EQU   *
```

The three operand S/370 instructions may also be used (where *operand3* follows *operand1* in both forms), as in

```
        IF CLM,R1,M3,cond,D2(B2)
```

and

```
        IF ICM,R1,M3,D2(B2),cond
```

Compound predicates may be formed by using the boolean operators AND and OR. Since the complement of a *condition* is 15 – *condition,* a NOT operator is unnecessary. In compound predicates we want only as many basic predicates to be tested as are necessary to determine the value of the predicate. We also want basic predicates to be tested in the order written. Hence, in A AND (B OR C) we test A first. If A is false, the whole predicate is false. Otherwise, we next test B. If B is true, then the whole predicate is true. Otherwise, we must test C, which now is the value of the predicate. The example

```
        IF 12,AND,                                            X
              (CLI,3(R5),EQ,C'%'),OR,                         X
              (AR,R6,R9,P) THEN
          group1
        ELSE
          group2
        ENDIF
```

should generate the code

```
         BC     15-12,L#2
         CLI    3(R5),C'%'
         BC     8,L#1
         AR     R6,R9
         BC     15-2,L#2
L#1      EQU    *
            group1
         B      L#3
L#2      EQU    *
            group2
L#3      EQU    *
```

Note that the operators associate to the right, so that the implied grouping of A OR B AND C OR D is A OR (B AND (C OR D)). In order to associate to the left, we use the operators ANDIF and ORIF. Thus, A OR B ANDIF C OR D has the implied grouping (A OR B) AND (C OR D). In other words, ANDIF and ORIF act as a closing parenthesis for the expression to their left and as an opening parenthesis for the expression to their right. Hence the example

```
         IF 12,AND,                                                X
                 (CLI,3(R5),EQ,C'%'),ORIF,                         X
                 (AR,R6,R9,P)  THEN
            group1
         ELSE
            group2
         ENDIF
```

generates the code

```
         BC     15-12,L#1
         CLI    3(R5),C'%'
         BC     8,L#2
L#1      EQU    *
         AR     R6,R9
         BC     15-2,L#3
L#2      EQU    *
            group1
         B      L#4
L#3      EQU    *
            group2
L#4      EQU    *
```

Sometimes more than one instruction is needed to set the condition code in a basic predicate of a compound predicate. To do this you simply write the instructions in the desired order, omitting the condition subfield for all but the last instruction of the basic predicate. Each instruction must be enclosed in parentheses. Thus, for example,

```
         IF (TM,FLAGBYTE,X'80',O),AND,                                X
               (LH,R3,COUNT),                                         X
               (LTR,R3,R3,P),ORIF,                                    X
               (LH,R3,SIZE),                                          X
               (CH,R3,LE,MAXSIZE) THEN
            group
         ENDIF
```

expands into

```
         TM    FLAGBYTE,X'80'
         BC    15-1,L#1
         LH    R3,COUNT
         LTR   R3,R3
         BC    2,L#2
L#1      EQU   *
         LH    R3,SIZE
         CH    R3,MAXSIZE
         BC    15-13,L#3
L#2      EQU   *
            group
L#3      EQU   *
```

As a further convenience we provide the macro ELSEIF. It is equivalent to using ELSE followed by IF except that only one ENDIF is required to close the initial IF instead of an ENDIF for each of the contained IF's. Thus,

```
         IF pred1 THEN
            group1
         ELSEIF pred2 THEN
            group2
         ELSEIF pred3 THEN
            group3
         ELSE
            group4
         ENDIF
```

is equivalent to

```
IF pred1 THEN
   group1
ELSE
   IF pred2 THEN
      group2
   ELSE
      IF pred3 THEN
         group3
      ELSE
         group4
      ENDIF
   ENDIF
ENDIF
```

The IF-ELSEIF- . . . -ELSEIF-ELSE-ENDIF figure provides a form of SELECT-CASE mechanism for use when the case numbers (predicates) cannot be evaluated by the assembler.

B.2 THE SELECT-CASE FIGURE

The SELECT-CASE figure is implemented by the macros SELECT, CASE, DEFAULT, and ENDSEL. The PL/I version

```
SELECT(intg-expr);
      CASE(a):         group1;
      CASE((b,c)):     group2;
      DEFAULT:         group0;
ENDSELECT;
```

is coded in Assembly Language as

```
code to load register Rx with value of intg-expr
SELECT Rx
   CASE a
      group1
   CASE b,c
      group2
   DEFAULT
      group0
ENDSEL
```

where *Rx* specifies a general register and *a, b, c* etc. are positive integers or macro-time variables (SET*x* variables for S/360 AL) with positive integer values. Cases may be given in any order. The optional default group represents case 0 and any missing cases.The example

```
        SELECT Rx
          CASE 3
             group3
          CASE 5,2
             group2
          DEFAULT
             group0
        ENDSEL
```

expands into

```
        SLA    Rx,2            to index branch table
        BNP    L#4             Rx ≤ 0, use default
        C      Rx,L#1
        BH     L#4             Rx > max case, use default
        B      L#5-4(Rx)       into branch table
L#1     DC     A(L#6-L#5)      branch table length
L#2     EQU    *               case 3
            group3
        B      L#6
L#3     EQU    *               cases 2,5
            group2
        B      L#6
L#4     EQU    *               default
            group0
        B      L#6
L#5     EQU    *               branch table
        B      L#4             case 1
        B      L#3             2
        B      L#2             3
        B      L#4             4
        B      L#3             5
L#6     EQU *
```

Note that register *Rx* is destroyed by SELECT but may be used as a work register by the case groups.

The SELECT macro has two additional options,

```
        SELECT Rx,POWER=n,CHECK=yn
```

where *n* is a nonnegative integer representing a power of two and *yn* is either YES or NO. The POWER option (default value 0) requires all cases to be multiples of 2***n* and adjusts the initial shift instruction accordingly. The CHECK option (default YES) specifies whether or not to generate the tests for $Rx < 0$ and $Rx >$ maximum case. The example

```
SELECT Rx,POWER=3,CHECK=NO
   CASE 24                          3 * 2**3
      group3
   CASE 40,16                       5*8, 2*8
      group2
ENDSEL
```

generates the code

```
        SRA     Rx,3-2          to index branch table
        B       L#3(Rx)         into branch table
L#1     EQU     *               case 24
            group3
        B       L#5
L#2     EQU     *               cases 16,40
            group2
        B       L#5
L#3     EQU     *               branch table
        B       L#4             case 0
        B       L#4             8
        B       L#2             16
        B       L#1             24
        B       L#4             32
        B       L#2             40
L#4     EQU     *               default
L#5     EQU     *
```

B.3 THE CONDITIONAL LOOP FIGURES

The DO-WHILE figure is implemented by the macros WHILE and ENDWHILE. You code the PL/I version

```
DO WHILE(predicate);
     group;
END;
```

in Assembly Language as

```
WHILE predicate DO
   group
ENDWHILE
```

where *predicate* is the same as for the IF macro. Thus the example

```
WHILE CH,R5,LE,=H'10000' DO
   group
```

```
        ENDWHILE
```

expands into

```
        B      L#2
L#1     EQU    *
          group
L#2     EQU    *
        CH     R5,=H'10000'
        BC     13,L#1
```

Note that the predicate is saved by the WHILE macro and expanded by the ENDWHILE macro. Depending on the capabilities of your macro processor, the size and complexity of the predicate may have to be restricted as compared to what is allowed for the IF macro.

The REPEAT-UNTIL figure is implemented by the macros REPEAT and UNTIL. The PL/I version

```
REPEAT;
    group;
UNTIL(predicate);
```

is coded in Assembly Language as

```
        REPEAT
          group
        UNTIL predicate
```

where *predicate* is the same as for the IF macro. Hence the example

```
        REPEAT
          group
        UNTIL  (TM,FLAGBYTE,X'80',O),OR,                 X
               (C,R6,GT,CUTOFF)
```

generates the code

```
L#1     EQU    *
          group
        TM     FLAGBYTE,X'80'
        BC     1,L#2
        C      R6,CUTOFF
        BC     15-2,L#1
L#2     EQU    *
```

The LOOP-EXITIF-ENDLOOP figure is implemented by the macros LOOP, EXITIF, and ENDLOOP. You code the PL/I version

```
LOOP;
      group1;
EXITIF(predicate);
      group2;
ENDLOOP;
```

in Assembly Language as

```
LOOP
  group1
EXITIF predicate
  group2
ENDLOOP
```

where *predicate* is the same as for the IF macro. As in PL/I there may be more than one EXITIF in the loop. Thus, the example

```
LOOP
  group1
EXITIF  CLI,CHARBUF,EQ,C'#'
  group2
EXITIF  (SH,R2,=H'5',M),AND,                                  X
        (LTR,R3,R3,M)
  group3
ENDLOOP
```

expands into

```
L#1  EQU   *
       group1
     CLI   CHARBUF,C'#'
     BC    8,L#3
       group2
     SH    R2,=H'5'
     BC    15-4,L#2
     LTR   R3,R3
     BC    4,L#3
L#2  EQU   *
       group3
     B     L#1
L#3  EQU   *
```

B.4 THE ITERATIVE-DO FIGURE

The ITERATIVE-DO figure is implemented by the macros DO and ENDDO. Although the figure could be implemented strictly in terms of separate add, compare, and branch on condition instructions, we prefer to use the special S/360 instructions BXLE, BXH, and BCT, each of which performs incrementing (decrementing), comparison, and conditional branching within one instruction. Via its various options, the DO macro provides appropriate iteration code for practically all iterative loops.

The simplest form of iterative loop is to execute the loop *n* times. You specify this form by the TIMES parameter, as in

```
DO TIMES=(Rx,n)
  group
ENDDO
```

where *Rx* denotes a general register and *n* denotes the number of times to execute *group*. *Rx* must be specified, but *n* is optional. This form of loop uses the BCT instruction, which decrements *Rx* by 1 and branches if the result is nonzero. Hence the PL/I equivalent is

```
Rx = n;   /* only when n specified */
DO Rx = Rx TO 1 BY -1;
      group;
END;
```

The loop initialization code depends on whether *n* is an integer constant, and if so, its magnitude. We will describe the different forms of initialization after discussing the various kinds of iterative loops. The example

```
DO TIMES=(Rx,#ITEMS)
  group
ENDDO
```

generates the code

```
      L     Rx,#ITEMS
      LTR   Rx,Rx
      BNP   L#2
L#1   EQU   *
        group
      BCT   Rx,L#1
L#2   EQU   *
```

Notice that an initial test for $n > 0$ is made before executing *group*. The DO macro option CHECK=*yn*, where *yn* is either YES or NO (default YES), specifies whether to make an initial test before executing *group* or to allow *group* to be executed once regardless of the initial value of the iteration variable (register) *Rx*. If we had used

```
DO TIMES=(Rx,#ITEMS),CHECK=NO
```

in the above example, the expanded code would be

```
        L     Rx,#ITEMS
L#1     EQU   *
          group
        BCT   Rx,L#1
```

Note that when *n* is an integer constant, the DO macro knows how many times the loop is to be executed and thus can omit the initial test from the expanded code. For example,

```
        DO TIMES=(Rx,50)
          group
        ENDDO
```

expands into

```
        LA    Rx,50
L#1     EQU   *
          group
        BCT   Rx,L#1
```

even though CHECK is YES. Likewise,

```
        DO TIMES=(Rx,0)
          group
        ENDDO
```

generates

```
        B     L#1
          group
L#1     EQU   *
```

The CHECK option may also be used with any of the kinds of iterative loops discussed below.

The general form of iterative loop is expressed in Assembly Language as

```
        DO FROM=(Rx,i),BY=(Ry,j),TO=(Rz,k)
          group
        ENDDO
```

where *Rx, Ry,* and *Rz* are general registers and *i, j,* and *k* are the initial, increment, and cutoff values, respectively. The equivalent PL/I form is

```
Rx = i;   /* optional */
Ry = j;   /* optional */
Rz = k;   /* optional */
DO Rx = Rx BY Ry TO Rz;
     group;
END;
```

The loop is terminated by (i.e., ENDDO expands into) a BXLE or BXH instruction or by an add, compare, conditional branch sequence, depending on the values of the DO macro parameters. Note that the hardware restrictions on BXLE and BXH require that *Rz* be an odd-numbered register and that $y = z-1$ or $y = z$. *Rx* must always be specified, although not all of *Ry, Rz, i, j,* and *k* need be given.

The BXLE and BXH instructions add *Ry* to *Rx* and compare the result with *Rz*. BXLE branches if the result is less than or equal to *Rz*, whereas BXH branches if the result is higher. Thus, BXLE will usually terminate incrementing (ascending) loops and BXH will usually terminate decrementing (descending) loops. To obtain one of these loop terminators, either *Ry* or *Rz* must be specified. If you give only one of *Ry* and *Rz*, then $y = z-1$ is assumed for the other. (Note: the BXLE (BXH) instruction specifies *Rx* and *Ry* and the hardware determines *Rz* from *Ry*.) Each of the values *i, j,* and *k* is optional. A BXH instruction will be generated if the BY value *j* is negative numeric (i.e., a negative integer constant) or if the FROM value *i* and the TO value *k* are both numeric and $i > k$. Otherwise, a BXLE terminates the loop. Thus the example

```
        DO FROM=(Rx,=A(LAST)),BY=(Ry,-4),TO=(Rz,=A(FIRST))
          group
        ENDDO
```

generates the descending loop

```
        L      Rx,=A(LAST)
        LH     Ry,=H'-4'
        L      Rz,=A(FIRST)
        CR     Rx,Rz
        BL     L#2
        AR     Rz,Ry
  L#1   EQU    *
          group
        BXH    Rx,Ry,L#1
  L#2   EQU    *
```

What we really want is a BXHE terminator. The AR *Rz,Ry* instruction compensates for having to use BXH instead. The descending loop

```
        DO FROM=(Rx,0),TO=(Rz,-50)
          group
        ENDDO
```

expands into

```
        SR     Rx,Rx
```

```
        LH    Rz,=H'-50'
        AR    Rz,Rz-1
L#1     EQU   *
          group
        BXH   Rx,Rz-1,L#1
```

Note that since the BY parameters *Ry* and *j* were omitted, the macros assumed that $y = z-1$ and that *Ry* was already initialized. Although CHECK is YES, the initial value check was not generated since the macros know it would always be passed. As our last BX example, the ascending loop

```
        DO  FROM=(Rx,8),BY=(Ry,8),TO=(,LAST)
          group
        ENDDO
```

generates the code

```
        SR    Rx,Rx
        LA    Ry,8
        L     Ry+1,LAST
        BXH   Rx,Ry,L#2
L#1     EQU   *
          group
        BXLE  Rx,Ry,L#1
L#2     EQU   *
```

Because *i* and *j* are both numeric, a BXH is used for the CHECK option instead of a CR, BH sequence.

If *Ry* and *Rz* are both omitted from the DO macro, the loop is terminated by an add, compare, conditional branch sequence of instructions. However, *j* and *k* must both be specified; only *i* is optional. This form of loop termination needs only one register, whereas the BX form usually needs three. As before, if *j* is negative numeric or if *i* and *k* are both numeric and $i > k$, then a descending loop terminated by BNL is generated. Otherwise, the loop is ascending and is terminated by BNH. Thus the descending loop

```
        DO  FROM=(Rx,8(,BR)),BY=(,-2),TO=(,-50)
          group
        ENDDO
```

becomes

```
        L     Rx,8(,BR)
        B     L#2
L#1     EQU   *
```

```
              group
         AH   Rx,=H'-2'
L#2      CH   Rx,=H'-50'
         BNL  L#1
```

and the ascending loop

```
         DO FROM=(Rx,(Ra)),BY=(,(Rb)),TO=(,100000),CHECK=NO
              group
         ENDDO
```

expands into

```
         LR   Rx,(Ra)
L#1      EQU  *
              group
         AR   Rx,(Rb)
         C    Rx,=F'100000'
         BNH  L#1
```

Note that *i*, *j*, or *k* is enclosed in parentheses to specify a register containing the appropriate value rather than the value itself. The generated code can be further optimized by replacing the add instruction by BCTR when $j = -1$ or by LA when $1 \leq j \leq 4095$ and $0 \leq i \leq k \leq 2^{24} - 1$ and *Rx* is not R0. Likewise, the compare instruction can be omitted when $k = 0$ since the add instruction gives the same condition code.

In the above discussion of the general ITERATIVE-DO loop we said that a descending loop is generated if *j* is negative numeric or if *i* and *k* are numeric and $i > k$, and that otherwise the loop is ascending. In order to allow descending loops where *i*, *j*, and/or *k* are nonnumeric, we provide a positional parameter *d* (which must precede the keyword parameters), as in

```
         DO d,FROM=(Rx,i),BY=(Ry,j),TO=(Rz,k)
```

If *d* is omitted, the choice of direction is based on *i*, *j*, and *k* as stated above. If *d* is UP, an ascending loop terminator (BXLE or BNH) is generated, regardless of *i*, *j*, and *k*. Likewise, if *d* is DOWN, a descending loop terminator (BXH or BNL) is generated, regardless of *i*, *j*, and *k*. Thus the descending loop

```
         DO DOWN,FROM=(Rx,A),BY=(Ry,B),TO=(,C)
              group
         ENDDO
```

expands into

```
        L     Rx,A
        L     Ry,B
        L     Ry+1,C
        CR    Rx,Ry+1
        BL    L#2
        AR    Ry+1,Ry
L#1     EQU   *
          group
        BXH   Rx,Ry,L#1
L#2     EQU   *
```

All of the above iterative loops use integer arithmetic (fixed-point instructions) for controlling the loops. The option FLOAT=*p*, where *p* is E or D causes the short (E) or long (D) precision floating-point load, add, and compare instructions to be used instead. *Rx* should denote a floating-point register *Fx*, while *Ry* and *Rz* should be omitted (since there are no floating-point BX instructions). As before, UP or DOWN may be used to force an ascending or descending loop. Likewise, when the positional parameter *d* is omitted, the direction is determined from *i*, *j*, and *k*. The loop is descending if *j* is a negative integer or floating-point number or if *i* and *k* are integers and $i > k$. Otherwise, the loop is ascending. For example, the descending loop

```
        DO  FROM=(Fx,100),BY=(,-1E-2),TO=(,LAST),FLOAT=E
          group
        ENDDO
```

generates the code

```
        LE    Fx,=E'100'
        B     L#2
L#1     EQU   *
          group
        AE    Fx,=E'-1E-2'
L#2     CE    Fx,LAST
        BNL   L#1
```

while the ascending loop

```
        DO  FROM=(Fx,0),BY=(,16(,BR)),TO=(,+0.1),FLOAT=D
          group
        ENDDO
```

expands into

```
        SDR   Fx,Fx
        B     L#2
```

```
L#1   EQU   *
        group
      AD    Fx,16(,BR)
L#2   CD    Fx,=D'+0.1'
      BNH   L#1
```

Note that the macros require positive floating-point constants to begin with '+' so that they may be easily distinguished from *displacement(index,base)* values by looking at only the first character.

You should be aware that floating-point representation and arithmetic is not exact; it is subject to truncation and roundoff errors. For example, since 0.1 cannot be represented exactly in binary, the loop

```
DO  FROM=(Fx,+0.1),BY=(,+0.1),TO=(,10),FLOAT=E
    group
ENDDO
```

may not be executed exactly the 100 times you casually expect. Suppose that the machine representation of 0.1 is slightly less, say 0.099. Then the loop actually runs from 0.099 by 0.099 to 10. Assuming no further truncation and roundoff losses in adding the increment to the current controlled variable (*Fx*) value, then *Fx* contains 9.9 during the 100th pass through the loop. At the end of this pass *Fx* is incremented to 9.999, which is still less than 10. Hence, a 101st pass occurs. Likewise, if the machine representation of 0.1 is slightly larger than 0.1, then fewer than 100 passes are possible. In other words, you should use integer iterative loops when the exact number of passes through the loop is important.

We have illustrated the different forms of register initialization in the preceding ITERATIVE-DO examples. In the following summary, let *Rw* denote *Rx, Ry, Rz* and let *m* denote *i* (or *n*), *j*, *k*, respectively. If *m* is omitted, *Rw* is presumed already initialized. If *m* is an integer constant, then an SR, LA value, LH halfword literal, or L fullword literal instruction is generated, depending on the value of *m*. If *m* is enclosed in parentheses, it denotes a register containing the value, so an LR instruction is generated. Any other form for *m*, such as a literal, displacement(index,base), identifier, or expression, becomes the operand of an L instruction. Similar rules apply to the add and compare instructions and to the floating-point option.

As an added convenience we allow the EXITIF macro to be used for additional conditional exits from ITERATIVE-DO loops. It is especially useful in linear table searches. Thus, Example 3 of Chapter 2 could be expressed in Assembly Language as

```
         code to initialize TABLE and KEY
TABLE@   DSECT
KEY@     DS      CL5
DATA@    DS      CL50
LENGTH@  EQU     *-TABLE@
PROGRAM  CSECT
         USING   TABLE@,R7
         LM      R7,R9,=A(TABLE,LENGTH@,TABLE+(N-1)*LENGTH@)
         DO  FROM=R7,BY=R8,TO=R9
         EXITIF  CLC,KEY,EQ,KEY@
         ENDDO
         IF  CR,R7,LE,R9  THEN
            MVC     DATA,DATA@
         ELSE
            MVI     DATA,C' '
            MVC     DATA+1(L'DATA-1),DATA
         ENDIF
         DROP    R7
         ...
KEY      DS      CL5
DATA     DS      CL50
N        EQU     number of table entries
TABLE    DS      CL(N*LENGTH@)
```

the LM through ENDDO part of which expands into

```
         LM      R7,R9,=A(TABLE,LENGTH@,TABLE+(N-1)*LENGTH@)
         CR      R7,R9
         BH      L#2
L#1      EQU     *
         CLC     KEY,KEY@
         BC      8,L#2
         BXLE    R7,R8,L#1
L#2      EQU     *
```

B.5 IMPLEMENTATION CONSIDERATIONS

In this section we discuss in a general way the implementation of the above macros. Our primary concern is with the local and global information structures required. We then conclude with a discussion of the macro and assembly time facilities needed in an assembler to support this implementation. A quick review of Appendix A at this point would be helpful. Our implementation is based on OS/360 Assembler F.

Since the structured figures may be nested, we need at least one stack. When the beginning macro of a figure (IF, SELECT, DO, etc.) is expanded, the current status of the enclosing figure is saved on the stack and the new figure's status is initialized. Likewise, after we expand the ending macro of the figure (ENDIF, ENDSEL, ENDDO, etc.), we pop the stack to restore the enclosing figure's status. With Assembler F it is easiest to use a separate stack for each kind of information item, rather than one stack for each figure, as in Appendix A, or one stack for everything. The stacks are implemented by arrays.

As in Appendix A, we need a unique number generator for generating unique labels for the expanded figures. Whereas in Appendix A we generated one number for each occurrence of a figure, here we generate a new number for each label. This is because macros with compound predicates, such as IF, may generate an arbitrary number of labels, depending on the complexity of the predicate. In general, all labels created by one macro of a figure (for example, DO) which may be used by a later macro of the same figure (for example, ENDDO) form part of the figure's status information and must be saved on a stack when figures are nested. In the following discussion we say that a label is *created* when we obtain a new unique label from the unique label generator; *defined* when an EQU * card for the label is generated; *referenced* when the label is used as an instruction operand (as in BC 2,L#*1*); and *used* when it is either defined or referenced.

The basic IF-THEN-ELSE figure is quite simple. The global information consists of one label, which is created and referenced by the IF macro. If there is no ELSE part, the label is defined by ENDIF; otherwise, it is defined by ELSE. Now, ELSE must also create and reference a replacement label, which is likewise defined by ENDIF. The optimization of compound predicates (predicates containing the boolean operators AND, OR, ANDIF, and ORIF) is the only difficult problem. The problem is a local one, however, in that the complexity of the predicate affects only the IF macro and not the ELSE and ENDIF macros. The following algorithm for compound IF predicates is due to Kessler.[2]

We perform a left-to-right scan of the basic predicates (instructions) and operators. When we are scanning a basic predicate, we generate the instruction contained in it and save the condition code. When we scan an operator, we generate a BC instruction based on the saved condition and the particular operator. We also take other actions as specified below. We begin by creating two labels and assigning them to *L1* and *L2*. *L1* will be defined when the next ORIF is scanned or else by the ELSE or ENDIF macro. *L2* will be defined when the next ANDIF is scanned or else at the end of the IF macro expansion. We also initialize two indicators, *AND-indicator* and *OR-indicator,* to be off. Table B.2 describes the actions invoked by the operators when they are scanned.

We provide the ANDIF and ORIF operators as one possible solution to the limitations of Assembler F's macro facilities. Assembler F does not recognize sublists within sublists. Hence we must write

IF (((*bp1*),AND,(*bp2*)),OR,((*bp3*),AND,(*bp4*)))

as

IF (*bp1*),AND,(*bp2*),ORIF,(*bp3*),AND,(*bp4*)

where *bp1, . . . ,bp4* are basic predicates. With macro assemblers, such as Assembler H, which do not restrict sublist nesting, you can eliminate ANDIF and ORIF and use fully parenthesized expressions instead.

The SELECT-CASE figure is easier to implement. The SELECT macro

Table B.2

Operator	*Action*
AND	turn on *AND-indicator* generate branch on condition false to *L1*
OR	turn on *OR-indicator* generate branch on condition true to *L2*
ANDIF	turn on *AND-indicator* generate branch on condition false to *L1* if *OR-indicator* is on then generate *L2* EQU * create and assign a new label to *L2* turn off *OR-indicator*
ORIF	turn on *OR-indicator* generate branch on condition true to *L2* if *AND-indicator* is on then generate *L1* EQU * create and assign a new label to *L1* turn off *AND-indicator*
end of predicate	generate branch on condition false to *L1* if *OR-indicator* is on then generate *L2* EQU * forget *L2* pass *L1* on to ELSE or ENDIF macro

creates three labels which are used by the other macros of the figure—that is, they are global information items. The labels define the default group (or end of figure), the branch table, and the end of the figure. The POWER and CHECK options are also global items. Lastly, SELECT initializes two global stacks to be empty. One stack will contain the case numbers and the other will contain the corresponding case labels. The CASE macro creates and defines a case label. It also adds the case numbers and case label to the respective stacks. The DEFAULT macro defines the default label and indicates to ENDSEL that it has done so. The ENDSEL macro defines the branch table label, generates the branch table using the case number and case label stacks, defines the default label if DEFAULT did not, and defines the end-of-figure label.

The conditional loop figures are similar to the IF-THEN-ELSE figure in implementation. The WHILE macro creates two global labels, one which it defines as the start of the loop, and one which is defined by ENDWHILE at the start of the predicate at the end of the loop. WHILE must also pass the predicate to ENDWHILE. In Assembler F assembly time character variables (SETC variables) are restricted to a maximum length of eight characters. This limits the size and complexity of the predicate which can be passed. An alternative to passing the predicate is to have WHILE create the predicate code and pass that to ENDWHILE instead. Assembler H allows a maximum length of 255, which effectively eliminates any size restrictions. The REPEAT macro creates and defines one global label, which is referenced by UNTIL. The LOOP macro creates two global labels, one which it defines as the start of the loop, and one which is referenced by EXITIF and defined by ENDLOOP as the end of the figure.

We use the same algorithm for UNTIL compound predicates as for IF, since both macros generate code which branches if the compound condition is false and drops through to the next instruction if the condition is true. However, WHILE (or ENDWHILE) and EXITIF generate code which branches if the compound condition is true. The algorithm for WHILE and EXITIF is essentially the IF algorithm with the following modifications: *L1* will be defined when the next ORIF is scanned or else at the end of the ENDWHILE or EXITIF macro expansion. *L2* will be defined when the next ANDIF is scanned or else by the WHILE macro as the start of the loop or by ENDLOOP as the end of the figure. The actions for AND, OR, ANDIF, and ORIF are the same as for IF. However, the end of predicate action becomes

> generate branch on condition true to *L2*
> if *AND-indicator* is on then generate *L1* EQU *

Note that for UNTIL (WHILE, EXITIF), it is the final value of *L1* (*L2, L2*) which must be equated to the corresponding global label for the start (start, end) of the figure.

Although the specifications for the ITERATIVE-DO figure are rather long, the figure is fairly straightforward to implement. There are basically four types of DO loops—loops terminated by BCT, by BXLE or BXH, by a fixed-point add-compare-branch sequence, and by a floating-point add-compare-branch sequence—and all four types may be treated similarly. Each type of loop consists of an initialization part, a zero times through test, and a terminator (increment, compare, and conditional branch). Since the exact global information which DO must pass to ENDDO depends on the type of loop, we find that the easiest way to convey the information is to have the DO macro create and save on a global stack the instructions which replace ENDDO. Thus, DO does all the work locally; ENDDO merely outputs the saved instructions. This same instruction stack may be used by other macros as well, in particular WHILE and ENDWHILE. The only other complications are the special-case optimizations peculiar to each type of loop. If EXITIF is allowed with ITERATIVE-DO loops, the exit label (to which EXITIF branches) is a global label created by DO, referenced by each EXITIF, and defined by ENDDO at the end of its expansion.

A reasonable implementation of the above structured programming macros requires the following macro and assembly time facilities: You must have integer arithmetic and character string variables, the arithmetic operations of addition and subtraction, and the string operations of concatenation, substring extraction, and length determination. Global variables are necessary, whereas local variables are necessary only when recursive macros are used; the above macros are not recursive. You must be able to handle lists and sublists of macro operands, to determine their size, and to extract list elements. Stacks are necessary to accommodate nesting of the structured figures. Integer and character string arrays probably provide the easiest implementation of stacks, and are useful for other aspects of an implementation as well. In order to allow the macros to generate alternative expansions based on their parameters, you need the usual equality and inequality relations for comparing integers and character strings, along with a facility for conditional branching within a macro definition. Lastly, you should have a way to communicate errors to the macro user.

The PL/I F preprocessor and Assembler F satisfy most of the above requirements. Although PL/I F lacks a string length function and arrays of integers and strings, it does allow essentially unlimited-length strings. It does not provide a decent error message mechanism, which is why the implementation given in Appendix A has no error checking. The most irritating restriction in Assembler F is the limitation of character string variables to a maximum length of eight characters. This complicates the implementation of the instruction stack used by WHILE–ENDWHILE and DO–ENDDO, since we must use separate stacks for the first eight, the second eight, etc. characters of an instruction operand. If you do not have a suitable macro assembler available, we suggest that you implement a macro preprocessor. In the long run it is better than hand simulating the structured figures, and certainly better than unstructured coding. Definitions of the above macros for use with OS/360 Assembler F are available from the authors.

NOTES

Chapter 1

1. McCracken, D. D. Revolution in programming: an overview. *Datamation* 19, 12 (December 1973), 50-52.

2. Boehm, B. W. Software and its impact: a quantitative assessment. *Datamation* 19, 5 (May 1973), 48-59.

3. Ingalls, D. The execution time profile as a programming tool. In R. Rustin (ed.), *Design and Optimization of Compilers*. Prentice-Hall, Englewood Cliffs, N. J., 1972, 107-128.

4. Dijkstra, E. W. The humble programmer. 1972 ACM Turing Award Lecture; *Comm. ACM* 15, 10 (October 1972), 859-866.

5. Mills, H. D. *How to Write Correct Programs and Know It*. IBM Corp., Gaithersburg, Md., FSC 73-5008, 1973.

6. Mills, H. D. On the development of large reliable programs. *Proc. 1973 IEEE Symposium on Computer Software Reliability,* IEEE, New York, 1973, 155-159.

7. Dijkstra, E. W. A constructive approach to the problem of program correctness. *BIT* 8 (1968), 174-186.

8. Böhm, C., and Jacopini, G. Flow diagrams, Turing machines and languages with only two formation rules. *Comm. ACM* 9, 5 (May 1966), 366-371.

9. Dijkstra, E. W. The humble programmer. *Ibid.*

Chapter 2

1. Dijkstra, E. W. Notes on Structured Programming. In O.-J. Dahl, E. W. Dijkstra, and C. A. R. Hoare, *Structured Programming*. Academic Press, London, 1972.

2. Mills, H. D. *How to Write Correct Programs and Know It*. IBM Corp., Gaithersburg, Md., FSC 73-5008, 1973.

3. Hoare, C. A. R. An axiomatic basis for computer programming. *Comm. ACM* 12, 10 (October 1969), 576-580, 583.

4. Dijkstra, E. W. *A Simple Axiomatic Basis for Programming Language Constructs*. Technological University Eindhoven, EWD 372-0, 1973.

5. Wirth, N. *Systematic Programming: An Introduction*. Prentice-Hall, Englewood Cliffs, N. J., 1973.

Chapter 3

1. Bohm, C., and Jacopini, G. Flow diagrams, Turing machines and languages with only two formation rules. *Comm. ACM* 9, 5 (May 1966), 366-371.

2. Mills, H. D. *Mathematical Foundations for Structured Programming*. IBM Corp., Gaithersburg, Md., FSC 72-6012, 1972.

3. *IBM System/360 Operating System PL/I (F) Language Reference Manual*. IBM Corp., Form C28-8201.

Chapter 4

1. Mills, H. D. Top-down programming in large systems. In R. Rustin (ed.), *Debugging Techniques in Large Systems,* Prentice-Hall, Englewood Cliffs, N. J., 1971, 41-55.

2. Gardner, M. Mathematical games. *Scientific American,* 223, 4 (October 1970), 120-123.

3. Goodenough, J. B., and Eanes, R. S. *Program Testing and Diagnosis Technology*. SofTech, Inc., Waltham, Mass., Contract DAAA 25-72C-0667, 1973.

4. Gardner, M. Mathematical games. *Scientific American,* 227, 2 (August 1972), 106-109.

Chapter 5

1. Aron, J. D. The "Super-programmer project." In J. N. Buxton and B. Randell (eds.), *Software Engineering Techniques*. NATO Sci. Affairs Div., Brussels, 1970, 50-52.

2. Aron, J. D., *Ibid.*

3. Baker, F. T. Chief programmer team management of production programming. *IBM Systems Journal* 11, 1 (1972), 56-73.

4. Baker, F. T. System quality through structured programming. *Proc. AFIPS 1972 FJCC,* Vol. 41, AFIPS Press, Montvale, N. J., 339-343.

5. Mills, H. D. *Chief Programmer Teams Principles and Procedures*. IBM Corp., Gaithersburg, Md., FSC 71-5108, 1971.

6. Baker, F. T., and Mills, H. D. Chief programmer teams. *Datamation* 19, 12 (December 1973), 58-61.

7. Mills, H. D. On the development of large reliable programs. *Proc. 1973 IEEE Symposium on Computer Software Reliability,* IEEE, New York, 155-159.

Chapter 6

1. Weiderman, N. H. *Synchronization and Simulation in Operating System Construction.* Ph.D. Thesis, Cornell University, 1972.

2. Shaw, A. C., and Weiderman, N. H. A multiprogramming system for education and research. *Proc. IFIP Cong. 1971,* North-Holland Publ. Co., Amsterdam, 1972.

3. *IBM System/360 PL/I Language Specifications.* IBM Corp., Form Y33-6003.

4. Shaw, A. C. *The Logical Design of Operating Systems.* Prentice-Hall, Englewood Cliffs, N.J., 1974.

Appendix B

1. Kessler, M. M. *Assembly Language Structured Programming Macros.* IBM Corp., Gaithersburg, Md., 1972.

2. Kessler, M. M. *Ibid.* Appendix II.

REFERENCES

Aron, J. D. The "Super-programmer project." In Buxton, J. N., and Randell, B. (eds.), *Software Engineering Techniques*. NATO Sci. Affairs Div., Brussels, 1970, 50-52.

Ashcroft, E., and Manna, Z. The translation of "go to" programs to "while" programs. *Proc. IFIP Congress 1971,* Booklet TA-2, North-Holland Publ. Co., Amsterdam, 1971, 147-152.

Baker, F. T. Chief programmer team management of production programming. *IBM Systems Journal* 11, 1 (1972), 56-73.

———. System quality through structured programming. *Proc. AFIPS* 1972 *FJCC,* Vol. 41, AFIPS Press, Montvale, N.J., 339-343.

———, and Mills, H. D. Chief programmer teams. *Datamation* 19, 12 (December 1973), 58-61.

Benson, J. P. Structured programming techniques. *Proc. 1973 IEEE Symposium on Computer Software Reliability,* IEEE, New York, 143-147.

Boehm, B. W. Software and its impact: a quantitative assessment. *Datamation* 19, 5 (May 1973), 48-59.

Böhm, C., and Jacopini, G. Flow diagrams, Turing machines and languages with only two formation rules. *Comm. ACM* 9, 5 (May 1966), 366-371.

Cheng, L. L. *Some Case Studies in Structured Programming*. The MITRE Corp., Bedford, Mass., MTR-2648 VI, 1973.

Conway, R., and Gries, D. *An Introduction to Programming*. Winthrop, Cambridge, Mass., 1973.

Cooper, D. C. Bohm and Jacopini's reduction of flow charts. *Comm. ACM* 10, 8 (August 1967), 463, 473.

Dahl, O.-J., Dijkstra, E. W., and Hoare, C. A. R. *Structured Programming*. Academic Press, London, 1972.

Dijkstra, E. W. A constructive approach to the problem of program correctness. *BIT* 8 (1968), 174-186.

———. *A Short Introduction to the Art of Programming*. Technological University Eindhoven, EWD 316, 1971.

———. *A Simple Axiomatic Basis for Programming Language Constructs.* Technological University Eindhoven, EWD 372-0, 1973.

———. Co-operating sequential processes. In Genuys, F. (ed.), *Programming Languages.* Academic Press, New York, 1968, 43-112.

———. GoTo statement considered harmful. *Comm. ACM* 11, 3 (March 1968), 147-148.

———. The humble programmer. 1972 ACM Turing Award Lecture; *Comm. ACM* 15, 10 (October 1972), 859-866.

Donaldson, J. R. Structured programming. *Datamation* 19, 12 (December 1973), 52-54.

Floyd, R. W. Assigning meanings to programs. In Schwartz, J. T. (ed.), *Mathematical Aspects of Computer Science.* American Mathematical Society, Providence, R.I., 1967, 19-32.

Freeman, P. Functional programming: testing and machine aids. In Hetzel, W. C. (ed.), *Program Test Methods.* Prentice-Hall, Englewood Cliffs, N.J., 1973, 49-56.

Gardner, M. Mathematical games. *Scientific American,* 223, 4 (October 1970), 120-123.

———. Mathematical games. *Scientific American,* 224, 2 (February 1971), 112-117.

———. Mathematical games. *Scientific American,* 227, 2 (August 1972), 106-109.

Goodenough, J. B., and Eanes, R. S. *Program Testing and Diagnosis Technology.* SofTech, Inc., Waltham, Mass., Contract DAAA 25-72C-0667, 1973.

———, and Ross, D. T. *The Effect of Software Structure on Software Reliability, Modifiability, Reusability, and Efficiency: A Preliminary Analysis.* SofTech, Inc., Waltham, Mass., Contract DAAA 25-72C-0667, 1973.

Henderson, P., and Snowdon, R. An experiment in structured programming. *BIT* 12 (1972), 38-53.

Hoare, C. A. R. An axiomatic basis for computer programming. *Comm. ACM* 12, 10 (October 1969), 576-580, 583.

———. Proof of a program: FIND. *Comm. ACM* 14, 1 (January 1971), 39-45.

———. Proof of a structured program: 'The sieve of Eratosthenes.' *The Computer Journal,* 15, 4 (November 1973), 321-325.

Hopkins, M. E. A case for the GOTO. *Proc. ACM* 1972 *Annual Conference,* ACM, New York, 1972, 787-790.

IBM System/360 Operating System Assembler Language. IBM Corp., Order No. GC28-6514.

IBM System/360 Operating System PL/I (F) Language Reference Manual. IBM Corp., Form C28-8201.

Ingalls, D. The execution time profile as a programming tool. In Rustin, R. (ed.), *Design and Optimization of Compilers.* Prentice-Hall, Englewood Cliffs, N.J., 1972, 107-128.

Kelly, J. R., and McGowan, C. L. *Structured programming extensions to PL/I*. Brown Univ. CCIS Tech. Report No. 73-88, 1973.

Kelly, J. R., and Wilcox, T. R. *BCPL/360 Reference Manual*. Dept. of Computer Science, Cornell Univ., Ithaca, N.Y., 1970.

Kernighan, B. W., and Plauger, P. J. *The Elements of Programming Style*. McGraw-Hill, New York, 1974.

Kessler, M. M. *Assembly Language Structured Programming Macros*. IBM Corp., Gaithersburg, Md., 1972.

Knuth, D. E. An empirical study of FORTRAN programs. *Software —Practice and Experience* 1, 2 (1971), 105-133.

———. *Structured Programming with GO TO Statements*. Stanford Computer Science Department report STAN-CS-74-416, 1974.

———, and Floyd, R. W. Notes on avoiding "GO TO" statements. *Information Processing Letters* 1, 1 (February 1971), 23-31.

Kosaraju, S. R. Analysis of structured programs. *Proc. Fifth Annual ACM Symp. Theory of Computing,* (May 1973), 240-252.

Leavenworth, B. M. Programming with(out) the GOTO. *Proc. ACM* 1972 *Annual Conference,* ACM, New York, 1972, 782-786.

Ledgard, H. F. The case for structured programming. *BIT* 13 (1973), 45-57.

Liskov, B. H. A design methodology for reliable software systems. *Proc. AFIPS* 1972 *FJCC,* Vol. 41, AFIPS Press, Montvale, N.J., 191-199.

———, and Towster, E. *The Proof of Correctness Approach to Reliable Systems*. The MITRE Corp., Bedford, Mass., MTR-2073, 1971.

———, and Zilles, S. Programming with abstract data types. Proc. of a Symposium on Very High Level Languages, *SIGPLAN Notices* 9, 4 (April 1974), 50-59.

London, R. L. Proving programs correct: some techniques and examples. *BIT* 10 (1970), 168-182.

Martin, J. J. The 'natural' set of basic control structures. *SIGPLAN Notices* 8, 12 (December 1973), 5-14.

McCracken, D. D. Revolution in programming: an overview. *Datamation* 19, 12 (December 1973), 50-52.

———, and Weinberg, G. M. How to write a readable FORTRAN program. *Datamation,* 18, 10 (October 1972), 73-77.

McGowan, C. L., and Kelly, J. R. *Top-Down Segmented Structured Programming*. Brown Univ. CCIS Tech. Report No. 73-91, 1973.

———, and Misra, J. *Program Inverses*. Brown Univ. CCIS Tech. Report No. 73-73-2, 1973.

McHenry, R. C. *Management Concepts for Top Down Structured Programming*. IBM Corp., Gaithersburg, Md., FSC 73-0001, 1973.

Miller, E. F., and Lindamood, G. E. Structured programming: top-down approach. *Datamation* 19, 12 (December 1973), 55-57.

Mills, H. D. *Chief Programmer Teams Principles and Procedures*. IBM Corp., Gaithersburg, Md., FSC 71-5108, 1971.

———. *How to Write Correct Programs and Know It*. IBM Corp., Gaithersburg, Md., FSC 73-5008, 1973.

———. *Mathematical Foundations for Structured Programming*. IBM Corp., Gaithersburg, Md., FSC 72-6012, 1972.

———. On the development of large reliable programs. *Proc. 1973 IEEE Symposium on Computer Software Reliability*, IEEE, New York, 1973, 155-159.

———. Top-down programming in large systems. In Rustin, R. (ed.), *Debugging Techniques in Large Systems*. Prentice-Hall, Englewood Cliffs, N.J., 1971, 41-55.

Myers, G. J. *Composite Design: The Design of Modular Programs*. IBM Corp., Poughkeepsie, N.Y., TR 00.2406, 1973.

Naur, P. Programming by action clusters. *BIT* 9 (1969), 250-258.

———. Proof of algorithms by general snapshots. *BIT* 6 (1966), 310-316.

Neely, P. M. *Fundamentals of Programming*. Computation Center of the University of Kansas, Lawrence, Kansas, 1973.

Parnas, D. L. A technique for software module specification with examples. *Comm. ACM* 15, 5 (May 1972), 330-336.

———. On the criteria to be used in decomposing systems into modules. *Comm. ACM* 15, 12 (December 1972), 1053-1058.

Randell, B. Towards a methodology of computing system design. In Naur, P., and Randell, B. (eds.), *Software Engineering*. NATO Scientific Affairs Division, Brussels, 1969, 204-208.

Shaw, A. C. *The Logical Design of Operating Systems*. Prentice-Hall, Englewood Cliffs, N. J., 1974.

———, and Weiderman, N. H. A multiprogramming system for education and research. *Proc. IFIP Cong. 1971*, North-Holland Publ. Co., Amsterdam, 1972.

Snowdon, R. A. PEARL—a system for the preparation and validation of structured programs. In Hetzel, W. C., (ed.), *Program Test Methods*. Prentice-Hall, Englewood Cliffs, N.J., 1973, 57-73.

Stevens, W. P., Myers, G. J., and Constantine, L. L. Structured design. *IBM Systems Journal* 13, 2 (1974).

Sullivan, J. E. *Extending PL/I for Structured Programming*. The MITRE Corp., Bedford, Mass., MTR-2353, 1972.

Weiderman, N. H. *Synchronization and Simulation in Operating System Construction*. Ph.D. Thesis, Cornell University, 1972.

Weinberg, G. M. *The Psychology of Computer Programming*. Van Nostrand Reinhold, New York, 1971.

———, Yasukawa, N., and Marcus, R. *Structured Programming in PL/C*. Wiley, New York, 1973.

Wirth, N. Program development by stepwise refinement. *Comm. ACM* 14, 4 (April 1971), 221-227.

———. *Systematic Programming: An Introduction*. Prentice-Hall, Englewood Cliffs, N.J., 1973.

Wulf, W. A. A case against the GOTO. *Proc. ACM 1972 Annual Conference*, ACM, New York, 1972, 791-797.

———. Programming without the goto. *Proc. IFIP Congress 1971,* Booklet TA-3, North-Holland Publ. Co., Amsterdam, 1971, 84-88.

Zurcher, F. W., and Randell, B. Iterative multi-level modeling—a methodology for computer system design. *Proc. IFIP Congress 1968, Booklet* D, North-Holland Publ. Co., Amsterdam, 1968, 138-142.

INDEX